**Endorsed for
Pearson Edexcel
Qualifications**

Chinese
for Advanced Subsidiary Level

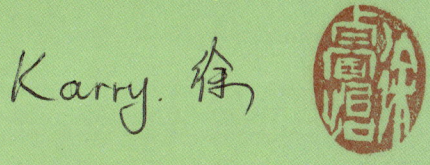

Xiaoming Zhang

Eileen Lee

Cypress Book Co. UK Ltd.

Chinese for Advanced Subsidiary Level

Xiaoming Zhang   Eileen Lee

Editor: Xue Mei
Cover Design: Seagull Design, SHUICHANGLIU DIGITAL PRINTING CO., LTD
Cover photo © Adobe Stock, Gui Yong Nian

First published in Great Britain in 2018 by Cypress Book Co. UK Ltd.
Unit 6, Provident Industrial Estate
Pump Lane
Hayes UB3 3NE
United Kingdom
Tel: 0044 (0)20 8848 0572
E-mail: info@cypressbooks.com

Find us at www.cypressbooks.com

Text copyright © 2018 by Xiaoming Zhang, Eileen Lee

The moral rights of the authors have been asserted.

All rights reserved. No part of this publication may be reproduced or transmitted by any means, electronic, mechanical, photocopying or otherwise, without the prior permission of the publisher.

ISBN: 9781845700379

Printed in China 2018

About the Authors

Eileen Lee BSc, PGCE, is a qualified teacher in Britain in the upper primary sector (aged 7–13). She taught Chinese first as a mother tongue, then as a heritage language in complementary schools for many years. With the teaching experience obtained in mainstream schools, she adapted the relevant practice to apply to complementary Chinese schools. She has taught at different levels and has prepared numerous pupils for both GCSE and A Level exams. She was the headteacher of a complementary school for five years. She has also taught Chinese as a Modern Foreign Language in independent schools to both native and non-native learners for over ten years. Eileen co-authored the *GCSE Chinese Revision Guide* (in two versions: Cantonese-traditional script Chinese, and Mandarin-simplified script Chinese) in 2004. She co-authored *Curriculum Guide for Chinese* in 2007 and its Cantonese version in 2009 published by CILT. She is the chief editor of and co-authored all the eight books in the *Let's Learn Chinese* series (from beginner level to GCSE). She also contributed to the *GCSE Revision Exercise Book, AS and A2 Revision Exercise Books*, all published by the UK Federation of Chinese Schools (UKFCS). She was the President of the UKFCS between 2002 and 2005 and served on its Education Committee from 1993 to 2018. Eileen received an award from the National Association for Teaching English and Community Languages to Adults in the year 2011–2012 in the category of 'community language teacher who has made a positive contribution to their organisation through sharing their practice, eg teaching ideas, materials and approaches'. She was an Education Adviser to the UKFCS from 2014 to 2018. Eileen was an external examiner of the GCSE (2003 specification) Chinese Paper for Speaking. She was also a moderator and team leader of the GCSE (2009 specification) Chinese Paper for Speaking until 2012. Eileen is a regular presenter and trainer in workshops run by the UKFCS at its annual conferences and to teachers of its member schools in the UK.

Xiaoming Zhang BA, has over thirty-five years of experience in teaching Chinese both in China and the UK. She obtained a BA in Chinese Language and Literature from Shanghai Normal University. After graduation, she worked in a prestigious high school, and then in a college in Shanghai. Later she became a lecturer in Chinese language and literature before coming to the UK. She has been teaching Chinese as a foreign language in Wycombe Abbey School for nearly twenty years and helped the school to establish the successful Chinese Department. Apart from her publications and teaching awards obtained in China, in 1997 she co-authored *Basic Chinese: A Grammar and Workbook* and *Intermediate Chinese*, both published by Routledge. In 2006 and 2007 Xiaoming authored *Chinese for A Level* published by Cypress Book Company UK. Limited in both traditional and simplified Chinese scripts. In the following year she co-authored *Chinese for AS*, again published by Cypress Book in both Chinese scripts. She also published many articles about Chinese teaching and researches in the overseas edition of the *People's Daily* and the *Chinese Learning and Teaching Journal*.

Acknowledgements

The authors would like to thank the following friends and family for their contribution towards the production of this book:

Wu Yunhong for proof-reading Units 1–4 of this book and for all her practical and useful comments;

Yin-fung Au for proof-reading the Introduction of Unit 5 and for his recommendations for re-organising its structure;

Joe Au for proof-reading the whole book and for his invaluable suggestions;

Our publisher Cypress Books for their support and confidence in our work;

And finally our husbands Sam and Joe for their support and encouragement, as well as a regular supply of tea and snacks.

Endorsement Statement

In order to ensure that this resource offers high-quality support for the associated Pearson qualification, it has been through a review process by the awarding body. This process confirms that this resource fully covers the teaching and learning content of the specification or part of a specification at which it is aimed. It also confirms that it demonstrates an appropriate balance between the development of subject skills, knowledge and understanding, in addition to preparation for assessment.

Endorsement does not cover any guidance on assessment activities or processes (e.g. practice questions or advice on how to answer assessment questions), included in the resource nor does it prescribe any particular approach to the teaching or delivery of a related course.

While the publishers have made every attempt to ensure that advice on the qualification and its assessment is accurate, the official specification and associated assessment guidance materials are the only authoritative source of information and should always be referred to for definitive guidance.

Pearson examiners have not contributed to any sections in this resource relevant to examination papers for which they have responsibility.

Examiners will not use endorsed resources as a source of material for any assessment set by Pearson.
Endorsement of a resource does not mean that the resource is required to achieve this Pearson qualification, nor does it mean that it is the only suitable material available to support the qualification, and any resource lists produced by the awarding body shall include this and other appropriate resources.

Contents

Foreword ix
About this book x
Suggestions on how to use this book xiii

ONE
当代华人社会变迁

Unit One   家庭
Chapter 1   我的家 5
Chapter 2   三代人 12
Chapter 3   无奈的"小皇帝" ... 20
Chapter 4   中国社会的老龄化 ... 27

Unit Two   教育与工作
Chapter 5   上学读书 37
Chapter 6   望子成龙 45
Chapter 7   职场百态 54
Chapter 8   工作与生活的平衡 ... 64

TWO
中国文化

Unit Three   中国文化
Chapter 9   辞旧迎新 78
Chapter 10   清明祭祖 86
Chapter 11   漫谈端午 94
Chapter 12   中秋佳节 102
Chapter 13   中国的传统习俗 110

Unit Four   中国文化——文化活动
Chapter 14   好读书　读书好
　　　　　　读好书 121
Chapter 15   电影 130
Chapter 16   电视 138
Chapter 17   怡人的音乐 146

vii

THREE
文学作品与电影

Unit Five 文学与电影 如何分析文学作品与电影

Chapter 18 《一只叫凤的鸽子》（作者：曹文轩，2014）...... 163
Chapter 19 《城南旧事》〈惠安馆〉（作者：林海音，1960）...... 165
Chapter 20 《城南旧事》〈爸爸的花儿落了〉（作者：林海音，1960）...... 168
Chapter 21 《请投我一票》（导演：陈为军，2007）...... 170
Chapter 22 《天水围的日与夜》（导演：许鞍华，2008）...... 173

Appendices

- **Appendix I**
  Transcripts of listening exercises 176
- **Appendix II**
  Keys to the listening exercises 189
- **Appendix III**
  Useful expressions for speaking and writing 195
- **Appendix IV**
  Guide to tackling speaking exams 197
- **Appendix V**
  Guide to writing responses to literary texts 203
- **Appendix VI**
  Guide to translating texts 205
- **Appendix VII**
  Vocabulary list 212

Foreword

In recent years there has been an increase in the production of and demand for higher level Chinese course books. This is due to the rise in the number of students studying Chinese up to GCSE level and beyond. Schools which have been teaching Chinese to GCSE level need course books to cater for students who continue with their study of Chinese post GCSE.

Edexcel, the examining board, whose specification (Specification September 2017 GCE Chinese 8CN0) this book addresses, has revised its A level examinations to incorporate new tests of the four skills. Furthermore, it has also changed some of the content and format of the assessment. As a result, new approaches and new materials are needed to help to prepare students for the new examination. This book aims to do just that.

The authors of this book regard it as a very useful teaching tool to lead the student of Chinese from GCSE to AS level as far as vocabulary, grammar and cultural content are concerned. This book can also be used for the Pre-U, IB and HSK examinations. Students taking Chinese studies at university level may find this book useful as additional reading materials.

About this book

This book consists of 5 Units. Units 1–4 correspond to the two main themes of Chinese society and Chinese culture. Alongside the two main themes, Unit 5 covers three literary texts and two films which are specified in the new syllabus.

Each of the two main themes is sub-divided into sub-themes. Theme One covers family, education and employment. Theme Two covers Chinese traditions and cultural activities. Units 1–4 are thus organised accordingly, as shown on the Contents page.

Features of Units 1–4

- Each Unit starts with an introduction which gives brief background information on the sub-theme concerned. It is presented in both Chinese and English for ease of comprehension.
- The Unit is then sub-divided into chapters, with each chapter covering one topic and featuring various aspects of it, and the starting point is always a text. There are at least three short texts in each chapter. They can be a survey report, an advertisement, a letter, an interview, a news report, a web page, or a diary entry etc, to give students the vocabulary and register needed to tackle the topic.
- A vocabulary list is given after each text to help the student understand the new essential words and phrases. The number of new characters introduced in each unit has been carefully limited to one that the student can manage and not feel overwhelmed by.
- Comprehension exercises then follow to test what information has been conveyed. There are additional speaking and writing exercises which are to be completed in the lesson. This approach provides opportunities for the student to jot down notes in Chinese, and to engage in class discussion in Chinese.
- Each chapter also highlights some of the grammatical structures in the Grammar List of Edexcel's Specification September 2017. Both vocabulary and grammar structures are practised extensively. This, we feel, is one of the great strengths of the book. The vocabulary and structures appear first and, once mastered, become the essential tools the student needs to attempt the new speaking and listening tasks which then follow.
- These tasks are presented in the same way as in the Edexcel examinations, to familiarise students with the examination format thus giving them additional confidence. Students are then guided through continuous writing tasks with all the necessary vocabulary, structures and information to help them.

- Another great strength of the book is its introduction of the literary texts and films early in the school term. Teachers and students do not have to wait until Unit 5 to start to work on the literary texts and films. Speaking and short writing tasks based on the relevant content of them will be linked to the related topics of the themes from day one, so that the student gets a head start on the study of the literary texts and films.
- Information on Chinese culture and society is contained in all the chapters. This has the dual purpose of providing additional reading materials, as well as related knowledge to the student.

Features of Unit 5
Literary works and films
- The Unit starts with an introduction and guidance on how to analyse literary works and films with examples from the specified texts and films in the syllabus. It is presented in both Chinese and English for ease of comprehension.
- The Unit has five chapters, each of which covers a literary text or a film.
- Each chapter begins with an introduction of the author or director (in the case of a film), followed by a description of the plot of the literary work or the film.
- There is an outline of the writing style or filming technique used by the author or director for students to discuss and analyse.
- Each chapter finishes with questions related to the plot and the writing style or filming technique for students to discuss in class and to write about.

Appendices
There are seven appendices at the end of the book. They provide very useful information and guidance for teachers and students when practising the four skills.

Appendix I: It contains the transcripts of the listening exercises in Units 1–4.

Appendix II: It provides suggested keys to the listening exercises in Units 1–4. Appendices I and II, along with the accompanying audio recordings online, would make this book also suitable for self study.

Appendix III: This is a list of phrases for expressing opinions for speaking and writing. These phrases are very useful to include in speaking and writing practice.

Appendix IV: This appendix gives advice on how to deal with speaking questions in the exam. It contains two sample tasks with detailed suggestions of how to construct the responses.

Appendix V: Similarly this appendix shows students how to write responses to literary texts or films.

Appendix VI: This is another practical appendix which gives students useful guidance on how to translate texts. It provides step-by-step advice on ways to tackle translation tasks, whether from Chinese to English or from English to Chinese. Examples are used to illustrate the suggestions.

Appendix VII: This is a vocabulary list at the end of the book that directs the student back to the Unit in which the character first appeared.

Suggestions on how to use this book

We have set out this book in what we consider to be the most useful and logical order. We explain this below in a general way for those who feel they need some guidance and explanation. Nothing is set in stone. It is what we as teachers have found works.

- The introduction at the beginning of each Unit gives a general idea of what is to come in the subsequent chapters. The student can read it first before coming to the lessons as it is written in both Chinese and English. The teacher can then use it for preliminary discussions and to set the scene for teaching later.
- The texts in each chapter serve as starting points for teaching and learning the topic. In addition, the illustrations accompanying the texts can provide interesting focal points to lead into discussions.
- Each chapter's Chinese vocabulary list can then be studied and examined from the point of view of composition, radicals, pronunciation, stroke order etc, and the need to just learn them stressed. The function given for each word is always as it appears in the text.
- A reading aloud of the text follows and then the comprehension exercise is done quickly to check if the information has been fully understood. The questions are usually in exam-style.
- The information on Chinese culture and society in each chapter can be used as homework for reading. However, the speaking and writing exercises should be conducted in the classroom to provide opportunities for teacher-student and student-student interaction.
- Although the literary texts and films are dealt with separately in Unit 5, it is practical and logical to start introducing them early in the school term. Whenever the topic is relevant and can be linked up with the literary texts or the films, speaking and short writing tasks are set for the student to practise in the classroom. Therefore, the student must start to study these works right from the beginning.
- In the later exercises of each chapter, in which the student is asked to choose character groups from several possibilities, the contexts in which the choices are placed become more complex: the phrase becomes a sentence and then a paragraph. This is to help the student to become more confident with a more complex structure.
- Once the students have mastered the vocabulary and the sentence patterns, they are ready to attempt the speaking exercise. They should be referred to the page

of suggestions on how to express their opinions (see Appendix III) to help them with this task and be encouraged to keep a list of such expressions as they meet them throughout the course. They should also be reminded that there is much in the preceding text and chapter which will help them: students often forget that they can recycle and dwell on what they feel they do not know. For the first speaking exercises in Chapter 1 of Unit 1, we have given annotated sample answers in Appendix IV. We have done the same with the first writing exercises in Chapter 18 of Unit 5, for which we have given annotated sample answers in Appendix V.

- The listening tasks can be done before or after the speaking task, but both should have been done before the writing exercise. These should be attempted at the end as by this time the student has already read, studied, spoken and listened to the relevant Chinese words. This could perhaps be used as a basis for class discussion and suggestions and then written out as an individual time-constrained assignment later.
- Translation exercises from Chinese to English and English to Chinese can be set as quick class tests of how the student is coping or as group work in class, or simply as homework. It would be useful if the student is guided to read the suggestions on how to translate texts in Appendix VI at the beginning of the course as translation exercises are included in all the chapters from Units 1–4.
- Other types of exercises have been inserted into the Units from time to time so that there is enough variety to prevent the chapters from becoming a predictable repetition of the same types of tasks. The variety is to keep the students motivated by presenting them with new challenges, and to get them to interact with materials that they can relate to.

* A summary of the changes made to the Edexcel 2009 Specification is outlined below.

根据 Specification September 2017 GCE Chinese 8CN0，我们可以看出，新的 AS 考试从内容到形式都有较大的改变。

内容
1. 增添了在"当代华人社会的变迁"的大前提下，华人家庭结构和代沟以及家庭计划和人口老龄化、工作机会以及工作和生活的平衡。
2. 强调了有关电影、电视、音乐和阅读的文化活动一定要与中国文化有关。
3. 引进了文学作品《一只叫凤的鸽子》、《城南旧事》中的《惠安馆》和《爸爸的花儿落了》，以及电影《请投我一票》和《天水围的日与夜》。

形式

1. 听力：过去的听力只有最后一道题是用中文回答中文问题，其他的都是用英文回答英文问题。新的考试除了一道题是中文选择题外，其他都需要用中文回答中文问题；最后一题要求根据听到的中文对话与英文题目，用英文写概要。
2. 阅读理解：过去只有一道题要求考生用中文回答中文问题，其他的题目都是用英文回答英文问题。新的考试要求所有的题目都是用中文回答中文问题。
3. 写作：过去要求用 180—200 字写一篇命题作文，超过字数的部分不给分。新的考试会根据大纲规定的三个短篇小说和两部电影共设B、C两部分，考生必须在B部分或者C部分选择一题写一篇分析文章。每道题在提供要点的同时规定了论题，新大纲建议文章字数在 225—300 之间，超过字数的部分考官也照看不扣分。
4. 口语：过去只要求考生根据分配到的一个口试题，准备 15 分钟，然后根据英文短文的内容和用英文写的要点，自己独自用中文连续表达 4—6 分钟。现在每位考生需要做两个口试题，而且两个都是问答题，题目和要求都是用中文写的。考生在分配到两道题目后，准备时间一共 15 分钟。

    第一个口试答题需要对话 7—9 分钟。问题 1 要求考生说出短文的概要；问题 2 要求考生回答根据短文第一部分内容提出的问题；问题 3 要求考生回答根据短文第二部分内容提出的问题；问题 4 则要求在短文主题的基础上，拓开讨论与之相关的文化与社会问题。第二个口试题需要对话 5—6 分钟。前一半时间由考官按照答题卡上规定的问题逐一提出，让考生回答；后一半时间，考官会在同样的主题下拓开去，继续提出问题。在做这两个口语考试的过程中，考官都会期待考生能展开思路、提出问题，并表达自己的观点与看法。
5. 翻译：Paper1 中有把中文短文翻译成英文的考题，Paper3 中有把英文短文翻译成中文的考题。

一

Unit One 家庭

- Chapter 1　我的家
- Chapter 2　三代人
- Chapter 3　无奈的"小皇帝"
- Chapter 4　中国社会的老龄化

Unit Two 教育与工作

- Chapter 5　上学读书
- Chapter 6　望子成龙
- Chapter 7　职场百态
- Chapter 8　工作与生活的平衡

当代华人社会变迁

第一单元　家庭

这个单元覆盖了关于家庭结构、人口老龄化、代沟、家庭计划的话题。

• 家庭结构

在过去的30年间，华人社会在人口与家庭结构方面发生了很多变化，并且变化一直在继续着。自从1978年中国政府推行了计划生育政策以来，典型的中国家庭结构已经演变成了由两三个人组成的小家庭。

第二类家庭结构是单亲家庭。随着现代离婚率的提高，这类家庭的数量正在增加。最近的统计显示，第三类家庭结构也多起来了，那就是祖孙家庭。追溯原因，大概与男女社会地位的变化有关系。

在当代华人社会，男女得到了平等待遇，他们有受教育和就业的平等机会。"男主外、女主内"的家庭模式发生了变化，女人跟男人一样，也有追求事业的愿望。这个趋势使得夫妻要共同承担家庭责任，双方都外出工作，挣钱养家，在家也一起分担家务活。

然而，当他们有了孩子后，照看孩子就成了一个问题。妻子可能会回归家庭，或者他们上班时可以将孩子送到托儿所，下班回家时照顾他们。不把孩子送到托儿所的夫妻可能会让自己的父母来照顾孩子，所以，在白天，祖孙家庭相当普遍。

在中国农村，祖孙家庭的数量也在增加。许多夫妻去城里打工，养育孩子的问题更为严重。他们很多时候只能把孩子留下，让祖父母或外祖父母照顾，而他们只有在春节时才能回家，和孩子相处的时间很短。

• 人口老龄化

当代华人社会的另一个变化是人口老龄化。随着生活水平的提高和医疗条件的改善，人的寿命延长了；再加上出生率的下降，人口老龄化进程加快。现在，老人要么在家里由自己的孩子来照顾，要么去养老院由护工照顾。"养儿防老"的传统思想已发生了变化，不少老年父母不再坚持要子女在家供养自己，而愿意选择在养老院养老。

• 代沟

随着人的寿命延长，不同辈份之间的互相交往也多了。在不同时代出生长大的人们，他们的生活方式、行为举止、思想观念等，显然都会有很大的差异。这种"代沟"一向都有。然而，在科技巨变、信息爆炸的互联网时代，加之独生子女是历史上非常独特的一个群体，家庭中的代沟问题就凸显出来了。

- **家庭计划**

20世纪80年代推行的独生子女政策是为了控制人口增长，可是，现在由于老龄化开始影响中国的可持续发展，中国政府从 2016 年开始，放宽了独生子女政策，一对夫妻可以生两个孩子。虽然有了选择，可是不少年轻夫妻反而不愿生两个孩子，有的甚至不愿意生孩子。

Unit 1 focuses on family, covering topics such as family structures, generation gap, family planning, and ageing population.

• Family structures

In the last three decades, Chinese society has undergone many changes in population as well as in family structure, and the changes are ongoing. Since 1978 when the Chinese government implemented the one-child policy, the typical Chinese family structure has evolved to become small family units of two to three members.

The second type of structure is the single-parent family. In recent years the rate of divorce has gone up, leading to a rise in this type of family structure. Furthermore, according to recent statistics, a third type of structure is also on the increase, and that is grandparents-grandchildren families. The underlying cause for this is probably related to the change in the status of both sexes in Chinese society.

As men and women are treated more equally in modern Chinese society, both genders have equal opportunities to receive education and to enter into employment. The "traditional" role of women being the homemaker has begun to change to one in which women, like men, have aspirations to pursue their careers. There is a trend for husband and wife to share their responsibilities in supporting the family by bringing in money from work, as well as doing domestic chores at home.

However, when they have children, childcare becomes an issue. The wife may revert back to the homemaker role. Alternatively they may send their children to a nursery when they work during the day, and look after them when they come home from work. Couples who don't send their children to a nursery may have them looked after by their grandparents. As a result, grandparents-grandchildren families are quite common in the day time.

In the Chinese countryside, this type of family structure is also on the rise. The issue of childcare is more acute as many couples go to work in the cities. They leave behind their children for the grandparents to look after. They return home only for the Spring Festival, when they can only spend a short time with their children.

• Ageing population

Another change in contemporary Chinese societies is the ageing population. With improvements in living standards and health provision, life expectancy has increased. Coupled with the fall in the birth rate, the process of the ageing population in China has sped up rapidly. Elderly people are either looked after by their children at home or go into a care home to be looked after by carers. This change also reflects a shift from the traditional thinking of grown-up children taking care of their elderly parents to one in which the elderly parents are willing to choose to go into a nursing home.

• Generation gap

With the higher life expectancy, there is a higher likelihood for different generations to interact with each other. Obviously people born and brought up in different times have different lifestyles, behave and think differently. This kind of generation gap has always existed. However, in a world of fast technological changes and information explosion on the Internet, coupled with the unique historical existence of the onlychild, the issue of generation gap among families stands out even more.

• Family planning

The one-child policy in the 1980s was to control population growth in China. However, in view of the ageing population affecting the development of the country, the Chinese government relaxed the one-child policy in 2016, allowing couples to have two children. Although young couples have this choice now, many of them choose not to have two children, or not to have children at all.

1 我的家

短文一 Text One

现代家庭生活

一名妇女杂志的美国记者来到上海，想了解中国现代家庭的生活状况。今天她采访了一位在图书公司当编辑的陈女士。

记者：陈女士，您可以介绍一下自己的家庭吗？
陈：可以。我和我丈夫结婚八年了，我们有一个六岁的儿子。丈夫是设计师，儿子今年上一年级。
记者：你们每天的生活是怎样安排的？
陈：我们的生活节奏快极了！每天早上六点半我们就起床了，丈夫做早饭，我照顾儿子洗脸、刷牙、穿衣服。吃完早饭，丈夫送孩子到学校，我去上班。因为我早上班，就可以早一点儿下班。学校放学时，我就到学校接孩子，再到市场买菜。回到家先休息一会儿，然后我总是一边做饭，一边看孩子做作业。如果他有什么问题，我就给他讲解。丈夫七点才下班回家。晚饭后，他陪孩子温习功课，我就继续做家务。晚上也没有时间做休闲活动，因为我们都已经很累了。
记者：那么，周末你们都做些什么呢？
陈：周末上午，孩子要学钢琴，下午去体操班。我和丈夫就只能利用孩子上课外班的时间去打羽毛球、游泳或者逛街等。晚上有时候我们一家人会去看电影，或者在家看电视。
记者：谢谢您接受我的采访。

生词

妇女	fùnǚ	women
了解	liǎojiě	to understand
家庭	jiātíng	family
状况	zhuàngkuàng	situation; condition
编辑	biānjí	editor
节奏	jiézòu	rhythm
讲解	jiǎngjiě	to explain
才	cái	not until
陪	péi	to accompany
逛街	guàngjiē	to window-shop

R 读完上面的短文，回答下面的问题。Answer the following questions in Chinese.

1. 陈女士的工作是什么？
2. 陈女士的丈夫做什么工作？
3. 你认为陈女士夫妇每天的生活节奏怎么样？为什么？
4. 陈女士每天除了上班以外，还要做什么？请举例说说。
5. 陈女士夫妇什么时候才能做休闲活动？解释原因。

短文二 Text Two

单亲家庭

李海心和女儿王小玲住在台北。两年前海心跟丈夫离婚了。她的三个兄弟姐妹都在海外居住，见面的机会很少。海心在一家鞋店工作，店主对店员还算不错，知道海心是单亲妈妈，上下班时间可以让她自己选择，只要先跟店主说好了就行。

海心的女儿是中学三年级学生，学习成绩一直都很好，但是近来交了一些新朋友，海心觉得女儿的行为举止和思想观念都好像变了。她每晚都花很长时间在网上跟朋友聊天，周末又常常外出，也不告诉母亲她去哪里。

每当海心问她去哪里的时候，她总是说："不要你管，你不懂，也不明白我。"这真的让海心十分担心。幸好海心姐妹的孩子都比小玲大，她们都经历过子女青春期遇到的问题，所以海心可以跟她们谈谈。现在资讯发达，有什么事情，海心都会跟她们在网上沟通，请教处理方法，经常得到很有用的建议和支持。

生词

离婚	líhūn	to divorce
兄弟姐妹	xiōngdì jiěmèi	brothers and sisters; siblings
海外	hǎiwài	overseas
居住	jūzhù	to live; to reside
单亲	dānqīn	single parent
行为举止	xíngwéi jǔzhǐ	behaviour
思想观念	sīxiǎng guānniàn	thinking; concept
变	biàn	to change
幸好	xìnghǎo	luckily
经历	jīnglì	to experience
青春期	qīngchūn qī	puberty
遇到	yùdào	to encounter
资讯	zīxùn	information
发达	fādá	developed
请教	qǐngjiào	to ask for advice
处理	chǔlǐ	to deal with
建议	jiànyì	suggestion
支持	zhīchí	support

R 读完上面的短文，判断正误。Write True (T), False (F) or Not Mentioned in the text (NM) in the brackets.

1. 李海心住在上海。 （ ）
2. 李海心的丈夫在海外生活。 （ ）
3. 她的女儿王小玲是中学生。 （ ）
4. 王小玲的表哥和表姐不住在台湾。 （ ）
5. 李海心是一家鞋店的店主。 （ ）
6. 王小玲周末常常外出，李海心不知道她去哪里。 （ ）
7. 李海心会在网上跟她的姐妹谈关于子女青春期遇到的问题。 （ ）
8. 王小玲的学习成绩从来都不好。 （ ）

S 在短文一和短文二所介绍的家庭中，你认为哪一位父亲／母亲在教养子女方面最辛苦？为什么？
Which parent in Text One and Text Two has the most difficult time with their children? And why?

短文三　Text Three

生词		
照顾	zhàogù	to look after
会计师	kuàijìshī	accountant
收入	shōurù	income
减少	jiǎnshǎo	to reduce
工作量	gōngzuò liàng	workload
外佣	wàiyōng	foreign domestic helper
负责	fùzé	responsible
夫妻	fūqī	husband and wife
看望	kànwàng	to visit
郊外	jiāowài	countryside
辛苦	xīnkǔ	hard
实现	shíxiàn	to realise
追求	zhuīqiú	to pursue
事业	shìyè	career
愿望	yuànwàng	wishes
满意	mǎnyì	satisfactory

三代同堂

黄明英和她丈夫陈大新住在香港。他们有一儿一女，大新的父母也跟他们住在一起，帮着照顾孩子。明英和大新都是会计师，收入不错。为了减少父母的工作量，他们请了一位外佣，负责洗衣、做饭、打扫等家务。

这样，下班回家，夫妻就能有时间帮孩子温习功课，陪孩子玩。可是周末一到，主人要给外佣放假，父母也会去看望大新的姐妹，或者去郊外走走。明英夫妇就不得不自己照顾孩子，还要做家务，所以他们总说：周末比平时更忙！

不过，明英觉得他们的生活虽然很忙，也很辛苦，但是因为有父母和外佣的帮助，她能实现追求事业的愿望，所以她还是感到满意的。

R Highlight as many 词 as you can find in all three texts which are names of family members or relatives, e.g. 丈夫.

W Write down any 词或短句 from all three texts which have something to do with house chores and childminding.

S 在上面三篇短文所介绍的家庭中，你认为哪一家的生活最忙？哪一家的主人最辛苦？为什么？Which family in the three given texts has the busiest lifestyle? And why?

Unit One 家庭

Snippet

According to the Office for National Statistics in the UK, there were 18.9 million families in the UK in 2016, of which 12.7 million were married or civil partner couple families—the most common type of family structure. The second largest family type was the cohabiting couple family at 3.3 million families, followed by 2.9 million single-parent families.

根据英国国家统计局的统计，英国在 2016 年共有1890（一千八百九十）万个家庭，其中的1270（一千二百七十）万是夫妻或者法定伴侣——这是最普遍的家庭结构；第二大结构是同居伴侣，有330（三百三十）万；然后是单亲家庭，有290（二百九十）万。

Find similar statistics for your country and make a bar chart with your findings.

S Choose from the films 《请投我一票》and《天水围的日与夜》 for this exercise. Describe the family structures in the film you watch.

W Draw up a table and compare different aspects of lives in the different structures. Present your findings to the class in Chinese.

Film (please tick one): ☐《请投我一票》 ☐《天水围的日与夜》

Head of family	Structure type	Family member	Marital status	Number of children	Job of parents

句式学习

1. 为了……

The preposition 为了 is combined with a noun, pronoun, a subject-predicate phrase or other parts of speech to form a prepositional phrase. It functions as an adverbial modifier of purpose or cause. It may occur before a subject.

例句：❶ 为了健康，我们要少吃肉，多运动。
❷ 为了了解中国，这位美国记者来到了北京。
❸ 海心为了教育好青春期的女儿，经常上网请教自己的兄弟姐妹们。

2. 只要……就……

This is a conditional compound sentence. It can be used before the subject as well as after the subject, expressing the idea that so long as such a condition exists, the result may arise. But it does not exclude the possibility that some other condition may give rise to the same result.

例句：❶ 只要 + 不是周末或假期，他们每天早上六点半 + 就 + 要起床。

❷ 妈妈 + 只要 + 女儿的行为举止和思想观念变了，就 + 会担心。

3. Subject + 不得不 + (adverbial) verb

This is used to form the double negative sentence pattern to emphasise the action.

例句：❶ 海心离婚以后，什么事情都 + 不得不 + 自己处理。

❷ 放学时，陈女士要去学校接孩子回家，所以她 + 不得不 + 早点儿去上班。（早点儿 is used as an adverb here.）

4. Subject + 好像 + observation

This sentence structure can be used to express "seems". If it is used without a subject, it has the meaning of "it seems that..." in English. This could then be followed by an entire statement.

例句：❶ 她的兄弟姐妹 + 好像 + 都在海外居住。

❷ 好像 + 快要下雨了。

5. 才

In this sentence structure 才 is used to give the idea that an action or event happens only at a certain point in time but not before.

例句：王工程师的儿子身体不好，二十五岁 + 才 + 上大学。

练习

1. 请在三篇短文中找出用以上句式的句子。
2. 请用上面的句式造句。Make up sentences using the sentence patterns above.

S 口语练习

短文 在传统中国家庭中，通常都是"男主外，女主内"。丈夫在外工作赚钱养家，而妻子则在家做饭、打扫、照顾孩子。现在男女平等，特别是在城市里，很多夫妻白天都要工作。两人工作，家庭收入多了，可是下班回家做家务成了一个很大的负担。现在有些高收入家庭，妻子也会选择不出去工作，回归家庭。

Unit One 家庭

论点 夫妻两人都工作对家庭好。

1. 短文的主要意思是什么？
2. 根据短文，丈夫和妻子都工作会有什么问题？
3. "夫妻都工作对家庭好。"你同意这个论点吗？为什么？
4. 在有钱的家庭，妻子不出去工作。你觉得这样好吗？为什么？

W 写作练习

请写一篇 150 字左右的短文，可以考虑以下几点。

题目 成成的家

1. 在《请投我一票》中，成成是谁？
2. 他的家庭有几口人？父母做什么工作？
3. 你觉得他和父母的关系怎么样？

L 听力练习

1. 请听小英跟马克的一段对话，然后用中文回答下面的问题。
   ❶ 小英的妈妈什么时候生日？
   ❷ 小英准备怎样庆祝她妈妈的生日？
   ❸ 小英家有几口人？他们是谁？
   ❹ 小英的爸爸住在哪里？

2. Listen to the conversation again and summarise the make up of Mark's family in English. You are not required to write in full English sentences. You must give three details for question (a) and two details for question (b).
   (a) Summarise how many people there are in Mark's family and who they are.
   (b) Summarise what Mark said about buying birthday presents for the family.

G 词语练习

根据英文，选字组词。

采　问
访（　）　to visit
（　）访　to interview

医　刷
牙（　）　dentist
牙（　）　toothbrush

节　演
（　）奏　rhythm
（　）奏　to perform (play a musical instrument)

相　顾
照（　）　to take care of
照（　）　to take a photo

Chapter 1 我的家

继 连
(）续 to carry on
(）续 continuous

本 讯
资（ ） information
资（ ） capital (financial)

辑 主
编（ ） editor
（ ）编 editor-in-chief

结 离
（ ）婚 to marry
（ ）婚 divorce

念 看
观（ ） concept
观（ ） to watch

达 展
发（ ） to develop
发（ ） developed

国 书
（ ）籍 books
（ ）籍 nationality

弹 拉
（ ）钢琴 to play the piano
（ ）小提琴 to play the violin

G 选词填空

1. 意见　选择　建议　支持　帮助

在学校教师的（　　）下，大新的孩子（　　）参加了体操班。大新和他的妻子都特别（　　），希望自己的孩子不但学习好，同时身体也好。

2. 资料　资讯　沟通　发达　交通

现在的网络越来越（　　），大家在手机上可以看到很多新的（　　），跟居住在海外的朋友（　　）也方便极了。

T 翻译练习

1. Translate the following paragraph into English.

我家有五口人：爸爸、妈妈、姐姐、弟弟和我。爸爸每天一早就去上班，妈妈照顾我和弟弟吃完早饭以后，就先送我们上学，然后自己去上班。姐姐在大学读书，不住在家里，放假的时候才回家。

2. 把下面的一段文字翻译成中文。

My best friend Mark comes from a single-parent family. His parents divorced three years ago and he lives with his dad now. His dad is an engineer. He goes to work early every morning. Mark can look after himself. After breakfast, he takes a bus to school. He can even prepare dinner for his dad and himself in the evening.

11

2 三代人

短文一　Text One

- 外祖母：李美云
- 母亲：张家乐
- 外孙女：王清

■ 祖辈生涯

李美云今年88岁了。她有六个兄弟姐妹，婚姻都是父母包办的。自从结婚后，她就一直与丈夫住在北京胡同的一个四合院里，到现在有六七十年了。居住的房子已经有点儿破旧，左右邻居也都是普通劳动者，有理发的，有修车的。

她虽然生过五个孩子，但是过去的医疗条件不好，只活下来了两个。她丈夫以前开过一间杂货店，后来生意不好就关门了。美云只能通过帮人洗衣服、做家务来赚钱养家。

美云曾经生活在战争年代，还经历过不少政治运动，现在能够安享晚年，她感到十分幸福满足。她经常骄傲地说："我父母是大字不识的农民，我也是一个文盲，谁能想到我的后代都是大学生？！"

生词

婚姻	hūnyīn	marriage
包办	bāobàn	arranged
胡同	hútòng	lane; alley
四合院	sìhéyuàn	courtyard house
破旧	pòjiù	dilapidated
邻居	línjū	neighbour
普通	pǔtōng	ordinary
劳动者	láodòngzhě	manual worker
理发	lǐfà	have a haircut
修车	xiūchē	to repair cars
医疗条件	yīliáo tiáojiàn	medical condition
活	huó	to live (Here the sentence means "only two survived".)
开	kāi	to run (Here the sentence means "to own and run a business".)
杂货	záhuò	groceries
养家	yǎngjiā	to provide for the family
曾经	céngjīng	once before
战争	zhànzhēng	war
政治运动	zhèngzhì yùndòng	political movement
安享晚年	ānxiǎng wǎnnián	to enjoy old age
幸福	xìngfú	happy
骄傲	jiāoào	proud
农民	nóngmín	peasant
文盲	wénmáng	illiterate

短文二　Text Two

幸福的一代

张家乐是李美云的女儿，她和丈夫是在大学读书时相识相爱的。那时，大学毕业生的工作都是由国家负责分配的。她是一位化学工程师，丈夫是一位建筑师。他们在二十六岁时结婚，只有一个女儿。

现在他们住在一栋大楼的顶层公寓里，室内布置得非常现代化：一台电视机的大屏幕占了客厅墙的三分之一。每个人都很享受全家人在一起看电视的时间。

生词

相爱	xiāng'ài	to fall in love
负责	fùzé	be responsible for
分配	fēnpèi	to allocate
建筑师	jiànzhùshī	architect
一栋	yídòng	a block of (building)
顶层	dǐngcéng	top floor
公寓	gōngyù	apartment
布置	bùzhì	to decorate
屏幕	píngmù	screen
占	zhàn	to occupy
墙	qiáng	wall
享受	xiǎngshòu	to enjoy

短文三　Text Three

现代的年轻人

王清是张家乐的独生女儿，南京大学日语系的毕业生。她一毕业就被一家日本电脑公司聘用了，现在是推销部门的主任。她二十九岁结婚，丈夫是在一个电子产品展览会上认识的。她丈夫曾到英国留过学，现在是一家手机公司的总经理。

夫妻俩都不打算生儿育女。王清说："中国现在的年青人，在不久的将来，估计都需要供养四到六个老人。如果再生儿育女，负担实在太大了，不如做个'丁克族'！"

生词

独生	dúshēng	single child
系	xì	department (as in a university)
聘用	pìnyòng	to employ
推销	tuīxiāo	sales
部门	bùmén	department (as in a company)
主任	zhǔrèn	person in-charge
产品	chǎnpǐn	product
留学	liúxué	to study abroad
总经理	zǒngjīnglǐ	general manager
俩	liǎ	both
生儿育女	shēng'ér yùnǚ	to bear and rear children
负担	fùdān	burden
实在	shízài	really
丁克族	dīngkèzú	a group of people with double income and no kids

短文四 Text Four

代沟

王清每个月都会与外祖母和母亲见面，大家一起吃饭聊天。上一代对下一代有很多叮嘱，可是下一代不爱听，有时大家还会争论起来。

李美云：王清，看来你从来不打扫房间啊，到处都是乱七八糟的！家乐，你也不教教自己女儿应该怎样处世做人？唉！

张家乐：王清，你花钱花得实在太多了！买的东西全都不实用。你应该把钱存起来养老。还有，别每隔半年、一年就换工作，为什么不能安心在一个公司好好工作呢？

王　清：你们怎么这么唠叨？时代不同了，现在社会安定，条件好，有钱就要享受生活，难道要等自己老了，吃不动、玩不动了才享受吗？

生词

叮嘱	dīngzhǔ	to urge someone to do or not to do something
争论	zhēnglùn	to argue
乱七八糟	luànqī bāzāo	messy
处世做人	chǔshì zuòrén	to conduct oneself in society
实用	shíyòng	practical
存	cún	to save up (money)
养老	yǎnglǎo	to provide for old age
换	huàn	to change
安心	ānxīn	to settle down
唠叨	láodao	be garrulous
安定	āndìng	stable

R 读完四篇短文，回答下面的问题。Answer the following questions in Chinese.

1. 李美云和张家乐分别住在什么样的房子里？
2. 李美云和她丈夫是怎样赚钱养家的？
3. 列举出四篇短文中受过教育的人物。
4. 张家乐和王清的职业分别是什么？

R 读完四篇短文，在下面每句的括号里写出正确的答案。
Write True (T), False (F) or Not Mentioned in the text (NM) in the brackets.

1. 李美云现在有两个子女。　　　　　　　　　　　　（　）
2. 李美云的邻居是店主。　　　　　　　　　　　　　（　）
3. 这三代人都受过高等教育。　　　　　　　　　　　（　）
4. 张家乐的丈夫是电脑工程师。　　　　　　　　　　（　）
5. 王清是一家日本公司的职员。　　　　　　　　　　（　）
6. 王清和她丈夫是在英国认识的。　　　　　　　　　（　）
7. 李美云每个月都跟她女儿和外孙女见面。　　　　　（　）
8. 王清的丈夫在一家手机公司工作。　　　　　　　　（　）

Chapter 2 三代人

R Highlight as many 词 which have something to do with family relationships as you can find in the text, e.g 丈夫.

R Highlight any 词或短句 which have something to do with either past history or the modern world.

W / S The three generations of women are quite different in many respects. List as many of them as you can, then compare and discuss your list in the class.

S Who uses the following comments to describe whom?
1. 不懂得享受美好的生活。
2. 忽略了家务活。
3. 浪费金钱。
4. 不忠于雇主。
5. 忽略了对孩子的教导。
6. 太担心未来的生活。

What other differences are there between different generations? For example, how they see the past, the present time, and the future. How about their lifestyles?
◆ 她们对过去、现在及将来的生活有什么看法？
◆ 她们的生活方式是怎样的？

S Find out from your grandparents and parents how they used to live. Draw up a table and compare different aspects of life in the two different societies. Present your findings to the class in Chinese.

	Family	Education	Marriage	Job	Outlook in life
爷爷	Lived with his parents and grandparents and had 7 siblings	None	Arranged by parents	Worked in a shop	Earned enough money to support the family

15

Unit One 家庭

 《四世同堂》, written by a very famous Chinese writer 老舍 (Lao She), is a novel about a family of four generations, all living under the same roof. Do you think different generations living together is common in the modern world? What advantages or disadvantages do you think there are to this way of living? Write down at least two points for each in Chinese.

Advantages	Disadvantages

 你赞成这种居住方式吗？为什么？如果可以选择，你会选择跟父母和祖辈一起住吗？为什么？

句式学习

1. **自（从）……后，便／就……**
   To indicate that since the happening of something, it has been....
   例句：自从园丁生病后，花园里的花草就一直没有人管理。

2. **分数 Fractions**
   Numeration of fractions normally follows the pattern "X 分之 Y", where "X" is the denominator and "Y" is the numerator. For example, 1/10 means 十分之一, 2/3 means 三分之二.
   例句：中国人口占世界总人口的五分之一。

3. **百分比**
   Percentage is read as "百分之 × ". For example, 95% means 百分之九十五.
   例句：中国现在的文盲人口不到百分之八。

4. **"全"和"所有、都"的不同用法**
   "全" has the meaning of whole or all.
   例句：全家人去参观电子展览会。
   You can also say 所有家人都去参观电子展览会 or 家人都去参观电子展览会；however, you can't use 都 to modify a noun, so you can't say 都家人去参观电子展览会.

5. **是……的**
   This sentence pattern is used to emphasise the time, place or manner of

an action which took place in the past. 是 is placed before the word group which is emphasised.

例句：存钱为了将来养老用。

But to emphasise the purpose of saving up money, you can say 存钱是为了将来养老用的。（目的 purpose）

例句：❶ 独生子女政策是1978年开始的。（时间 time）
　　　❷ 总经理是从电脑公司来的。（地点 place）
　　　❸ 他是坐地铁上班的。（方式 manner of action）

6. "被"字句

In Chinese, a sentence in which the predicate verb is preceded by the phrases 被, 让 or 叫 + object is called the 被-sentence. The subject of 被-sentence is the receiver of an action.

例句：❶ 这辆汽车被那位工人修好了。
　　　❷ 她被一家建筑公司聘用了。

7. 难道

This phrase is used to give force to a rhetorical question.

例句：❶ 你们这代人都是独生子女，难道你不是吗？
　　　❷ 你的房间乱七八糟的，难道你从来不打扫吗？

练习

1. 请在四篇短文中找出用以上句式的句子。
2. 请用上面的句式造句。Make up sentences using the sentence patterns above.

S 口语练习

短文 最近有一个关于"代沟"的调查发现，大部分学生觉得父母太唠叨，有76%的学生表示在穿衣服的问题上跟父母有代沟。比如，有的学生买了时尚的牛仔裤，父母不理解为什么新裤子上有这么多破洞。超过一半的学生表示喜欢用零用钱买自己喜欢的东西，可是父母希望他们买有用的东西。学生们最不能接受的是父母偷看自己的日记和微信等。

论点 产生代沟的责任在父母。

1. 短文的主要意思是什么？
2. 根据短文，学生对父母的哪些方面不满意？
3. "产生代沟的责任在父母。"你同意这个论点吗？为什么？
4. 中国传统观念认为子女应该听从父母的，你同意吗？为什么？

Unit One 家庭

W 写作练习

请写一篇 150 字左右的短文，可以考虑以下几点。

题目 英子的家

1. 在《爸爸的花儿落了》中，英子的家里有几口人？
2. 英子的家里是谁做家务的？
3. 英子和爸爸的关系怎么样？

L 听力练习

1. 请听小英跟她妈妈的一段对话，然后用中文回答下面的问题。
   ❶ 小英的爷爷什么时候过生日？
   ❷ 小英的妈妈打算怎样庆祝他的生日？
   ❸ 小英有什么反应？
   ❹ 小英后来有什么建议？

2. Listen to the conversation again and summarise the reasons given by Xiao Ying about her work in English. You are not required to write in full sentences. You must give three details for question (a) and two details for question (b).
   (a) Summarise the tasks Xiao Ying has to do on a daily basis.
   (b) Summarise the tasks Xiao Ying has to do in general.

G 词语练习

根据英文，选字组词。

姻 服 礼

婚（　） wedding
婚（　） marriage
婚（　） wedding dress

民 住 留

居（　） to reside
居（　） resident
居（　） to live

近 座 居

邻（　） neighbour
邻（　） nearby
邻（　） adjacent seat

药 疗 科

医（　） medical courses
医（　） medical treatment
医（　） medicine

理 筑 正

修（　） to repair
修（　） to revise
修（　） to construct

文 色 眼

（　）盲 colour blindness
（　）盲 illiteracy
（　）盲 blindness

曾　已　圣
(　) 经　Bible
(　) 经　once before
(　) 经　already

家　育　父
养 (　)　adoptive father
养 (　)　to bring up
养 (　)　to keep family

老龄　城市　现代
(　) 化　urbanization
(　) 化　aging
(　) 化　modernisation

屏　闭　开
(　) 幕　opening
(　) 幕　closing
(　) 幕　screen

责　担　重
负 (　)　be responsible for
负 (　)　to bear a burden
负 (　)　burden

主　用　员
雇 (　)　to employ
雇 (　)　employer
雇 (　)　employee

G 选词填空

快乐　分配　布置　享受　推销　部门　买卖

王小安在一家电脑公司工作。她是一位 (　) 经理，除了需要给其他职工 (　) 工作，还要负责 (　) 公司的电脑产品。她住在市中心的一栋公寓里，客厅 (　) 得又漂亮又现代，她很 (　) 现在的生活，感到很满足。

T 翻译练习

1. Translate the following paragraph into English.

    根据一些心理学家的分析，代沟的出现，很多时候是因为父母对子女管得太多，例如在听音乐、穿衣服、交朋友、读书和选择职业等方面，父母过分担心，让子女觉得没有自由。

2. 把下面的一段文字翻译成中文。

    A well-known family counsellor suggests some ideas for closing the generation gap. She says regular communication is the key. If parents and their children communicate and share life experiences with each other regularly, they can maintain a much better relationship among themselves.

family counsellor:
家庭调解师 Jiātíng tiáojiěshī;
家庭辅导员 Jiātíng fǔdǎoyuán

3 无奈的"小皇帝"

短文一　Text One

计划生育政策

爸爸妈妈
爷爷奶奶　　外公外婆

中国政府在20世纪80年代大力推行计划生育，鼓励一对夫妻只生一个孩子，并且为独生子女提供各种福利。这项政策取得了很大的成效，但是独生子女的教育却成为一个严重的问题。

"小皇帝"这个词是指那些被宠坏了的孩子，其中多半是独生子女。

生词

政府	zhèngfǔ	government
大力	dàlì	vigorously
推行	tuīxíng	to pursue
计划生育	jìhuà shēngyù	family planning
福利	fúlì	benefit
项	xiàng	(a measure word)
政策	zhèngcè	policy
成效	chéngxiào	result; effect
教育	jiàoyù	education
严重	yánzhòng	serious
小皇帝	xiǎo huángdì	little emperor
宠坏	chǒnghuài	to spoil (a child)
独生子女	dúshēng zǐnǚ	only child

Snippet

The Chinese government began its birth control policy in 1978. Posters of different designs were used in this mass campaign to encourage people to practise birth control. Look at poster number 1: its caption is 实行计划生育，贯彻基本国策. The message is to get the people to think of the country's well-being. Now look at the three posters on the next page and discuss in the class what methods the Chinese government used to try to achieve its aim.

生词

控制	kòngzhì	to control
快速	kuàisù	rapid

20

Chapter 3 无奈的"小皇帝"

为了控制人口快速增长，中国政府在1978年开始实施计划生育政策，鼓励人民少生孩子。看这些宣传海报，说说当时中国政府是怎么鼓励人民计划生育的。

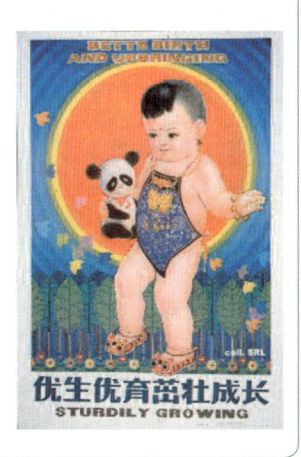

短文二 Text Two

地铁报 第240期 2010年8月20日
地址：东海市三角街商业大厦84号5楼
电话：1839450

四二一综合症日益严重

李天明

30多年来，由于计划生育政策，中国产生了一个特别的人群——独生子女。

这些独生子女有祖父母、外祖父母和父母共同的宠爱，没有跟兄弟姐妹相处的机会。他们中间出现了"小皇帝""小公主"。有的衣来伸手、饭来张口，什么家务也不会做，也不愿意学着做；有的认为别人对他们好是应该的，养成了自私任性、以自我为中心的性格；有的吃得太好，营养过剩，得了肥胖症；有的只能接受表扬，受不了批评；有的从小缺少一起玩耍的兄弟姐妹和其他同龄人，产生了孤独自闭的心理问题……专家把这些毛病叫作"四二一综合症"。

根据最近一项社会调查报告，这一群体的"四二一综合症"不但影响了他们自身的健康成长，还影响了他们的学习、工作、婚姻和家庭等。

生词

综合症	zōnghézhèng	syndrome
日益	rìyì	increasingly
产生	chǎnshēng	to produce; to come into being
人群	rénqún	group
相处	xiāngchǔ	to get along with
公主	gōngzhǔ	princess
伸手	shēnshǒu	to stretch out one's hand
张口	zhāngkǒu	to open one's mouth
养成	yǎngchéng	to form (a habit)
自私	zìsī	selfish
任性	rènxìng	wilful
性格	xìnggé	personality
营养	yíngyǎng	nutrition
过剩	guòshèng	excess; surplus
肥胖症	féipàngzhèng	obesity
表扬	biǎoyáng	praise
批评	pīpíng	criticism
缺少	quēshǎo	lack of
同龄人	tónglíngrén	peer
孤独自闭	gūdú zìbì	solitary; unsociable
心理	xīnlǐ	mentality
毛病	máobìng	trouble; shortcoming
根据	gēnjù	according to
调查	diàochá	survey
自身	zìshēn	oneself

Unit One 家庭

短文三 Text Three

海外华文报 2016年4月16日

中国政府放宽独生子女政策

中国政府在20世纪80年代推行的计划生育政策，虽然收到了控制人口快速增长的成效，暂时缓解了社会的医疗、教育和就业等压力，让不少家长可以用全部的精力与财力来培养一个孩子。这些孩子得到的照顾和教育通常比多子女家庭的好。可是，现在发现，"四二一综合症"不但影响了孩子的成长，而且对社会的负面影响也比较大。

再加上现在面临着人口老龄化对中国经济发展的影响，中国政府在2016年初改变了计划生育政策，准许每对夫妻生两个孩子。不过，一些年轻夫妇现在习惯了享受高收入、又不用养育孩子的好处，他们很多都选择不生孩子，加入丁克族，追求事业的发展。

生词

放宽	fàngkuān	to relax
暂时	zànshí	temporarily
缓解	huǎnjiě	to alleviate
就业	jiùyè	employment
精力	jīnglì	energy
培养	péiyǎng	to nurture; to foster
负面	fùmiàn	negative
面临	miànlín	be faced with
老龄化	lǎolínghuà	ageing
经济	jīngjì	economy
准许	zhǔnxǔ	to allow
养育	yǎngyù	to raise (a child)

R 读完三篇短文，回答下面的问题。Answer the following questions in Chinese.

1. 中国政府在20世纪80年代推行的计划生育政策是什么？取得了什么成效？
2. 独生子女政策带来了什么问题？
3. "四二一综合症"的具体表现是怎样的？
4. 《地铁报》文章的作者李天明认为"四二一综合症"带来了什么后果？
5. 你对李天明的说法有什么看法？为什么？
6. 中国政府在2016年推行了什么生育政策？为什么？

R 读完两篇报纸文章，在下面每句的括号里写出正确的答案。
Write True (T), False (F) or Not Mentioned in the text (NM) in the brackets.

1. 一项社会调查报告说独生子女经常生病。 ( )
2. "四二一"指的是祖父母、外祖父母，再加上父母。 ( )
3. 独生子女都想做家务，可是父母不让他们做。 ( )
4. 独生子女容易发胖，因为他们吃得太好，营养过剩。 ( )
5. 现在的年轻夫妇很多都选择不生孩子，要把精力放在事业上。 ( )
6. 独生子女都有"以自我为中心"的性格。 ( )
7. 中国政府为独生子女家庭提供各种福利。 ( )
8. 从2016年开始，中国政府给每个家庭生孩子的自由。 ( )

S Both《请投我一票》and《天水围的日与夜》have an only child in the films. Describe the behaviour and lifestyle of each of them. Do you think they match the descriptions of the "四二一综合症"? Discuss in the class which child matches the descriptions most closely.

S 你认为独生子女政策与二孩政策各有什么优点或者缺点？在课上讨论一下，然后用中文填写下面的表格。

W

	优点	缺点
80年代的独生子女政策		
2016年的二孩政策		

W Write an eye-catching caption in Chinese for a poster for each of the following subjects:
1. Discourage women from having children too early in life.
2. Extoll the virtues of women staying at home to look after children.
3. Extoll the virtues of women having independent financial means.
4. Encourage female students to study science.
5. Encourage male students to study childcare.

句式学习

1. **不但……并且……** furthermore

   It usually indicates a coordinate compound sentence.

   例句：30多年前，中国政府<u>不但</u>推行计划生育政策，<u>并且</u>提倡晚婚晚育。

2. **不但……而且……** not only, but also

   In a progressive compound sentence, the second clause is a step further from what is said in the first.

   例句：目前中国的大城市里，有些夫妻<u>不但</u>不生两个孩子，<u>而且</u>有的连一个孩子都不愿意生。

3. **让／叫／请 + somebody to do something**

   In Chinese, there is a kind of sentence with a verbal predicate composed of two verbal constructions, in which the object of the first verb is at the same time the subject of the following verb. Such sentences are called pivotal sentences.

Unit One 家庭

例句：❶ 有些父母不让孩子做家务。
　　　❷ 妈妈说现在政策变了，叫女儿再生一个孩子。
　　　❸ 张老师请班长候选人表演才艺。

4. **由于**

　　由于 means the same as 因为, to indicate reason and combine with 所以.

　　例句：**1a** 由于中国人口老龄化，所以社区需要有更多的居家养老中心。
　　　　　1b 因为中国人口老龄化，所以社区需要有更多的居家养老中心。
　　　　　However, 由于 can combine with 因此、因而；but 因为 cannot.
　　　　　❷ 由于有些独生子女缺乏团队精神，因此不能与别人合作。

5. **Verb + 不得**

　　Complement placed after a verb to express impossibility or inability; cannot; be unable to.

　　例句：有些年青人听 + 不得 + 别人的批评。

6. **动词重叠**

　　Verbs denoting actions can be duplicated. This is usually used when one wishes to indicate that the action is of very short duration.

　　例句：❶ 请你说说"四二一综合症"的病征是什么。
　　　　　❷ 妈妈，让我试试怎么用洗衣机吧。

练习

1. 请在三篇短文中找出用以上句式的句子。
2. 请用上面的句式造句。Make up sentences using the sentence patterns above.

S 口语练习

短文 中国的独生子女，尤其是 90 后，他们是在中国经济快速发展的时代出生长大的。很多人在家里什么家务也不用做。有的子女希望学习做饭、打扫房间，父母也不同意。一般来说，他们的任务就是好好学习，将来有个好工作。只要这样，父母就满意了。

　　可是专家说，从小做家务可以让孩子提高动手能力，降低学习压力，跟父母更加亲近。

论点 孩子应该学习做家务。

1. 短文的主要意思是什么？
2. 根据短文，有的父母为什么不同意孩子做家务？
3. "孩子应该学习做家务。"你同意这个论点吗？为什么？
4. "孩子做家务可以跟父母更加亲近。"你同意吗？为什么？

W 写作练习

请写一篇 150 字左右的短文，可以考虑以下几点。

题目 成成的家

1. 在纪录片《请投我一票》中，成成是谁？
2. 他妈妈在他竞选班长中起了什么作用？
3. 他身上有哪些独生子女的特点？

L 听力练习

1. 听四位朋友谈他们做独生子女的经验和感受，然后用中文回答下面的问题。
   ① 陈明亮为什么说他的压力很大？
   ② 王小玲的妈妈担心什么？
   ③ 李大山的父母认为什么最重要？
   ④ 张莉的爷爷奶奶在家是怎样照顾她的？

2. Listen to this Chinese podcast about only children again and summarise the feelings of these four friends. You are not required to write in full English sentences. You must give three details for question (a) and two details for question (b).
   (a) Summarise how Chen Mingliang, Wang Xiaoling and Li Dashan feel about being only children.
   (b) Summarise why Zhang Li says she enjoys being an only child.

G 词语练习

根据英文，选字组词。

综　肥胖　自闭

(　) 症　syndrome
(　) 症　autism
(　) 症　obesity

扬　现　演

表 (　)　performance
表 (　)　behaviour
表 (　)　praise

许　备　确

准 (　)　to prepare
准 (　)　accurate
准 (　)　to allow

调　检　看

(　) 查　survey
(　) 查　to check
查 (　)　to look over

营　育　培

养 (　)　to raise (a child)
(　) 养　nutrition
(　) 养　to nurture

剩　节　河

过 (　)　to celebrate a festival
过 (　)　to cross a river
过 (　)　excess

Unit One 家庭

独 儿 单

孤（　）loneliness
孤（　）alone
孤（　）orphan

过 济 验

经（　）economy
经（　）to pass by
经（　）experience

正 负 临

（　）面 positive
（　）面 negative
面（　）be faced with

就 事 毕

（　）业 career
（　）业 employment
（　）业 graduation

治 策 府

政（　）government
政（　）policy
政（　）politics

少 点 课

缺（　）be absent from a lesson
缺（　）shortcoming
缺（　）be short of

G 选词填空

1. 让　要　的　得　从　为

现在很多（　）中国来（　）留学生都是独生子女。在英国，他们（　）自己做饭，可是常常做（　）不太好吃。他们真的需要培养自立能力。

2. 推广　推行　鼓励　日益　福利　幸福

中国政府应对（　）严重的人口老龄化问题，从 2016 年开始（　）二孩政策。为了（　）年轻的夫妻生两个孩子，还给生二孩的夫妻提供一项（　），那就是增加生育假期。

T 翻译练习

1. Translate the following paragraph into English.

张马田家有父母，还有爷爷、奶奶，可是没有兄弟姐妹。他是独生子女，常常觉得很孤独。每天一放学，他就去兴趣班，星期一是画画，星期二是拉小提琴，星期三是打篮球……总之每天都要去，他觉得很累。有时候他真想有一个弟弟或妹妹，可以一起在家玩耍。

2. 把下面的一段文字翻译成中文。

Mary lives in London with her parents and an older sister, Lily. She is very glad that she is not an only child because she loves having an older sister who looks after her when her parents are out. They get on very well together. Lily helps her with her homework. She also reads with her and talks about the stories in the books. Lily can play the piano very well and she teachs Mary to sing while she plays.

26

4 中国社会的老龄化

短文一 Text One

■ 退休一族

黄山和李林一退休就去报名读老年大学了。黄山参加了书法班，李林参加了摄影班。他们没有上过大学，但是相信"活到老，学到老"，希望退休以后还能圆一个梦，圆一个大学梦。

他们有空时，在院子里除了种花草以外，还种了一些青菜、香菜和西红柿，红红绿绿的，又好看，又好吃。

晚上，黄山喜欢和朋友们一块打太极拳，或者下棋、打麻将；李林却爱逛商店，或者跳广场舞。她说，跳舞不但是让人放松的娱乐活动，也是锻炼身体的一个好办法。

黄山和李林有时候会和朋友们一起去外地旅游。最近，他们正在准备出国看世界，去了解不同的文化。

随着生活水平的提高，思想观念的改变，老人退休后不只是买菜做饭，照顾孙子、孙女了，他们的晚年生活变得丰富多彩起来了。

生词		
社会	shèhuì	society
退休	tuìxiū	to retire
报名	bàomíng	to enrol
摄影	shèyǐng	photography
圆梦	yuánmèng	to make a dream come true
种	zhòng	to grow
香菜	xiāngcài	coriander
西红柿	xīhóngshì	tomato
打太极拳	dǎ tàijí quán	to practise Tai Chi
下棋	xiàqí	to play chess
打麻将	dǎ májiāng	to play Mahjong
放松	fàngsōng	to relax
娱乐	yúlè	entertainment
锻炼	duànliàn	to exercise
外地	wàidì	parts of the country other than where one is
随着	suízhe	in pace with; in the wake of
丰富多彩	fēngfù duōcǎi	rich and varied

R Highlight in the text as many 短语 as you can, which are to do with common activities pensioners do, e.g. 上老年大学.

Unit One 家庭

短文二 Text Two

谈"养儿防老"

很久以来，中国人一直有一个传统观念，那就是"养儿防老"。父母有养育子女的责任，子女长大成人以后，也有照顾父母老年生活的义务。因此，过去还有"多子多福"的说法。子女越多，父母越幸福。

根据最新的统计，目前中国60岁以上的老人已经超过两亿，而且老龄化的进程正在不断加快，估计到2030年，中国60岁以上的老人会占全国人口的四分之一。

现在大多数家庭都是独生子女，夫妻两人除了要外出工作，养育自己的孩子以外，如果还要照顾双方家庭的老人，几乎是不可能的事情了。

不能"养儿防老"，那么父母老了，特别是当他们失去了生活自理能力以后，应该怎么办呢？

生词

养儿防老	yǎng'ér fánglǎo	to have children to prepare for old age
传统	chuántǒng	traditional
养育	yǎngyù	to bring up; to rear
责任	zérèn	responsibility
义务	yìwù	obligation
多子多福	duōzǐ duōfú	the more children, the more benefits
统计	tǒngjì	statistics
目前	mùqián	at present
亿	yì	a hundred million
进程	jìnchéng	process
不断	búduàn	continuous
加快	jiākuài	to quicken
估计	gūjì	to reckon
双方	shuāngfāng	both sides
几乎	jīhū	almost
失去	shīqù	to lose
自理	zìlǐ	to take care of oneself

R 读完短文一和短文二，回答下面的问题。Answer the following questions in Chinese.

1. 在第一段短文里，黄山和李林夫妇有什么梦想？
2. 黄山和李林各有什么爱好？
3. 根据第二段短文，谈谈中国家庭有什么传统观念？
4. 目前60岁以上的老人有多少？

W In your country / region where you live, what do elderly people do when they are unable to look after themselves? Make a list of the services available to them in Chinese. Compare your list with your classmates'.
在你的国家／你住的地区，那些没有自理能力的老年人怎么照顾自己？请用中文列出专为他们而设的服务，并在课堂上跟你的同学交流一下，然后互相做比较。

S Make a list of activities which you think are suitable for pensioners. Present this list to the class in Chinese. Discuss which ones are for exercising the brain and which ones are for exercising the body.

短文三　Text Three

老年人的前景

张雨是一位服装设计师，她工作忙极了。她的丈夫经常出差，儿子在一间住宿学校上学。她70多岁的母亲一个人住，最近身体没有以前好了。

张雨了解到，目前中国主要有居家养老、家庭养老和机构养老三种方式。因为独生子女面临的问题，家庭养老很难做到，而机构养老，包括养老院、老年公寓和托老所，床位少，不容易进。

她母亲所在社区的"居家养老服务中心"介绍说，年满60岁以上的独居老人可以申请"居家养老"服务，费用大约是她母亲退休工资的三分之二。每天有服务人员送热菜、热饭上门，帮助做些家务。如果老人生病了，他们还会派医护人员来打针、送药、量血压等。

现在张雨的母亲住在自己的家里，平时有人照顾，女儿一有空就去看望母亲。母女俩对居家养老都非常满意。

生词

服装	fúzhuāng	clothing
出差	chūchāi	be away on official business
住宿学校	zhùsù xuéxiào	boarding school
居家	jūjiā	stay-at-home
机构	jīgòu	organisation
方式	fāngshì	way
养老院	yǎnglǎo yuàn	old people's home
托老所	tuōlǎosuǒ	care centre for elderly people
床位	chuáng wèi	bed space
独居	dújū	to live alone
上门	shàng mén	to be delivered to the home
派	pài	to send
医护人员	yīhù rén yuán	medical staff
打针	dǎzhēn	to give injection
量血压	liáng xuè yā	to take blood pressure

W 你认为哪些福利／服务对老年人有帮助？在你的国家／你住的地区有这些福利和服务吗？请用中文把这些列出来，比较一下。
What benefits / services do you think would be good for elderly people? In your country / region where you live, are there such benefits / services? Make a list of each of the above in Chinese and compare.

R 读完上面三篇短文，在下面每句的括号里写出正确的答案。
Write True (T), False (F) or Not Mentioned in the text (NM) in the brackets.

1. 黄山和李林都是大学毕业生。　　　　　　　　　　　　（　　）
2. 黄山和李林不但种花草，还种菜。　　　　　　　　　　（　　）
3. 现在中国退休老人的生活丰富多彩。　　　　　　　　　（　　）
4. 中国一直有"多子多福"的传统观念。　　　　　　　　（　　）
5. 中国60岁以上的老人已经有两亿了。　　　　　　　　　（　　）

Unit One 家庭

6. 张雨是位服装设计师，经常要出差。　　　　　　　　　　（　）
7. 张雨的母亲是一位独居老人。　　　　　　　　　　　　　（　）
8. 目前，在中国要住进养老院很难。　　　　　　　　　　　（　）

Snippet

重阳节

农历九月初九是中国的传统节日——重阳节。中国人认为数字"六"是阴，"九"是阳，两个"九"就是"重阳"了。因为"九"跟"久"发音一样，有长久、长寿的意思。

1988年，中国政府把这一天定为"老人节"，希望全社会都能有尊敬老人、爱护老人、帮助老人的好风气。

这天，人们有吃重阳糕、喝菊花酒、登高望远、观赏菊花等习俗和活动。

The 9th day of the 9th month in the lunar calendar is the traditional Chinese Chong Yang Festival (重阳节). Chinese people think that the number "six" is Yin (representing the moon), and "nine" is Yang (representing the sun). Putting two nines together becomes "double Yang", which is called Chong Yang. Because "nine" has the same pronunciation as "long time" in Chinese, Chinese people like to use it to mean "longevity".

In 1988 the Chinese government named this day "Old People's Day", hoping that the good practice of respecting, caring for and helping elderly people would be developed.

On this day, Chinese people customarily eat Chong Yang cake, drink chrysanthemum wine, go up mountains to see views, and enjoy the chrysanthemum flowers, etc.

句式学习

1. 一……就…… as soon as...
   This is a successive compound sentence. Each clause tells that some actions and things have taken place in successive order. This order of each clause is definite and cannot be reversed.
   例句：老人<u>一</u>失去自理能力，<u>就</u>有医护人员照顾他。

2. 却 but, however, yet
   却 means the same as 可是，但是 or 不过 to express "but" "however" "yet".

However, they are used differently in the structure of a sentence.

A. If the subjects in both clauses of a sentence are different, 却 cannot come before a subject:

例句：❶ 很多<u>退休老人</u>喜欢跳广场舞，<u>她</u>却不喜欢。(You cannot say 却她不喜欢。)

But if 可是，但是，or 不过 is used, it comes before the subject.

❷ 很多<u>退休老人</u>喜欢跳广场舞，但是 / 可是 / 不过<u>她</u>不喜欢。(ou cannot say 她但是 / 可是 / 不过不喜欢。)

B. Both clauses of a sentence share the same subject:

❸ 她希望进养老院，却 / 但是 / 可是 / 不过没有找到合适的房间。

3. 随着…… along with…

例句：随着中国社会的老龄化，每个社区都需要"居家养老服务中心"。

4. A 没有 B + adjective

This type of comparison is used in negative sentences to indicate the extent to which two things are dissimilar.

例句：❶ 她父亲 + 没有 + 她母亲健康。

❷ 以前退休老人的生活 + 没有 + 现在的丰富多彩。

5. Adjective + 起来了 is getting + adjective

例句：养老院服务好 + 起来了。

练习

1. 请在三篇短文中找出用以上句式的句子。
2. 请用上面的句式造句。Make up sentences using the sentence patterns above.

S 口语练习

短文 中国传统的三代同住、四世同堂的家庭越来越少了。分开居住的子女由于工作忙，家务多，不能常回家看望父母。没有子女在身边的老人感到特别孤独。中国政府在 2013 年 7 月 1 日推出了一项新政策，规定家庭成员应该关心老年人的精神需要，成年子女必须常回家看望年老的父母。

31

Unit One 家庭

论点 子女应该常回家看望父母。

1. 短文的主要意思是什么？
2. 根据短文，现在的子女为什么不能常回家看看父母？
3. "子女应该常回家看望父母。"你同意这个论点吗？为什么？
4. "养儿防老"是中国人的传统观念，你同意吗？为什么？

W 写作练习

请写一篇 150 字左右的短文，可以考虑以下几点。

题目 谈谈梁婆婆

1. 在《天水围的日与夜》中，梁婆婆是谁？
2. 她的家庭是什么类型的？
3. 你觉得她的老年生活可怜吗？

L 听力练习

1. 请听大海跟他母亲的一段对话，然后用中文回答下面的问题。
   ❶ 为什么大海今天去看他妈妈？
   ❷ 大海的母亲觉得养老院怎么样？
   ❸ 大海的母亲爱好什么？
   ❹ 大海下个周末会和谁一起来看望母亲？

2. Listen to the conversation again and summarise the details given by Dahai's mother about her life in the nursing home. You are not required to write in full English sentences. You must give two details for question (a) and two details for question (b).
   (a) Summarise Dahai's mother's opinions about the nursing home.
   (b) Summarise the hobbies of Dahai's mother and her friends.

G 词语练习

根据英文，选字组词。

倒　休　步

退（　）　to retire
退（　）　to regress
（　）退　to go backward

摄　电　倒

（　）影　movie
（　）影　reflection
（　）影　photography

娱　快　音

（　）乐　music
（　）乐　happy
（　）乐　entertainment

时　地　着

随（　）　everywhere
随（　）　along with
随（　）　at any time

Chapter 4　中国社会的老龄化

会　区　团		家　义　任	
社（　）	society	（　）务	obligation
社（　）	community	（　）务	housework
社（　）	community group	（　）务	task

自　整　总		独　家　民	
（　）理	to take care of oneself	居（　）	resident
（　）理	Prime Minister	（　）居	to live alone
（　）理	to sort out	居（　）	to live at home

构　会　动		圆　做　想	
机（　）	organisation	（　）梦	to make the dream come true
机（　）	opportunity	（　）梦	to dream
机（　）	power-driven	梦（　）	a dream

G 选词填空

负责　托老　托儿　随着　出差　责任

李阳在一家药厂当经理，工作的（　　）非常重，经常要到外地（　　），有时候还要出国开会。

李阳妻子工作的公司离家不是很远，每天都是她送孩子去（　　）所，晚上再接孩子回家。

李阳的父亲一直跟他们一起住，现在年龄也越来越大了，一个人在家觉得很无聊，他希望去（　　）所。

T 翻译练习

1. Translate the following paragraph into English.

    这所老年大学有电脑班、书法班、摄影班和太极拳班等，其中电脑班特别受欢迎。老人们可以学习怎么上网买东西、看新闻，怎么用手机拍照、写信等。大家都觉得这样的退休生活丰富多彩。

2. 把下面的一段文字翻译成中文。

    In the past, young people would live with their parents after they got married. Their parents could help look after their children. When the parents became old and needed help, they could be looked after by the young couple.

    However, nowadays most young people send their children to a nursery. Elderly people are also willing to live by themselves and have their own lives.

33

第二单元　教育与工作

　　这个单元覆盖了有关学校生活、学生、工作机会，以及工作和生活的平衡等议题。

　　中国的入学年龄是六周岁。从 1986 年开始实施九年义务教育。公立中小学的入学，是根据学生家庭住址所属地区来进行分配的。截至 2016 年，收费的私立民办中学和国际学校已经占到中国中学的 10%。

　　中国每年都有 900 多万学生参加高考（相当于英国 13 年级末的 A-Level 考试），能不能进大学，能进什么样的大学，最后都主要由高考成绩决定。中国大学有重点和普通之分，现在也出现了民办大学以及中外合办的大学。

• 学校生活和学生

　　中国学生普遍学习刻苦，基础知识好。在国际奥林匹克学科大赛与国际学生能力评估中，中国学生经常得奖并获得很多好评。但他们也付出了很大的代价：作业负担重，考试压力大，没有时间做其他的事情。中国学生常被认为"脱离社会实践"和"缺乏创造性思维"。根据世界卫生组织 2017 年的调查报告，中国青少年的近视率高居世界第一。长期以来，学校、家庭乃至社会，大多以考试成绩来衡量学生的好坏，造成了一部分青少年焦虑、消沉、自卑等心理问题。

　　在过去的20多年里，中国课堂从传统的设置发展到多样化的电子化教学。互联网带来了教学法的改变，它不但提供了大量的学习资料，而且有各种各样的娱乐功能。学生几乎每人一部手机，他们花在网上的时间越来越多。互联网可以让学生开阔眼界，知识面得到扩展，但是也会使得有些学生沉迷于虚拟世界。

　　尽管有了这些先进的科学技术，中国的城市与农村，地区与地区之间的教育资源分配还不够均衡，城乡和区域之间的教育质量有较大的差距，有些贫困地区还有失学儿童。多年来，海内外关心教育的人士纷纷捐款，在中国各地建立了 5000 多所希望小学，让失学儿童能够走进学校，接受教育。随着中国经济的发展，政府每年给边远贫困地区的教育经费不断增加，区域之间的差距正在缩小。同时，城市里的不少大学生和高中生经常利用节假日，去边远贫困地区关心并帮助那里的学生，还有的把自己兼职赚的钱和省下来的零花钱拿去资助失学儿童。

• 工作机会

　　在如今的市场经济体制下，年轻人找工作比过去30年有了更多的选择。他们不但可以去私营企业，还可以自主创业或从事自由职业等。但同时，有些用人单位片面地注重学历、学位、经验，甚至有重男轻女的问题。因此，对于年轻人来说，找工作的机会并不均等。中国面临人口老龄化的问题，城市劳动力不足，同时大量年轻农民为了摆脱农村的贫困生活，来到城市当"农民工"。

• **工作和生活的平衡**

中国的传统观念总是强调工作，忽视生活。事实证明，工作和生活是一个硬币的两面。因此，一个人如果既会工作，又会生活，那么就能做到家庭和谐、身心健康，这样的人更容易有工作热情，也更能取得事业上的成功。

Unit 2 Education and Employment

Unit 2 focuses on topics relating to school life, student issues, employment opportunities, as well as work-life balance.

In China, school age starts at 6 years old. Since 1986 the Chinese government has implemented a 9-year compulsory education policy. Students are allocated to state primary and secondary schools according to their catchment areas. There are also private and international schools, which, up to 2016, amounted to 10% of Chinese secondary schools.

Each year more than 9 million students take part in the National College Entrance Examination (equivalent to A-Level exams at the end of Year 13 in the UK). The result of this exam determines whether a candidate will get a place in a university and what type of university. In China there are the "key point" universities and the "common" universities, which are all state-run. Nowadays there are also private universities and "China and foreign country joint-venture" universities.

• School life and student issues

Chinese students generally work hard and have a good foundation of knowledge. In both the International Science Olympiad, and the Programme for International Student Assessment, Chinese students often win prizes and have achieved the best results in maths, science and culture. However, these come at a high price: students have a lot of school work and the pressure to succeed in exams is tremendous. As a result they don't have much time for anything else. A Chinese student is typically described as "out of touch the society" and "lacking creative thinking". According to a survey by the World Health Organisation in 2017, myopia among Chinese youngsters is the worst in the world. For a long time exam results have been used to distinguish a good student from a bad one at school, at home and in society. This has led to severe psychological problems such as anxiety, depression and inferiority complex among some young people.

In the last twenty years or so the Chinese classroom has evolved from the traditional setup to one with many technological features. E-learning is bringing changes to the teaching style as well. The Internet not only provides an enormous amount of materials for learning, but also all kinds of functions for entertainment. Almost every student has a smart phone nowadays and they spend an increasing amount of time on the Internet. The Internet can widen a student's horizon and broaden their knowledge, but it can also lure unsuspecting students to become addicted to the world of the Internet.

Despite all these technological advances, educational resources are still very much unevenly distributed in Chinese cities and the countryside. The quality of education differs greatly among cities, towns and regions. There are children who are still deprived of education in poor areas. For many years, philanthropists at home and abroad concerned about this have contributed huge donations to China for building and running more than 5000 "Hope" primary schools, providing for the education of the poor children. The government has increased funding for these poor areas every year with the development of the Chinese economy, thus reducing the differences in education provision between regions. There are, at the same time, many university and high school students from cities who are willing to spend their holidays in the remote poor regions to help the children there. Some of them donate their hard-earned cash from part-time jobs to these educationally deprived children.

• Employment opportunity

In today's market economy, there are far more choices for young people seeking employment than thirty years ago. They can look for jobs in private enterprises, run their own business, or become a free-lancer. On the other hand, there are employers who only look at the applicants' academic qualifications, experiences, and even gender, with preference for male over female, leading to unequal opportunity for young people who look for a job. China is facing an ageing population. Cities do not have sufficient human resources. At the same time a large number of young peasants move to cities to become "peasant workers" in order to escape poverty in the countryside.

• Work-life balance

In Chinese tradition, the ethics of work is very strong, to the extent that other aspects of life are often neglected. People have begun to recognise that work and life are two sides of the same coin, and that they have to get the balance right between them. Hence there has been a new awareness about the importance of keeping fit through exercises, recreational activities and, in general, relaxing more.

5 上学读书

短文一 Text One

读书难

生词		
公立	gōnglì	state-run
初中	chūzhōng	junior high school
高中	gāozhōng	senior high school
走读	zǒudú	day pupil
住宿	zhùsù	boarding
必修	bìxiū	compulsory for study
语文	yǔwén	language and literature
选修	xuǎnxiū	opitional for study
高考	gāokǎo	college entrance examination
补习班	bǔxíbān	private tutorials
模拟	mónǐ	mock (exam)
重点大学	zhòngdiǎn dàxué	key university (similar to Russell Group or Ivy League universities)

　　北山中学是一所公立学校，有初中部和高中部。有的学生走读，有的住宿。张明是这所中学高中三年级的学生，除了必修的语文、数学、物理、化学、生物和英语以外，他还选修了法语。因为快要高考了，所以他不参加学校的任何课外活动。每天放学回家，只休息半个小时就开始做作业，晚上的时间也花在复习功课上。周末，他父母还让他参加补习班，做模拟考试题目。

　　张明觉得自己在中国考上重点大学的机会不大，因此他很希望能去美国上大学。可是，他父母的收入不高，实在没有能力供他去国外读书。

R 读完上面的短文，回答下面的问题。Answer the following questions in Chinese.

1. 张明今年读几年级？
2. 他学习哪些科目？
3. 不用上学的时候，他做些什么？
4. 对升大学，张明有什么想法？

短文二 Text Two

新时代的"孟母三迁"

生词		
输	shū	to lose
起跑线	qǐpǎo xiàn	starting line
租借	zūjiè	to rent
学区房	xuéqū fáng	catchment area housing
资源	zīyuán	resource
素质	sùzhì	quality (of people)
质量	zhìliàng	quality (of product)
国际	guójì	international
投资	tóuzī	to invest
移民	yímín	to emigrate
平等	píngděng	equal
穷困	qióngkùn	poor

现在中国有一句话,叫作"不要让自己的孩子输在起跑线上"。学生就读的公立中小学,是根据家庭居住的地区来安排的。于是,许多家长为了子女能上一所好学校,愿意花大价钱在名校附近地区购买或者租借"学区房"。

好学校的资源多,设施全,学生素质好,教学质量也高,他们的毕业生进名牌大学的机会要高得多。可是好学校太少,怎么办呢?

随着外国名校到中国来开办国际学校,经济条件好的家庭可以送子女去国际学校读书。有钱的家庭,在国外的好学校附近购房,到欧美发达国家投资移民。孩子留学,母亲陪读,"新时代的孟母"为了孩子,已经"三迁"到海外了。

教育应该是平等的,那么穷困家庭的孩子还有没有受到好教育的机会呢?

R 读完上面的短文,回答下面的问题。Answer the following questions in Chinese.

1. 公立学校一般是根据什么录取学生的?
2. 为什么很多家长认为名校比一般学校好?
3. 为了让孩子能到名校读书,许多家长会用什么方法?
4. 什么样的人被叫做"新时代的孟母"?

Snippet
孟母三迁

孟子年幼的时候，住在墓地附近，经常看到有人举办丧事，于是他也学着办丧事。他母亲觉得这样不好，就搬到别处去住了。

后来他们住的地方环境比以前的好，但是离他们家不远有一个市场。孟子每天都从市场走过，他看到屠夫杀猪、宰羊、卖肉，也学着叫喊，扮屠夫做买卖。孟母更觉得这里不适合孟子读书，于是又再搬家。

Where do you think Mencius' mother moved them to now? Discuss in the class in Chinese.

W 根据现代社会的情况，编写新版"孟母三迁"的故事。

短文三　Text Three

一封家书

生词		
陌生	mòshēng	strange
留学生	liúxué shēng	student studying abroad
舒适	shūshì	comfortable
家乡	jiāxiāng	home country
情绪	qíngxù	mood
低落	dīluò	low
总算	zǒngsuàn	on the whole
耐心	nàixīn	patience
格外	géwài	especially
辩论	biànlùn	debate

亲爱的爸爸妈妈：

你们好！

我到英国差不多有三个月了。面对陌生的环境，我们一起来的几个留学生真的有点不习惯。现在所有事情都要我们自己做，我也没有在家里时的那种舒适生活了：放学回家妈妈做好美味的饭菜给我吃，爸爸每个周末还给我收拾房间。

前几天是中秋节，我们几个留学生相约在学校的球场赏月。因为大家都是第一次远离家乡，在国外过中秋节，我们非常想家，情绪很低落，几乎都要哭了！

在学习方面，我总算能够应付。学校的老师对学生很负责，很有耐心，对我们几个留学生格外照顾。

三点半以后学校有合唱、戏剧、辩论、摄影等兴趣小组的活动，在运动方面则有各种球类训练。我除了参加篮球队和网球班以外，周末还做跑步训练。

明天我们有一个英语考试，等我收到考试成绩后再给你们写信。

敬祝

身体健康！

小芬上

9月27日

Unit Two 教育与工作

R 读完小芬的信，回答下面的问题。Answer the following questions in Chinese.

1. 小芬在哪里留学？
2. 她是一个人到那里留学的吗？
3. 小芬在家的时候，她父母是怎样照顾她的？
4. 小芬怎样度过中秋节？
5. 她对新学校的印象怎么样？
6. 她参加了哪些课外活动？

W You, being 小芬, write a letter (180-200 characters) to your parents again, telling them:

1. The result of your English test and why you think you didn't do well;
2. What you think of the teaching methods in this school and why you are finding it hard to adjust;
3. How you spend time in the evening and what new friends you have made;
4. How you look forward to a forthcoming theatre trip with the school.

Snippet

孔子

Confucius (孔子) is a pioneer of schools for ordinary people, as opposed to schools only for the aristocracy and the landed gentry. He advocated 有教无类, which means that whatever your background, as long as you want to learn, you should be given the opportunity to do so. He also emphasised 因材施教, which means that teachers should teach pupils in accordance with their aptitude. These educational tenets are still very appropriate in the modern world. 孔子 is the father of 儒家, one of the most important philosophies in China.

S 在电影《请投我一票》里，老师组织了一次选举班长的活动。一方面是学生们学着怎么民主选举班长，一方面是三个候选人学着怎样拉票，再一方面就是家长怎样帮助自己的孩子拉票以及做竞选的准备。你在读小学或中学的时候，有过选举班长的经历吗？请在班上谈谈你的经验。你可以说说以下几点：

1. 这个竞选是选什么的？
2. 你是候选人还是投票人？
3. 候选人做了些什么去拉票？
4. 你觉得他们做得怎么样？为什么？

句式学习

1. **根据**

   This phrase tends to be formal and is preferably used when speaking about doing something following some official guidelines, such as a law, an official investigation, etc.

   例句：根据 + 中国的法律规定，每个公民必须接受九年义务教育。

2. **Adjective + 得多**

   This structure indicates the difference in quality or degree of the same thing as compared with its earlier or later period, e.g 好得多了，大得多了，长得多了.

   例句：跟以前相比，现在的医疗条件 + 好得多了，人的寿命 + 长得多了。

   It can involve a comparison of the same thing in two different situations.

   A + 比 + B + adjective + 得多

   例句：中国好学区的房价 + 比 + 其他地区的 + 贵 + 得多。

3. **Subject + 像 + observation**

   The similarity as stated in the first part of the sentence is normally explained in the rest of the sentence.

   例句：现在有些家长 + 像 + 中国古时候的孟母，一定要搬到好学区，让孩子进好学校。

4. **则 then**

   则 is often used in a successive compound sentence to contrast. 则 must appear in the second component sentence.

   例句：❶ 体育馆内有游泳池、网球场和乒乓球桌等，室外 + 则 + 有篮球场、足球场和棒球场。

   ❷ 这所住宿学校重视培养学生独立思考的能力，在饮食方面 + 则 + 特别重视学生的营养。

   ❸ 马克的生日会上，男士们在玩纸牌，女士们 + 则 + 全都去跳舞了。

5. **Subject + 对 + object + verb / adjective**

   例句：❶ 王明 + 对 + 这次高考 + 没有信心。

   ❷ 全社会 + 对 + 失学儿童的教育 + 十分重视。

> **练习**

1. 请在三篇短文中找出用以上句式的句子。
2. 请用上面的句式造句。Make up sentences using the sentence patterns above.

Unit Two 教育与工作

S 口语练习

短文 近十几年来，中国的家长都知道"不能让孩子输在起跑线上"。孩子刚会说话，就教他们读古典诗歌，学说英语；刚会拿笔，就让他们学习做数学题。因为在中国参加高考的时候，如果你有音乐、艺术或者运动等特长，可以加分，进大学的机会就多了，所以家长会从小带着孩子去参加不同的兴趣班、补习班。实际上，有时候，这些兴趣班是父母的选择，不是因为孩子自己感兴趣。

论点 孩子不能输在起跑线上。

1. 短文的主要意思是什么？
2. 根据短文，家长为什么要孩子从很小就参加兴趣班或补习班？
3. "孩子不能输在起跑线上。"你同意这个论点吗？为什么？
4. 中国家长认为孩子有兴趣特长很重要，你怎么看？

W 写作练习

请写一篇 150 字左右的短文，可以考虑以下几点。

题目 谈谈张家安

1. 在电影《天水围的日与夜》中，张家安是谁？
2. 谈谈他的暑假生活。
3. 他给你留下了一个什么样的印象？

L 听力练习

一、马文今天去参加东海中学的活动，因为他想来这所中学上高中。丽丽是高中毕业班的班长，带他参观了学校。

1. 听对话，然后在正确的答案前打 ☒。

   ❶ 东海中学今天有什么活动？
   - ☐ A 入学考试
   - ☐ B 开放日
   - ☐ C 新学生面试
   - ☐ D 运动会

   ❷ 丽丽觉得东海中学怎么样？（可以多选）
   - ☐ A 很多设备
   - ☐ B 很大
   - ☐ C 教学很好
   - ☐ D 体育课很好

   ❸ 丽丽常常去体育馆做什么？（可以多选）
   - ☐ A 打篮球
   - ☐ B 游泳
   - ☐ C 跑步
   - ☐ D 打网球

❹ 马文对明年有什么期望？（可以多选）
- ☐ A 有一位好的英语老师
- ☐ B 读物理课
- ☐ C 读化学课
- ☐ D 成为东海学校的学生

2. 再听一遍丽丽和马文的这段对话，然后用中文回答下面的问题。
   ❶ 马文喜欢哪个科目？
   ❷ 林老师是谁？
   ❸ 为什么同学们都爱上林老师的课？
   ❹ 丽丽说东海学校实验室的设备怎么样？

二、Listen to the conversation and summarise the details given by Xiaotian about his life in the new school. You are not required to write in full English sentences. You must give two details for question (a) and two details for question (b).

(a) Summarise how Xiaotian travels to school.
(b) Summarise what Xiaotian says about his lunch at school.

G 词语练习   根据英文，选字组词。

站　公　私

- (　) 立　privately run
- (　) 立　state run
- (　) 立　to stand

金　借　出

- (　) 租　for hire
- 租 (　)　to rent
- 租 (　)　rent

摄　电　星

- 影 (　)　movie star
- (　) 影　film
- (　) 影　photography

动　民　居

- 移 (　)　to shift
- 移 (　)　to emigrate
- 移 (　)　move one's residence

复　补　惯

- 习 (　)　habit
- (　) 习　to review
- (　) 习　tutoring

源　本　投

- (　) 资　investment
- 资 (　)　capital
- 资 (　)　resource

食　质　色

- 素 (　)　character / quality
- 素 (　)　vegetarian food
- 素 (　)　plain colour

耐　关　热

- (　) 心　to be concerned
- (　) 心　patience
- (　) 心　very keen on

Unit Two 教育与工作

学 地 郊
( ) 区 area
( ) 区 suburb
( ) 区 school district

舒 合 用
( ) 适 comfortable
( ) 适 suitable
适 ( ) be applicable

G 选词填空

1. 被 对 则 得 的 地 都

北山中学是一所很有名的公立学校，它的毕业生（　　）进了很好的大学。每年考试，学生都能取（　　）非常好（　　）成绩；在运动和音乐比赛中，学生（　　）能拿到很多奖牌，所以学生家长（　　）北山中学很满意。

2. 再 被 在 搬 陪读 移民 把

在中国，有些家庭的母亲不（　　）出去工作了。她们有的（　　）学区房住，有的（　　）到欧美国家去生活。这些母亲的主要任务都是（　　），照顾孩子的生活和学习，她们（　　）称为"新时代的孟母"。

T 翻译练习

1. Translate the following paragraph into English.

在英国，学生到了中学六年级（sixth form）可以选择读自己喜欢的学科。不过，学生读的科目要跟他们想去大学读的专业有关系。如果你要报考大学的物理系，那么物理和数学就是必修科目；如果你要去大学读医科，那么化学就是必修课。

教师给学生的作业经常是要求他们到图书馆或上网查找资料，然后整理、分析、完成一篇文章。

2. 把下面的一段文字翻译成中文。

Primary and secondary state schools in the UK usually start at 9 am and finish at 3.30 pm. Students can take part in all kinds of extra-curricular activities after school. There are drama, music, art and craft groups, school choirs, sports clubs, and debating societies which meet regularly.

Homework for primary school pupils is usually set for about 45 minutes to an hour every evening. However, secondary school students get more homework, which requires more time to complete.

6 望子成龙

短文一 Text One

From：小东
To：小林
Subject：何去何从

小林，我很想和你说说心里话，因为在家里我没有人可以商量，很苦恼。

最近我正在申请大学。我从小就喜欢树木花草，节假日最喜欢去的地方是植物园，而不是游乐园，所以我非常想报考园林专业。但是我的父母坚决反对，他们说我应该学习数学或者经济，毕业以后就可以进金融界工作，工资比园林职员要高得多。

我一点儿也不喜欢数学，可是又不想让父母生气和失望，我应该怎么办呢？

小东

生词

商量	shāngliang	to talk over
苦恼	kǔnǎo	vexed
植物园	zhíwùyuán	botanical garden
报考	bàokǎo	to enter for an exam
园林	yuánlín	landscape architecture
专业	zhuānyè	specialised; subject; discipline
坚决	jiānjué	determined
反对	fǎnduì	to oppose
金融界	jīnróngjiè	finance
生气	shēngqì	to be angry
失望	shīwàng	disappointed

R 读完上面的短文，回答下面的问题。Answer the following questions in Chinese.

1. 小林上大学后想读什么专业？
2. 他父母是什么态度？
3. 父母对小林的期望是什么？为什么？

W/S When you choose your university, which factors would you consider the most important? Discuss this in the class in Chinese. You can write down the factors first.

Unit Two 教育与工作

短文二 Text Two

学生的心声

《中学生报》的记者今天到东海中学采访，他请学生们谈谈大家是否感到幸福。

王丽明：我叫王丽明。现在家里的条件比以前好多了，我想要最新款的手机、最新潮的服装，妈妈都给我买，总之我要什么有什么。真幸福！

李　山：我叫李山。我很幸福，因为父母非常爱我。不过，当周末我想休息或者跟朋友外出，而父母还要我去补习班时，我就觉得一点儿也不幸福。

小　马：我是小马。我认为现在的中学生很不幸福。比如我，每天放学后都要去补习班，因为父母觉得我的考试成绩不够好，可能考不上重点大学。我最喜欢踢足球，可是已经半年没踢了。

兰　兰：我是兰兰。如果我的同学们都考上了重点大学，而我没考上，不但父母没有面子，自己也会很失望。人人都说考大学"压力山大"，本来我最喜欢看小说，妈妈说我现在只可以看跟高考有关的书。这样还哪里有什么幸福？！

生词		
是否	shìfǒu	is it not
新款	xīnkuǎn	new style
新潮	xīncháo	trendy
比如	bǐrú	for instance
不够好	búgòu hǎo	not good enough
面子	miànzi	face (as in reputation, prestige)
"压力山大"	yālì shāndà	pressure as big as a mountain

R 读完上面的短文，回答下面的问题。Answer the following questions in Chinese.

1. 王丽明为什么觉得自己现在很幸福？
2. 李山觉得幸福还是不幸福？为什么？
3. 小马的父母为什么要他上补习班？
4. 兰兰说她觉得考大学的压力很大，为什么？

Snippet
学业生涯

中国香港从 1978 年开始提供 9 年免费教育，一到高中，家长就要为孩子交学费了。

一般家长都希望自己的孩子进名校。从幼儿园、小学、中学，直到大学，学生在每个阶段都要通过入学考试，竞争很激烈，所以家长几乎都会为孩子找补习老师或者送他们去补习班。学生的休息和娱乐的时间确实是大大减少了。

Hong Kong government started to provide free education in 1978. Education is free for six years in the primary sector and three years in the lower secondary schools. Parents have to pay fees for the children's upper secondary education.

Parents generally wish to send their children to "prestigious" schools which have a selective policy. Nursery, primary and secondary school pupils have to take an entrance exam at each of these stages of education in order to get a place in the schools of their parents' choice. University is the same. The competition is severe, thus creating a trend for the parents to seek private tuition for their children. As a result, pupils' relaxation time is greatly reduced.

短文三　Text Three

<u>青少年无所不谈的天地</u>

加美：爸妈管我管得很严。晚上我一个人在房间里关上门的时候，他们会怀疑我是不是在喝酒、抽烟，甚至吸毒。其实我只是想有自己的时间和空间，静静地看看书或者听听音乐罢了，可是他们不信任我。

玛丽：不久前，同学给我介绍了一个电子游戏，刺激极了。我每天都玩，连应该做作业的时候也不愿意停下来。我知道这是不对的，可是停不下来，该怎么办呢？

大山：我今天穿了一条新买的牛仔裤跟同学们出去玩，可是他们都说我这裤子不好看，过时了。我很生气，为什么一定要新潮的服装才好看呢！

李丹：我快要上大学了。现在最担心的是在大学能不能交到好朋友，考试能不能得到好成绩，能不能把学习和社交生活平衡好。你有什么建议？

马克：我来自单亲家庭，妈妈的收入不高，没有能力供我上大学。最近我开始在周末去一家超市兼职。妈妈不太高兴，说这会影响我的学习。我不想让她担心，可是我真的需要赚钱，好把钱存起来将来上大学用。

生词

无所不谈	wúsuǒ bùtán	to talk about anything whatsoever
天地	tiāndì	world
严	yán	strict
怀疑	huáiyí	to suspect
抽烟	chōuyān	to smoke
吸毒	xīdú	to take drugs
其实	qíshí	in fact
刺激	cìjī	exciting
过时	guòshí	old fashioned
担心	dānxīn	to worry
社交	shèjiāo	social
平衡	pínghéng	to balance

Unit Two 教育与工作

R 上面是几位网友给"青少年天地平台"的短信，读完后回答下面的问题。

1. 加美觉得她父母对她怎么样？为什么？
2. 玛丽面临什么问题？
3. 大山对服装有什么看法？
4. 李丹对将去上大学有些什么担忧？
5. 为什么马克觉得需要做兼职？

S/W 跟你的同学在课上讨论上面的短信，然后选择一条，用 100—150 字给他／她写回信，提出建议。

Snippet

互联网

现在互联网确实很受欢迎，并被广泛使用。对于年轻一代来说，网络上的社交媒体让他们开阔眼界，扩大关系网。这种先进的技术有助于传播信息和新闻，但是也有坏处。社交网络可能会被滥用，造成不好的后果，例如，假新闻、色情信息、网络欺凌、种族仇恨邮件等。因此，英国学校制定了有关正确使用以及不可滥用信息技术的政策，以保证学生不受网上不当和非法活动的不利影响。

The Internet is certainly very popular and widely used nowadays. For the younger generation, the Internet has brought along the use of numerous social media, which greatly extend the scope and widen the circle of networking. This technological advancement has helped with the dissemination of information and news, but it also has drawbacks. Social networking can be abused in ways which have undesirable consequences, for example, fake news, pornography, cyber-bullying, racist hate-mail, to name just a few. Therefore UK schools set up their own policy related to the use or misuse of IT to make sure that students are not adversely affected by inappropriate and illegal online activities.

S 在电影《天水围的日与夜》里面，张家安中学毕业后有什么打算？
你可以说说以下几点：
1. 张家安对他中学会考的成绩有什么期望？
2. 他拿到会考成绩后，对未来的计划有什么改变？
3. 他的舅舅跟他说了什么？
4. 你觉得他舅舅一家人对他怎么样？为什么？

句式学习

1. "着"的用法

When used after a verb, the aspect particle 着 indicates the continuation of action.

例句：❶ 小东 + 戴着 + 一副太阳眼镜。

❷ 书桌上 + 放着 + 一台电脑。

If used in a negative sentence, it is 没（有）+ verb + 着.

❸ 小东 + 没戴着 + 眼镜，他 + 戴着 + 帽子。

❹ 卧室的窗户 + 没开着。

2. "把"的用法

把 is a marker for direct-object, indicating how an object (person or thing) is dealt with. It is always put after the subject of a sentence and before the verb.

例句：❶ 女儿请父母 + 把 + 自己的大学申请表看一下。

If there is an auxillary verb or a negative adverb in a 把 sentence, it must precede 把.

❷ 母亲对儿子说："你 + 应该 + 把 + 跟高考有关的题目都做一遍。"

❸ 她 + 还没有 + 把 + 这些作业做完。

3. 是否 whether or not; is or isn't

否 can be added after certain verbs to form an affirmative / negative sentence pattern.

例句：❶ 你的父母 + 是否 + 尊重你的私人空间？

❷ 学校 + 能否 + 给学生多一点户外活动的时间？

❸ 这些练习题你 + 会否 + 能在四点前完成？

4. 罢了

It is used as a modal particle, indicating "that's all", "nothing much".

例句：❶ 上大学只是中学毕业生的一个选择 + 罢了。

❷ 我这次能进名校只是运气好 + 罢了。

练习

1. 请在三篇短文中找出用以上句式的句子。
2. 请用上面的句式造句。Make up sentences using the sentence patterns above.

Unit Two 教育与工作

S 口语练习

短文 根据最近在香港的调查发现，超过 20%的中学生觉得父母不那么爱或者根本不爱自己，因为父母不尊重自己。比如，不管什么时候，不敲门就进他们的房间；随便翻看他们的书包、日记等。父母常说"人家的孩子考试又得了 100 分""人家的孩子数学比赛得奖了""人家的孩子进了重点大学"……这样的话让这些中学生很苦恼，觉得父母爱的是别人家的孩子。

论点 父母不尊重子女就是不爱子女。

1. 短文的主要意思是什么？
2. 根据短文，为什么有的学生觉得父母不爱自己？
3. "父母不尊重子女就是不爱子女。"你同意这个论点吗？为什么？
4. 有的华人父母喜欢用"别人家的孩子"来跟自己的孩子做比较。你觉得这样好吗？为什么？

W 写作练习

请写一篇 150 字左右的短文，可以考虑以下几点。

题目 谈谈英子

1. 在故事《爸爸的花儿落了》中，英子是谁？
2. 爸爸为什么有一天要打英子？
3. 爸爸打了英子以后，英子有什么变化？

L 听力练习

一、新学期开学，爱玛跟小红聊她们暑假做了什么。

1. 听对话，然后在正确的答案前打 ☒。

    ❶ 爱玛说她的暑假过得怎么样？
    - [ ] A 一般
    - [ ] B 很好
    - [ ] C 很无聊
    - [ ] D 十分好玩

    ❷ 爱玛在哪里工作？
    - [ ] A 超市
    - [ ] B 服装店
    - [ ] C 快餐店
    - [ ] D 图书馆

❸ 小红暑假做什么了？
  ☐ A 去旅游了
  ☐ B 打工
  ☐ C 上补习班
  ☐ D 考试
❹ 小红喜欢什么？
  ☐ A 运动
  ☐ B 旅游
  ☐ C 音乐
  ☐ D 历史

2. 再听一遍爱玛和小红的这段对话，然后用中文回答下面的问题。
  ❶ 爱玛为什么要在暑假里打工？
  ❷ 她用赚到的钱做什么？
  ❸ 小红为什么暑假还要去补习班？
  ❹ 小红喜欢去补习班吗？为什么？

二、Listen to the conversation and summarise the details given by Mary about her life in China. You are not required to write in full English sentences. You must give two details for question (a) and two details for question (b).

(a) Summarise where Mary learned to speak Chinese.
(b) Summarise what Mary is doing in China.

G 词语练习

根据英文，选字组词。

家 业 心

专（　）to concentrate
专（　）specialised field
专（　）specialist

决 定 强

坚（　）strong
坚（　）determined
坚（　）firm

钱 融 色

金（　）financial
金（　）golden colour
金（　）money

点 要 量

重（　）important
重（　）weight
重（　）key point

数 根 说

（　）据 according to
（　）据 data
据（　）it is said

中 级 当

（　）初 at the beginning
初（　）junior secondary school
初（　）elementary

51

Unit Two 教育与工作

恼 辛 味
苦（　　）distressed
苦（　　）bitter in taste
（　　）苦 laborious

希 失 远
（　　）望 disappointed
（　　）望 hope
（　　）望 to look into the distance

商 重 数
（　　）量 weight
（　　）量 quantity
（　　）量 to talk over

疑 念 关
怀（　　）to think of, to miss
怀（　　）to doubt or to suspect
（　　）怀 loving care

衡 公 安
平（　　）to balance
平（　　）safe
（　　）平 fair

新 流 热
（　　）潮 upsurge
（　　）潮 trendy
潮（　　）trend

G 选词填空

1. 放　存　给　界　做　修

每个周末，小玉白天去补习班选（　　）摄影，晚上去快餐店兼职赚钱。因为她希望将来进新闻（　　）工作，现在要把打工的钱（　　）起来，将来（　　）自己买一架好的照相机。

2. 意思　刺激　苦恼　现代　平衡　新潮

随着互联网新媒体的发展，网络不断推出（　　）的电子游戏，都有（　　）极了，小东总是玩得停不下来。可是学校每天的作业都很多，小东很（　　），不知道怎么（　　）学习与娱乐的关系。

3. 着　跟　过　把　被　在

母亲下班回家时，海平正坐（　　）沙发上，看（　　）一本非常有趣的小说。母亲生气极了，（　　）海平手里的书拿走了，还跟他说："你现在只可以看（　　）高考有关的书！"

T 翻译练习

1. Translate the following paragraph into English.

我是英国人，我太太是香港人。我们的儿子今年十一岁，刚在本地的一所公立学校读完五年级。九月份他就要上中学了，我们正在考虑，是让他去国际学校读书，还是继续上本地的公立中学。

R 招聘广告

随着市场经济化，私营企业可以自由刊登广告招聘职员。招聘广告各式各样：有些注重学历、学位、经验，有些强调年龄、性别，甚至外表。下面是两则招聘广告，请你分析它们的内容，并在班上讨论。

生词

私营	sīyíng	privately owned
企业	qǐyè	enterprise
刊登	kāndēng	to publish in a newspaper
招聘	zhāopìn	to advertise for a job vacancy
强调	qiángdiào	to emphasise

性别	xìngbié	gender
外表	wàibiǎo	appearance
则	zé	a measure word, it's used for an item of news or an advertisement
分析	fēnxī	to analyse

储备店长（5人）
1. 大专以上学历（能力强者可放宽要求），从事相关行业两年及以上工作经历。
2. 有良好的语言沟通能力和良好的服务态度。
3. 熟悉公司产品特点，汇总市场信息。

储备店长（5人）
1. 大专以上学历（能力强者可放宽要求），从事相关行业两年及以上工作经历。
2. 有良好的语言沟通能力和良好的服务态度。
3. 熟悉公司产品特点，汇总市场信息。

平面设计（5人）
20—35岁之间，形象气质佳，品行端正，有较强的沟通能力及执行力，有销售经验者优先。

平面设计（5人）
20—35岁之间，熟悉 形象气质佳，品行端正，有较强的沟通能力及执行力，有销售经验者优先。

咨询热线：000-123456789　　联系方式：181300729**　　联系方式：杨先生

ZHAO PIN 招聘 JOIN US 够胆你就来 加入我们成就梦想

平面设计
岗位职责：设计公司业务广告，公司形象宣传广告、公司办公用品等。
岗位要求：大专以上学历，年龄20—30岁，熟练使用Photoshop、CorelDRAW、InDesign、Illustrator排版软件。

市场营销
岗位职责：商业客户的开发、维护；客户广告设计的转达及复核等。
岗位要求：大专以上学历，年龄22—28岁。薪资待遇：无责任底薪（2500—3000元）+奖金。

发行专员
岗位职责：对市场进行监督和调查，投放刊物。
岗位要求：18—26岁，男，身体健康，吃苦耐劳。薪资待遇：2000—2500元。

客服专员
岗位职责：负责接听客户来访的咨询电话、记录、整理个人免费信息，并进行分类。
岗位要求：大专以上学历，年龄22—26岁，女性，普通话标准。

W / S When you choose your first job, which factors would you consider the most important? Discuss this in the class in Chinese. You can write down the factors first.

55

Unit Two 教育与工作

短文二 Text Two

农民工回乡创业

生词		
贫困	pínkùn	poor
耕地	gēngdì	cultivated land
面积	miànjī	area of land
贡献	gòngxiàn	contribution
转型期	zhuǎnxíngqī	transition period
劳动力	láodònglì	manual labour
创业	chuàngyè	to start an enterprise
麦草	màicǎo	straw
红火	hónghuǒ	flourishing

《明华经济日报》报道：因为中国有的农村地区经济不发达，农民生活贫困；有的地区人口多而耕地面积少，所以很多农村的年青人前往大城市打工。现在，有超过两亿的"流动工人"为中国的城市化做出了巨大的贡献。

近年来，中国经济进入转型期，不少手工业工厂关门了。有了一些工作经验的农民工开始回乡创业。他们不仅能为农村现代化的发展出力，同时还可以在自己家门口工作，照顾好家中老小。

本报记者最近采访了一位从广州打工十年后回到农村创业的林大新。

记者：请问，您在广州打工多年了，现在又回到农村，这是为什么？

大新：因为我的家人都在农村，过去我只有在春节的时候，才能回家看望他们。去年玩具厂关门了，我没了工作，就回到了农村。

记者：现在您怎么生活呢？

大新：我办了一个制作玩具的小工厂。我们的玩具都是用竹子和麦草做的，很受城里人的欢迎。现在我的收入比打工时高，而且可以每天跟家人在一起，我觉得很幸福。

记者：祝您的生意越来越红火！

R 读完上面的短文，回答下面的问题。Answer the following questions in Chinese.

1. 文章里提到的"流动工人"从哪里来？
2. 现在为什么不少手工业工厂关门了？
3. 农民工回乡创业有什么好处？
4. 林大新是谁？
5. 他为什么从广州回到了农村？
6. 他现在做的玩具有什么特点？

短文三 Text Three

电脑工程师与绿色蔬菜

生词		
浇水	jiāoshuǐ	to irrigate; to water (plants)
除虫	chúchóng	to get rid of pests
城镇	chéngzhèn	town
有机	yǒujī	organic
搭建	dājiàn	to build
大棚	dàpéng	big shed
种植	zhòngzhí	to grow; to cultivate
化肥	huàféi	chemical fertiliser
供不应求	gōngbú yìngqiú	demand over supply
热线	rèxiàn	hotline

陈树明原来在香港的一家电脑公司工作。虽然工程师的工资不错，可是工作时间长，压力很大，他总是觉得很累。两年前，他的健康出现了问题，因此在家休息养病。

他舅舅是新界的一个菜农，邀请树明到他的家里休养。就这样，树明常常跟着舅舅在田里种菜、浇水、除虫，有时候跟着舅舅把菜运到附近城镇的菜市场去卖。

树明喜欢这种生活，虽然辛苦，但是没有压力。特别是乡村清新的空气让人舒服，他的身体也好起来了。树明发现有机绿色蔬菜有着很大的市场需求。他建议舅舅搭建大棚，使用科学的方法来种植蔬菜，不使用农药和化肥，同时还尝试种植了一些新品种。

树明和舅舅生产的有机绿色蔬菜供不应求。于是，他给电脑公司发了辞职信，决定留在农村。树明还开了网上买菜热线，生意越做越好。他现在又健康又快乐，对生活满意极了。

R 读完上面的短文，回答下面的问题。Answer the following questions in Chinese.

1. 你觉得陈树明的健康为什么会出现问题？
2. 他为什么会去舅舅家住？
3. 树明为什么到了乡村，身体就健康起来了？
4. 文章中提到市场对什么需求很大？
5. 树明和舅舅种植的蔬菜有什么特点？
6. 树明把什么新科技带到了农村？

S/W 跟你的同学在课上讨论上面的短文，然后写一篇100—150字的短文，说说你喜欢在城市生活还是在乡村生活。

Unit Two 教育与工作

Snippet
世界工厂

　　三、四十年前，很多日用品和衣服都是在香港、台湾、新加坡等地区和国家生产的。近二十年来，中国的制造业蓬勃发展，现在更有了"世界工厂"之称。

　　中国全力发展经济，国内很多城镇乡村都开办了工厂，生产各式各样的物品。广东省就是其中的一个例子，它是世界上工厂最密集的地区。因此，它吸引了来自中国不同地区的"流动工人"，到这里的工厂寻找工作。

Many of our daily necessities and garments were manufactured in places such as Hong Kong, Taiwan and Singapore 30 to 40 years ago. In the past 20 years, China's manufacturing industry began to take off. Now it's even being named "workshop of the world".

China has gone all out to develop its economy. Factories are set up in cities and towns, turning out all kinds of products. Guangdong Province is just one such example. It has the highest concentration of factories in the world. As a result, it has attracted many "mobile workers" from all over China to seek work here.

S 在电影《天水围的日与夜》里面，贵姐的朋友梁婆婆的生活是怎样的？
你可以从以下几点谈一谈：

1. 她刚跟贵姐认识的时候，生活是怎样的？
2. 她没找到工作时，怎样维持生计？
3. 她后来是怎么找到工作的？
4. 开始工作以后，她有什么变化？为什么？

句式学习

1. 有 / 没有

The verb 有 and 没有 can be used to express comparison. This kind of comparison, when used in negative or interrogative sentences, expresses the extent to which two things are similar or dissimilar.

To say that something is not as ... as something else, you can use the following pattern:

A + 没（有）+ B + 这么 / 那么 + adjective

例句：**1a** 城市的空气 + 没有 + 乡村的 + 那么清新。(When the speaker is away from the countryside.)

1b 城市的空气 + 没有 + 乡村的 + 这么清新。(When the speaker is in the countryside.)

2a 中国现在的年轻人口 + 没有 + 几十年前的 + 那么多。

2b 中国几十年前的老龄人口 + 没有 + 现在的 + 那么多。

3 城市的空气 + 有没有 + 乡村的清新?

2. 地

地 is a structural particle which is used before a verb to show that what precedes. It is an adverbial modifier modifying the verb used.

例句：**1** 她认真地 + 解释自己辞职的原因。

2 林琳幸运地 + 得到了一份理想的工作。

3. 又 + adjective1 / verb1 + 又 + adjective2 / verb2

In Chinese, one uses 又……又…… to link coordinate verbs (verbal phrases) or adjectives (adjectival phrases) to underline that two situations or characteristics exist simultaneously. This usage is similar to "as well as".

例句：**1** 他们用竹子和麦草做的玩具又 + 环保 + 又 + 便宜。

2 他一毕业就被一家电动汽车厂聘用了，高兴得又 + 笑 + 又 + 跳。

Note: 和 should never be used to link adjectives or verbs.

练习

1. 请在三篇短文中找出用以上句式的句子。
2. 请用上面的句式造句。Make up sentences using the sentence patterns above.

S 口语练习

短文 在中国，有些 90 后缺少"做一行，爱一行"的精神。他们工作以后，会突然辞职，有的甚至不按照合同要求，说不上班就不来上班了。他们辞职或离职的原因各种各样：有的是因为不能和同事友好相处，有的是觉得工作压力大而工资不高，有的是因为受到了经理或老板的批评，也有的是因为找到了更好的工作。也有些年轻人辞职以后并不能马上找到自己理想的工作，于是就尝试自己创业当老板。

论点 年轻人应该"做一行，爱一行"。

1. 短文的主要意思是什么？
2. 根据短文，90 后辞职或离职有哪些原因？
3. "年轻人应该'做一行，爱一行'。"你同意这个论点吗？为什么？
4. 年轻人如果找不到自己理想的工作，可以自己创业当老板。你同意吗？为什么？

Glossary:
行业（hángyè）profession

Unit Two 教育与工作

W 写作练习
请写一篇 150 字左右的短文，可以考虑以下几点。

题目 谈谈《请投我一票》中罗雷的爸爸

1. 罗雷的爸爸是做什么工作的？
2. 他为帮助儿子拉选票做了什么？
3. 你认为罗雷的爸爸是不是一位好爸爸？为什么？

L 听力练习

一、小雨跟兰兰在聊她们未来的工作计划。

1. 听对话，然后在正确的答案前打 ☒。

    ❶ 兰兰曾经想到哪里工作？
    - ☐ A 毛衣店
    - ☐ B 时装店
    - ☐ C 服装厂
    - ☐ D 公园

    ❷ 兰兰现在决定做什么？
    - ☐ A 织毛衣
    - ☐ B 退休
    - ☐ C 做生意
    - ☐ D 管理公园

    ❸ 兰兰计划怎样经营她的网上毛衣店？（可以多选）
    - ☐ A 找服装厂帮她织毛衣
    - ☐ B 自己织毛衣
    - ☐ C 自己设计毛衣式样
    - ☐ D 请退休工人织毛衣

    ❹ 小雨答应兰兰什么？
    - ☐ A 帮她织毛衣
    - ☐ B 帮她找退休工人
    - ☐ C 成为她的第一个顾客
    - ☐ D 帮她找服装厂

2. 再听一遍小雨和兰兰的这段对话，然后用中文回答下面的问题。

    ❶ 兰兰为什么想自己开商店？
    ❷ 她上大学的时候读的是什么专业？
    ❸ 她喜欢研究什么？
    ❹ 为什么她要请退休工人？

二、Listen to the conversation and summarise the details given by Xiao Wang about his new job. You are not required to write in full English sentences. You must give two details for question (a) and two details for question (b).
(a) Summarise the way Xiao Wang's new job is better than his last one.
(b) Summarise why Xiao Wang is happy working in this supermarket.

G 词语练习

根据英文，选字组词。

辑　写　织
编（　　）　to compose
编（　　）　to weave
编（　　）　editor

胜　责　担
（　　）任　responsibility
（　　）任　be competent
（　　）任　to hold a post

地　种　牛
耕（　　）　cattle
耕（　　）　arable land
耕（　　）　to cultivate

面　体　极
（　　）积　volume
（　　）积　area
积（　　）　keen

业　场　员
职（　　）　staff
职（　　）　occupation
职（　　）　world of employment

挥　现　展
发（　　）　to discover
发（　　）　to unleash
发（　　）　to develop

业　意　造
创（　　）　to create
创（　　）　entrepreneurship
创（　　）　creative thinking

家　回　老
（　　）乡　hometown
（　　）乡　to go back to hometown
（　　）乡　fellow countryman from the same hometown

水　高　加
薪（　　）　salary
（　　）薪　high salary
（　　）薪　pay rise

界　表　向
外（　　）　appearance
外（　　）　outgoing
外（　　）　outside world

建　大　展
扩（　　）　to enlarge
扩（　　）　to expand
扩（　　）　to extend

职　退　别
辞（　　）　to bid farewell
辞（　　）　to resign
辞（　　）　to dismiss

Unit Two 教育与工作

农 中 西			虫 草 法		
( )药	Chinese medicine		除( )	to weed	
( )药	Western medicine		除( )	to control pests	
( )药	pesticide		除( )	division	

肥 学 变			释 决 放		
化( )	chemistry		解( )	to liberate	
化( )	fertiliser		解( )	to resolve	
( )化	change		解( )	to explain	

G 选词填空

1. 安定　挑战　热线　安分　有机　创意　创造

　　大牛高中毕业后,不愿意(　　)地当一个普通农民,他要(　　)自己。他用科学方法,种植(　　)蔬菜。他用新科技,开通买菜(　　),成为一位有(　　)的新农民。

2. 升职加薪　各种各样　关门倒闭　三三俩俩　供不应求　开门创业

　　随着中国经济的转型,职场上的高科技人才(　　),他们(　　)的机会相当多。不过同时,技术要求不高的手工业工厂纷纷(　　)了,不少人也失业了。政府办了(　　)的补习班,以帮助这些失业人员,重新回到职场。

3. 为　着　了　过　把　被　对　在

　　林琳今年就要从法学院毕业,进入职场了。她已经(　　)自己的简历放到网上(　　),希望能(　　)自己喜欢的公司看到,给她机会面试。她(　　)一家有名律师行做(　　)两个月的实习生,应该说她是有(　　)一些工作经验的大学生。

T 翻译练习

1. Translate the following paragraph into English.

　　美国大学毕业生福特去一家汽车公司面试。当他正要走进办公室面试的时候,看到地上有一张纸。他捡起来一看,原来是一张废纸,就把它扔进了墙角的纸篓里。然后他走到老板面前说:"我是来面试的福特。"老板说:"很好!福特先生,你被我们聘用了。""真的? 你还没有问我问题。"老板回答:"我认为像你这样能看见小事的人,将来自然能看到大事。只能看见大事的人,会忽略很多小事,是不会成功的。"

Glossary:
福特 (fútè) Ford

这位福特，就是今天美国福特公司的创始人(Founder)。

2. 把下面的这封求职信翻译成中文。

Dear Mr. Zhang,

I saw your advertisement for a tourist guide with Chinese-speaking tourists on the Internet today. I am very interested in doing this kind of work and will be available to start from the beginning of next month.

I studied Chinese for 4 years when I was at school. My reading and writing of Chinese is basic, but I can speak quite fluently. I have spent time on holiday in Shanghai and really enjoyed meeting the people there.

At university I studied English and Tourism. I would really like to get this job, as I can make good use of my Chinese language, as well as my knowledge of the history and culture of Britain.

Yours sincerely
Wang Jing

敬爱的张先生，

① 我今天在网上看见了你招聘会讲中文的导游的广告。我对这个工作很感兴趣，并且我可以在下月初开始这份工作。

② 我在学校时学了4年中文。我的阅读和书写只达到基础水准，但是我可以说得很流利。我曾在上海度过假，并且十分享受和当地人接触。

③ 我在大学学了英文和旅游业。我十分想要获得这份工作，因为我可以良好运用中文，我的历史知识以及英国习俗。

8 工作与生活的平衡

短文一　Text One

贤妻良母的一天

生词

管理员	guǎnlǐyuán	person in charge
匆匆	cōngcōng	hurriedly
抽空	chōukòng	to spare time
属于	shǔyú	belong to
支配	zhīpèi	to have control over
美满	měimǎn	perfectly satisfactory
标准	biāozhǔn	standard
贤妻良母	xiánqī liángmǔ	virtuous wife and good mother
出色	chūsè	outstanding
日复一日	rìfùyírì	day after day

　　我叫张海，是一名办公室管理员。我想说说自己的一天通常是怎样度过的。

　　我每天六点多就起床了，照顾一家人吃早饭。七点半前必须先送孩子上学，然后急匆匆地去上班，否则就会迟到。我的工作时间是上午九点到下午五点，吃午饭的时间，我还得抽空去买菜购物。

　　我一下班就去学校接孩子，送他去数学补习班。然后自己赶快回家做晚饭，打扫房间。等丈夫和孩子回家吃晚饭后，我得做家务，检查孩子的家庭作业，准备他第二天上学用的东西。九点左右，孩子洗澡、上床。十点以后我自己才有时间坐下来，看一会儿新闻，然后睡觉。

　　我常想：一天24小时，究竟有多少时间真正属于自己，让我可以自由支配，做些我想做的事情？我希望我的家庭美满幸福，希望成为一个标准的贤妻良母，我同时也希望做一个出色的办公室管理员。可是，日复一日，月复一月，年复一年，这种生活使我感到很累、很累！

R 读完上面的短文，回答下面的问题。Answer the following questions in Chinese.

1. 张海每天的上班时间有多长？
2. 吃午饭的时间她要做什么？
3. 她每天什么时候才可以休息？
4. 你觉得她能在成为一个出色的办公室管理员的同时，做一个标准的贤妻良母吗？为什么？
5. 你对她这种生活方式有什么想法？为什么？

Snippet
外佣

在香港、新加坡、台湾等国家和地区，很多家庭都聘用外籍女佣。雇主负责女佣的吃住，并付她们工资。根据最新的人口统计和移民纪录（2013），香港的470,000非华籍人口当中，外籍佣工占了三分之二。

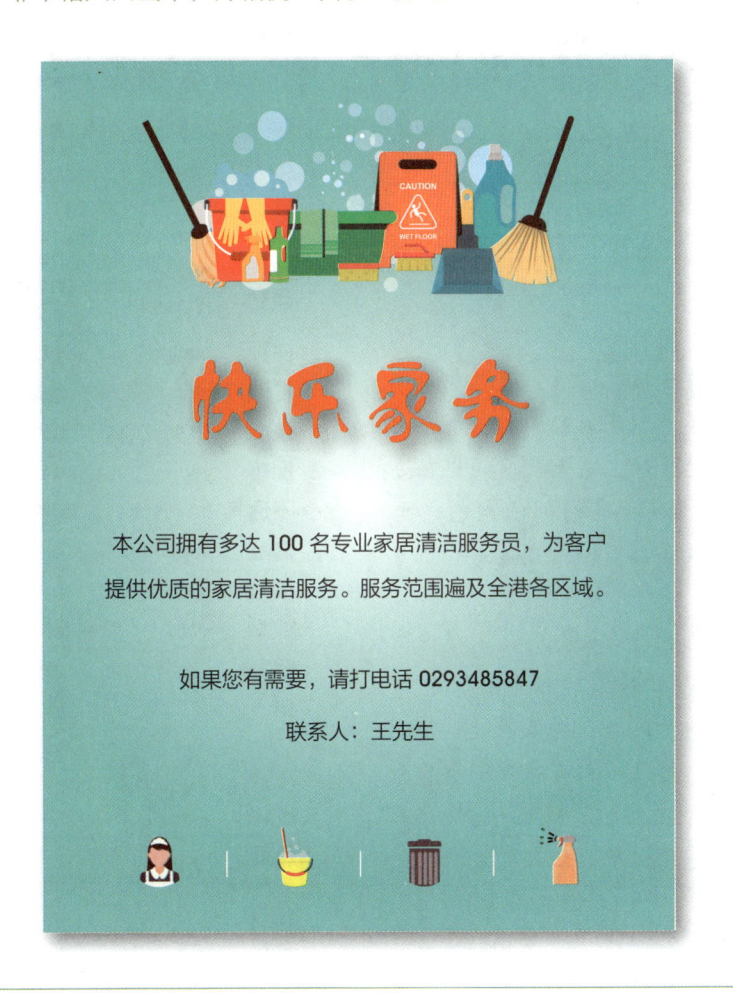

快乐家务

本公司拥有多达100名专业家居清洁服务员，为客户提供优质的家居清洁服务。服务范围遍及全港各区域。

如果您有需要，请打电话 0293485847

联系人：王先生

短文二　Text Two

谁来做家务

　　王雪心是一位生活指导师，她常常接触到不少像张海这样的职业妇女。王雪心认为职业妇女不一定都不能拥有自己的生活。她们可以要求丈夫分担做家务和照顾孩子的责任。如果经济条件不错，也可以请人来做家务。这样她们就可以有时间跟丈夫和孩子一起活动，也能有时间享受独处的时光，做自己想做的事情，比如娱乐、学习、休息等。

生词		
生活指导师	shēnghuó zhǐdǎoshī	life coach
接触	jiēchù	be in contact with
分担	fēndān	to share (responsibility)
独处	dúchù	be on one's own

S / W Discuss the following two scenarios in the class and choose one of them to write about.
1. 如果你是生活指导师，你会给张海什么建议？
2. 如果你未来的工作很忙，还要照顾家庭，你会怎样保持工作与生活的平衡？

短文三　Text Three

跑步通勤

　　《明华经济日报》报道：最近在中国的大城市出现了"跑步通勤"热。由于白领的生活越来越忙碌，每天长时间坐在办公室工作，晚上还要花时间上网、看电视，连走动的机会都很少，直接影响了身体健康。

　　为了给自己运动的机会，又不减少工作时间，很多人就从家跑步前往工作地点。他们认为跑步比坐拥挤又不透气的地铁或公共汽车更舒服。又有人说跑步后上班，头脑会更清醒、更有活力，能提升工作效率；跑步下班回家后让人更放松、更有精力，还能跟家人一起做休闲活动。

　　专家说"跑步通勤"集多方面的优点于一身：它把体育运动、节省交通费用、强身健体等合而为一，可说是"一石多鸟"。

生词		
跑步通勤	pǎobù tōngqín	"runcommute" refers to a run between one's home and workplace
白领	báilǐng	white-collar
忙碌	mánglù	busy
直接	zhíjiē	directly
拥挤	yōngjǐ	crowded
不透气	bú tòuqì	airless
清醒	qīngxǐng	alert
活力	huólì	energy
效率	xiàolǜ	efficiency
精力	jīnglì	vigour
集	jí	to incorporate
节省	jiéshěng	to save
强身健体	qiángshēn jiàntǐ	to strengthen the health and body
合而为一	hé'érwéiyī	to combine into one
一石多鸟	yìshí duōniǎo	to kill many birds with one stone

Chapter 8　工作与生活的平衡

R **上面是《明华经济日报》的一段报道，读完后回答下面的问题。**

1. 文章说在中国的大城市最近出现了什么新事物？
2. 为什么会出现这种新事物？
3. 这种新事物对什么人有好处？
4. 专家们对此有什么看法？
5. 你对这种新事物有什么想法？

Snippet

上班族的压力

最近的研究结果表明，现代的工作方式给上班族带来了很大的压力。虽然新科技、自由职业和个体经营的机会等使灵活的工作方式得到了发展和推广，但也导致了出现健康问题的可能。

一位经验丰富的医务专业人士说，很多人在家工作，这给了他们想要的灵活的工作时间，还有不必出门上班的便利。毫无疑问，这样的安排，帮助了那些既要工作，又要照顾家庭的人。然而，它会混淆工作和家庭生活，因为两者之间没有了明确的分界线。专业人士强调时间管理的重要性，以确保工作和生活的合理平衡。

Recent research findings indicate that modern work practices contribute to the high level of stress among the working population. Although new technology, freelancing, and self-employment opportunities etc. have enabled the development and spread of flexible working practices, they have also created problems which can lead to health issues.

An experienced medical professional says that lots of people work from home, which gives them the flexibility of the hours they want to work and the convenience of not having to travel to the workplace. This kind of arrangement, no doubt, has helped people who have to juggle between work and looking after a family. However, it can blur the demarcation of work and home life, as there is no clear cut-off point. She stresses the importance of time management to make sure that a healthy balance of work and life is maintained.

S 在电影《天水围的日与夜》里面，贵姐的生活是怎样的？她有属于自己的时间吗？

你可以从以下几点谈谈：

1. 她每天的工作时间有多长？
2. 不在超市工作时，她会做什么？
3. 她有什么休闲活动？
4. 你认为她的生活可以怎样改变？为什么？

Unit Two 教育与工作

句式学习

1. 否则

否则 can be used as an adverb, similar to the conjunction "otherwise" in English.

例句：❶ 一个人的工作压力不能太大，<u>否则</u>健康就会出现问题。

❷ 中国政府开放了二孩政策，<u>否则</u>将来人口老龄化问题就会更严重。

2. 先……再 / 然后……

This pattern is used for sequencing events, much like "first..., then..." in English. It can also include 然后, meaning "and after that".

例句：❶ 英子每天<u>先</u>去公司的健身房锻炼半个小时，<u>再</u>去办公室上班。

❷ 我建议你<u>先</u>让丈夫和你一起分担家务，<u>然后</u>让他分担培养孩子的责任，也让他做一些简单的打扫工作，这样你就能有多一点属于自己的时间。

3. 究竟

究竟 is used in a question to find out "actually or exactly" "what", "why"...

例句：❶ 听说现在越来越多的白领开始跑步通勤，<u>究竟</u>有多大的比例呢？

❷ 在寻找新工作的时候，<u>究竟</u>是选自己喜欢的工作好呢，还是选薪水高的好？

4. 连……都 / 也……

This sentence pattern is used to emphasise an unlikely or surprising event which serves to give more information or explanation related to the first clause. It is used in a similar way to "even" in English.

例句：❶ 她实在太累了，<u>连</u>吃饭的精力<u>都</u>没有。

❷ 很多职业妇女们除了上班，还要照顾家庭，几乎连 + 休闲的时间 + 都 + 没有。

❸ 随着城市人口老龄化和农民工回乡潮流的出现，饭店连 + 服务员 + 也 + 很难招聘到了。

练习

1. 请在三篇短文中找出用以上句式的句子。
2. 请用上面的句式造句。Make up sentences using the sentence patterns above.

口语练习

短文 为了帮助员工做到工作与生活的平衡，不少公司开始实行灵活的工作时间。员工可以根据生活和家庭的需要来决定和调节上下班的时间。例如可以在上班前先去健身房运动，可以抽时间去学校接送孩子，甚至提早下班去参加读书会或者看球赛等。结果员工上班的实际时间没有减少，而且工作效率更高。灵活的工作时间不但让员工满意，而且让雇主也感到满意。

论点 灵活的工作时间可以帮助员工做到工作与生活的平衡。

1. 短文的主要意思是什么？
2. 根据短文，为什么灵活的工作时间让雇主满意？
3. "灵活的工作时间可以帮助员工做到工作与生活的平衡。"你同意这个论点吗？为什么？
4. 请谈谈除了实行灵活的工作时间，员工还可以怎么做到生活与工作的平衡？

写作练习

请写一篇 150 字左右的短文，可以考虑以下几点。

题目 谈谈《请投我一票》中的家长们的工作

1. 这几位候选人的家长分别是做什么工作的？
2. 哪一位家长的工作时间最有灵活性？

听力练习

一、小花跟她叔叔在聊工作和生活的方式。
　　1. 听对话，然后在正确的答案前打 ☒。
　　　　❶ 小花说她叔叔的肚子怎么样？
　　　　　　☐ A 像皮球
　　　　　　☐ B 有啤酒肚子
　　　　　　☐ C 很不健康
　　　　　　☐ D 像她爸爸现在的肚子
　　　　❷ 小花叔叔现在在哪儿工作？
　　　　　　☐ A 家里
　　　　　　☐ B 办公室
　　　　　　☐ C 酒吧
　　　　　　☐ D 鞋店
　　　　❸ 他每天花很多小时坐着做什么？（可以多选）
　　　　　　☐ A 看电视
　　　　　　☐ B 用电脑工作

Unit Two 教育与工作

- [ ] C 辅导孩子的功课
- [ ] D 吃饭

❹ 小花的爸爸每天都做些什么活动？（可以多选）
- [ ] A 休闲
- [ ] B 工作
- [ ] C 运动
- [ ] D 跟朋友见面

2. 再听一遍小花和她叔叔的这段对话，然后用中文回答下面的问题。
   ❶ 小花的叔叔胖是因为他常常喝酒吗？为什么？
   ❷ 小花的叔叔对自己的生活方式满意吗？为什么？
   ❸ 小花的爸爸认为工作是最重要的吗？
   ❹ 小花的爸爸是怎样平衡工作和生活的？

二、Listen to an excerpt of an interview between a radio reporter and a health expert, Dr Li, about work-life balance. You are not required to write in full English sentences. You must give two details for question (a) and two details for question (b).

(a) Summarise the examples given by Dr Li about the different stages in life when people feel very busy.

(b) Summarise the suggestions Dr Li makes about how to cope with pressure from work.

G 词语练习

根据英文，选字组词。

过　假　程

度（　） to go on holiday
度（　） to spend (time)
（　）度 level

须　要　定

必（　） certainly
必（　） have to
必（　） necessary

配　持　付

支（　） to support
支（　） to pay money
支（　） to allocate

空　水　气

抽（　） to spare the time
抽（　） to extract water
抽（　） to extract air

属　关　是

（　）于 with regard to
于（　） hence
（　）于 to belong

准　记　明

标（　） to mark
标（　） mark; sign
标（　） standard

Chapter 8 工作与生活的平衡

管　经　整
(　) 理　to sort out
(　) 理　management
(　) 理　manager

触　近　受
接 (　)　contact
接 (　)　to accept
接 (　)　close to

透　空　生
(　) 气　air
(　) 气　angry
(　) 气　breathable

率　果　法
效 (　)　efficiency
效 (　)　to follow the example of
效 (　)　effect

指　辅　领
(　) 导　to coach
(　) 导　leadership
(　) 导　to guide

处　立　自
独 (　)　by oneself
独 (　)　independent
独 (　)　be on one's own

精　活　努
(　) 力　energy
(　) 力　diligent
(　) 力　vigour

担　配　数
分 (　)　distribution
分 (　)　to share
分 (　)　score

G 选词填空

1. 跑步通勤　贤妻良母　家庭妇女　一石二鸟　急匆匆　开车上班

　　王勤是一位职业妇女，不但工作非常努力、出色，而且把孩子和丈夫的生活照顾得很好，大家都说她是一位 (　　)。她每天都是 (　　) 地 (　　)。这样，既可以节省时间，又可以锻炼身体，真是 (　　)。

2. 被　把　正　在　得　对　跟

　　90 后 (　　) 纷纷进入职场。这代人大多数是独生子女，人们 (　　) 他们称作"小皇帝""小公主"。父母和祖父母往往 (　　) 他们过分宠爱，因此他们中有很多人变 (　　) 非常自我。长大工作了，他们不知道应该怎么 (　　) 同事相处。

T 翻译练习

1. Translate the following paragraph into English.

　　王山是一家玩具工厂的总工程师，每天的工作紧张极了。下班回家后还要看报告和分析，休息的时间不多，休闲活动就更不用说了。王山的家人都劝他不要

71

Unit Two 教育与工作

把工作带回家，可是他说，在办公室他根本就没有时间看文件，不带回家，他又怎么能把工作做好呢？

王山这样的工作方式持续了四年。后来，他生病了，而且病得很严重。休息了大半年才慢慢地好起来。经过这次打击后，他决定改变自己的工作态度和生活方式，还培养了对园艺的爱好。

现在，他下班回家以后，就在花园里种花养草，修剪树枝。人放松了，工作也变得愉快起来。

2. 把下面的一段文字翻译成中文。

A hobby is something you enjoy doing and which makes you feel relaxed or happy when you are doing it. If a hobby becomes an obsession then it means you spend too much time on it, to the point where you can no longer keep up with your responsibilities at work or home.

Health professionals stress that having a hobby is very important for a balanced lifestyle. There are many different types of hobbies, both indoors and outdoors. They can include collecting themed items and objects, engaging in creative and artistic activities, playing sports, or other amusements. Whatever your hobby is, it is always nice to do something completely different from work as a way to relax.

Unit Three 中国文化

- Chapter 9　辞旧迎新
- Chapter 10　清明祭祖
- Chapter 11　漫谈端午
- Chapter 12　中秋佳节
- Chapter 13　中国的传统习俗

Unit Four 中国文化——文化活动

- Chapter 14　好读书　读书好　读好书
- Chapter 15　电影
- Chapter 16　电视
- Chapter 17　怡人的音乐

中国文化

TWO

第三单元　中国文化

　　这个单元覆盖了中国的清明节、端午节、中秋节和春节这四个重要的节日，以及中国的传统习俗。

　　中国的传统节日和习俗跟农耕文明有密切的关系。古代的农事是以季节变化作为一个周期来运作的，分为春种、夏长、秋收、冬藏。一些祭祀与活动也是配合农业耕作的节奏而产生。本单元涵盖的四个节日比较均衡地出现在四个季节不是偶然的，而是让人们可以有阶段性的休息、娱乐来调剂终日繁忙的农耕生活。每个节日都有其自己的特点、起源、故事、习俗，以及特定的饮食和娱乐。不过，他们的共同点是强调全家人一起过节以及祭祀祖先或者神灵，都是为了驱邪或者祈福。

• 清明节

　　每年公历的 4 月 5 日前后是清明节，正是春分过后，气温逐渐升高，雨量增多，是春耕春种，植树造林的好时节。古时候，人们忙完春种后，亲朋好友们会结伴去郊野春游，借此增进亲情与友情。清明节还有插柳、荡秋千和放风筝的习俗，这是古人绿化环境、强身健体的好方法。清明节前的一两天是寒食节，本是一个扫墓的日子，由于两个节日接近，逐渐合二为一，从此清明节开始有了扫墓祭祖的风俗。

• 端午节

　　端午节是在农历的五月初五。夏至时节，天气湿热，病菌繁殖快，人容易得病。于是人们在端午节会大扫除，并用不同的方法来驱赶蚊蝇。端午原来是一个祛病防疫的节日，后来因为南方的一位爱国诗人屈原在这一天跳江自尽，于是有了端午节起源与屈原有关的说法。至于划龙舟，中国古代南方的图腾是龙，本来就有划龙舟祭祀图腾的习俗，粽子也是早就有的一种食品。现在故事演变成：划龙舟是为了去寻找屈原的尸体，粽子喂鱼是让它们不伤害屈原的尸体。

• 中秋节

　　中秋节在农历的八月十五，这是一个庆祝丰收的节日。人们在享受丰收果实的同时，还会感恩风调雨顺的天气和肥沃的土地。古代的中国人崇拜月亮，他们以圆圆的月饼做祭品，向月亮表示感谢。一家人在吃了团圆饭后，坐在星空下品尝月饼，欣赏明月。月亮里各种影影绰绰的形状激发了人们丰富的想象力，给我们留下了嫦娥和玉兔等关于中秋节的美丽传说。

- **春节**

春节从农历正月初一开始，过了元宵节才结束。在农耕社会中，这是一个农闲修整，同时为开春农耕做准备的阶段。在这个辞旧迎新的时候，感谢神灵祖先一年来的保佑，祈祷来年的丰收，是每一个家庭的大事，必须全体成员聚集在一起，表示重视。就这样，逐渐形成了春节期间全家团聚的习俗，以及通过祭祖、吃团圆饭、守岁、拜年、走亲访友等活动来增加彼此的亲情和友情。

- **中国的传统习俗**

除了中国的每个节日都有各自的习俗外，表示喜庆的红色，丧礼中穿戴白色，以及在婚礼中喝"改口茶"等，也都是中国独特的传统习俗。

进入21世纪的网络时代，西方的节日与习俗为中国的年轻人所接受，中国的传统习俗将发生怎么样的变化？我们应该如何保存传统习俗？这些都成为了新课题，需要我们思考。

Unit 3 Chinese Culture

Unit 3 focuses on the topics relating to the four most important Chinese festivals, namely the Qing Ming Festival, Dragon Boat Festival, Mid-Autumn Festival, and Spring Festival, and other customs.

Chinese traditional festivals and their customs are closely related to agriculture. In ancient times agricultural activities revolved around the four seasons and were generally divided into spring sowing, summer growing, autumn harvesting, and winter storing, thus completing a year's cycle. Some of the sacrificial rituals and activities also corresponded to the different stages of agricultural work. The above four festivals represented more evenly the division of the four seasons, throughout which people could rest and engage in leisurely activities as a change to busy agricultural life. Each festival has its own characteristics, origin, story, custom, food and entertainment. However, they also have something in common, and that is their emphasis on the whole family celebrating the festival together as well as paying respect to the ancestors and worshipping the super beings. They also want to drive away evil spirits and pray for happiness.

- **Qing Ming Festival**

The Qing Ming Festival falls on the 5th (before or after) of April, after the Spring Equinox,

Unit Three 中国文化

in the Gregorian calendar every year. Around that time the weather warms up and the rainfall increases. This is the best season for ploughing and sowing as well as planting trees. In ancient times, when peasants finished their work in the fields, they liked to organise outings with friends and relatives as a way to socialise. People also played on the swing and flew kites. These activities were good for protecting the environment and keeping fit. A day or two before the Qing Ming Festival, there was another festival called "Cold Food". This was a festival for sweeping the tomb. As both festivals were very close to each other, they were combined into one and since then the Qing Ming Festival began to assume the customs of sweeping the tomb and paying respect to the ancestors.

• Dragon Boat Festival

The Dragon Boat Festival falls on the 5th day of the 5th month of the lunar calendar. Around the Summer Solstice, the weather was hot and humid, a favourable condition for bacteria to grow fast, making people ill more readily. To combat this, people organised spring cleans during the Dragon Boat Festival. They used different methods to repel snakes and insects. The Dragon Boat Festival had been intended as a time for curing illnesses and epidemic prevention. Later on because of a patriotic poet by the name of Qu Yuan in southern China, who killed himself by jumping into a river, the incident became the legend associated with the festival. The Dragon was a totem in southern ancient China. Rowing dragon boats was the custom of worshipping the totem. Rice dumplings already existed then. Nowadays the legend has evolved into one in which people believe that the purpose of rowing a dragon boat is to look for Qu Yuan's body, and that throwing rice dumplings into the water is to feed the fish so that they will not harm his body.

• Mid-autumn Festival

The Mid-Autumn Festival falls on the 15th day of the 8th month of the lunar calendar. This was a time for celebrating harvest. People thanked the good weather and fertile land for their crops while enjoying the result of their hard labour. In ancient times, Chinese people used to worship the moon. They made round moon cakes as offerings to express gratitude to the moon. When families finished their reunion meal, they sat under the moon and enjoyed the moon cakes. The shadowy shapes in the moon inspired the Chinese imagination, which later created the story of Chang E and the jade rabbit.

• Spring Festival

The Spring Festival begins on the 1st day of the 1st month of the lunar calendar and lasts until the Yuan Xiao Festival which is on the 15th day of the same month. In agricultural society, this was a period of rest, repair, as well as preparation for ploughing the land in the New Year.

During this time it was important for the whole family to thank the spirits and ancestors for their protection throughout the year, and to pray for a good harvest in the coming year. The whole family got together to show the importance with which they regarded this matter. Gradually family reunions during the Spring Festival became an established custom. Paying respect to the ancestors, the family reunion dinner, seeing the New Year in, paying New Year's calls to friends and relatives are a way to enhance the relationship with each other.

· Chinese customs

Apart from the special customs for each festival, there are other customs such as using the colour red to represent joy and jubilation, white to express loss and sadness, and drinking tea not just as an everyday beverage but in a special ceremony at a wedding, which are quite unique in Chinese culture.

In the 21st century and in the world of the Internet, Western festivals and customs are accepted by the Chinese younger generation. How the Chinese traditions and customs will change and how they should be preserved have become emerging issues to be considered.

9 辞旧迎新

短文一　Text One

■ 春节联欢会

我们虽然居住在英国，可是这儿庆祝中国新年的活动越来越受到本地人的欢迎，过年的气氛非常热闹。昨天是农历的大年初一，我们的中文学校也举办了庆祝活动。

当学生们走到礼堂时，一位老师站在门口给大家发红包。礼堂里一片喜气洋洋。礼堂前挂着一对大红灯笼，一边的墙上倒贴着"福"字和十二生肖的图片，另一边墙上有一对春联："春回大地，福到人间"。老师、家长和学生们一见面就互相拜年，"恭喜发财""心想事成""学业进步"等祝贺语此起彼伏。学生们为庆新春准备了丰富多彩的节目：扇子舞、红绸舞、民歌演唱和功夫表演等，精彩极了，得到了大家的好评。

表演结束后，大家都兴高采烈地坐下来，享用家长们带来的新年食品，其中最受欢迎的就是饺子和年糕，每个人都吃得津津有味。

生词

气氛	qìfēn	atmosphere
农历	nónglì	lunar calendar
喜气洋洋	xǐqì yángyáng	full of joy
十二生肖	shí'èr shēngxiào	12 Chinese zodiac
春联	chūnlián	spring couplets
此起彼伏	cǐqǐ bǐfú	to rise or appear one after another
红绸舞	hóngchóu wǔ	red ribbon dance
好评	hǎopíng	good comments/ reviews
兴高采烈	xìnggāo cǎiliè	in high spirits; in great delight

R 读完上面的短文，回答下面的问题。Answer the following questions in Chinese.

1. 作者昨天在哪里参加了庆祝新春的活动？
2. 礼堂里墙上布置了一些什么？
3. 大家见面时说些什么祝贺语？
4. 庆祝会上有什么表演？
5. 大家觉得表演怎么样？
6. 表演结束后大家做了什么？

Snippet

挥春与春联

　　新春期间，中国人有写挥春的习俗。挥春写在红纸上，字数各有不同。单字最常见的是"福"，双字的有"大吉"，四个字的最多："迎春接福""龙马精神""如意吉祥""出入平安""年年有余""招财进宝""丰衣足食"等都是很常见的。挥春贴在墙上或门上，目的是祈求在新的一年有好运来临。

　　另外是春联。春联都是成对的，讲究上下联字数的相等，平仄的相调。很多都是贴在门上，期盼来年会给自己及家人带来好运。常见的春联有：

风调雨顺，国泰民安

爆竹一声除旧，春联万户更新

和和顺顺千家乐，月月年年百姓福

W Find more 挥春 and 春联 and write them down on red paper. They can be displayed in the classroom.

短文二　Text Two

年兽的传说

　　据说在很久很久以前，一只叫"年"，也叫"夕"的怪兽，总是在年末的时候出现。它到村子里去吃猪、牛、羊等，吃完了以后就吃人，村民们都害怕得不得了。不过，后来人们发现，怪兽害怕火光、巨响和红色。于是大家都穿上红衣服，在门上贴上红纸，敲锣打鼓，还放爆竹和烟花，怪兽被吓得逃跑了。这就是"除夕"的意思。人们开始舞龙舞狮，欢天喜地地庆祝赶跑了怪兽；同时，也兴高采烈地迎接新年的到来。

　　实际上，这只是一个古老的传说。年末是寒冷的冬天，很多地方是一片冰天雪地，森林里、山洞里的一些野兽找不到食物，就会到村子里来吃牲畜，甚至人。这些野兽就是传说中的"年"。

生词

传说	chuánshuō	legend
据说	jùshuō	it is said
怪兽	guàishòu	monster
年末	niánmò	end of year
巨响	jùxiǎng	huge noise
敲锣打鼓	qiāoluó dǎgǔ	to beat the gongs and drums
爆竹	bàozhú	fire cracker
吓	xià	to scare
逃跑	táopǎo	to flee
除夕	chúxī	New Year's Eve
欢天喜地	huāntiān xǐdì	wild with joy
实际上	shíjìshang	in reality
山洞	shāndòng	cave
野兽	yěshòu	wild animal
牲畜	shēngchù	livestock

短文三 Text Three

除夕

农历年的最后一天叫除夕，也叫大年夜。世界各地的华人都尽可能在除夕前赶回家，为了可以和家人团圆，一起吃年夜饭，一起辞旧迎新。

年夜饭不但要吃鱼，而且这道菜不能吃完，因为汉语中"鱼"和"余"是同音字，表示"年年有余"的意思。北方人要吃饺子，因为饺子的形状像金元宝，有富贵的意思；南方人要吃年糕，因为"糕"和"高"同音，表达人们期待"年年高升""高高兴兴"。吃了年夜饭，长辈会给小辈发红包，红包里的钱叫"压岁钱"。"岁"与"祟"是同音字，"祟"有"鬼怪"或"鬼怪害人"的意思，古人认为"压岁钱"可以让一切害人的东西远离孩子，保佑他们健康成长。

总之，华人在过年的时候，无论是食品，还是活动，都有驱邪祈福的意思。

生词

团圆	tuányuán	reunion
年夜饭	niányèfàn	meal eaten on New Year's Eve
辞旧迎新	cíjiù yíngxīn	to say farewell to the old and to welcome in the new
余	yú	surplus
金元宝	jīnyuánbǎo	gold ingot used as money in ancient China
富贵	fùguì	riches and honour
长辈	zhǎngbèi	older generation
祟	suì	evil spirit
压岁钱	yāsuìqián	money given to children as a Chinese New Year gift
保佑	bǎoyòu	to protect and bless
驱邪	qūxié	to drive away the evil spirits
祈福	qífú	to pray for happiness

R 读完上面的短文，回答下面的问题。Answer the following questions in Chinese.

1. 除夕是哪一天？
2. 为什么华人都希望在除夕前回家？
3. 年夜饭要吃什么？
4. 为什么长辈要给小辈红包？
5. 过年的时候，华人的食品和活动有什么特点？

S You are asked to speak in a class assembly in Chinese about the Chinese New Year. You must include the following:
1. 中国新年又叫什么？为什么？
2. 中国新年时，华人一般会有些什么活动？
3. 华人为什么觉得中国新年重要？
4. 讲一个你庆祝新年的经历。

Snippet
元宵是一种什么食品？

在元宵节，华人要吃一种传统的节日食品，这种食品在中国北方叫元宵，在南方叫汤圆。元宵不但可以在节日吃，平时也可以当点心吃。元宵有多种馅料，其中芝麻馅、豆沙馅最普遍。人们会在元宵节的晚上，也就是在春节过后第一次看到月圆时，大家吃元宵、汤圆，意喻团团圆圆、平平安安。

R / S 猜灯谜——灯谜是谜语的一种形式，猜灯谜是元宵节的活动之一。人们把写好的谜语贴在花灯上，让看灯的人一边赏灯，一边猜谜。谜语可以是猜字，也可以是猜事物。下面是几个谜语，你试试能否猜中。

1. 有时像圆盘，有时像小船，白天看不见，夜里才见面。　　　　　（猜一物）
2. 人在草木中。　　　　　　　　　　　　　　　　　　　　　　　（猜一字）
3. 左边缺点水，右边全是水。　　　　　　　　　　　　　　　　　（猜一字）
4. 外面看是绿的，里面看是红的，吃起来是甜的，吐出来是黑的。
　　　　　　　　　　　　　　　　　　　　　　　　　　　　　　（猜一物）
5. 这物长来真奇怪，肚子上面长口袋，孩子袋里吃和睡，跑得不快跳得快。
　　　　　　　　　　　　　　　　　　　　　　　　　　　　　　（猜一物）
6. 有面没有口，有脚没有手，虽有四只脚，自己不会走。　　　　　（猜一物）
7. 值钱不值钱，全在这两点。　　　　　　　　　　　　　　　　　（猜一字）
8. 两动物，站一起，一个有角，一个有尾，一个在山，一个在水。
　　　　　　　　　　　　　　　　　　　　　　　　　　　　　　（猜一字）

句式学习

1. 无论 / 不论……还 / 都 / 也……

无论 (wúlùn) means "no matter" and is generally used in the first part of the sentence. As with many other constructions, 还, 都 and 也 can be used in the second part of the sentence, making the whole sentence to emphasize

Unit Three 中国文化

that the action or decision will not change.

例句：❶ <u>无论</u>是国内的中国人，<u>还</u>是海外的华人，<u>都</u>特别重视在除夕吃团圆饭的习俗。

❷ <u>不论</u>来自哪个民族，大家<u>都</u>兴高采烈地去伦敦市中心参加庆祝春节的活动。

2. **总而言之/总之**

   总之 is a short term for 总而言之. It has the meaning of "first and last" or "in a word, in short", to be used for drawing a conclusion.

   例句：❶ 过年时候吃的东西有年糕、饺子、春卷、汤圆等等，<u>总之</u>，什么食品都好吃极了。

   ❷ 红绸舞、扇子舞、武术表演、民歌演唱……，<u>总而言之</u>，春节晚会的节目都非常精彩。

3. **Structure a: place + 有 + somebody/something**
   Structure b: place + verb + 着 + somebody/something

   The two structures above are different and their meanings are not exactly the same. Although both structures indicate the existence of somebody/something, **Structure b** gives additional information whereas **Structure a** does not.

   例句：
   - 1a 礼堂里 + 有 + 很多红灯笼。
   - 1b 礼堂里 + 挂着 + 很多红灯笼。
   - 2a 运动场上 + 有 + 成千上万的学生。
   - 2b 运动场上 + 站着 + 成千上万的学生。

练习

1. 请在三篇短文中找出用以上句式的句子。
2. 请用上面的句式造句。Make up sentences using the sentence patterns above.

S 口语练习

主题二 中国文化

次主题 传统

春节

你必须思考以下几点：
- 常见的春节食品。
- 为什么华人觉得回家吃年夜饭很重要？
- 华人怎么表示驱邪祈福的心愿？

W 写作练习

请写一篇 150 字左右的短文，可以考虑以下几点。

题目 谈谈《惠安馆》中的秀贞

1. 秀贞房间的墙上贴着一张什么画？请简单介绍一下。
2. 为什么这张年画一直贴在墙上？
3. 秀贞经常提到的小桂子是谁？

L 听力练习

一、请听健明和他外公外婆的一段对话，完成下面的练习。

1. 听对话，在正确的答案前打 ☒。

    ❶ 健明的小姨会请他吃什么？
    - [ ] A 年糕
    - [ ] B 面条
    - [ ] C 饺子
    - [ ] D 包子

    ❷ 外公外婆希望健明用红包里的钱去买什么？
    - [ ] A 手提电脑
    - [ ] B 手机
    - [ ] C 手套
    - [ ] D 手袋

    ❸ 外公说他和健明的外婆只想什么？
    - [ ] A 只想发财
    - [ ] B 只想年轻
    - [ ] C 只想身体好
    - [ ] D 只想工作顺利

    ❹ 中国人过年吃鱼是表示希望什么？
    - [ ] A 高高兴兴
    - [ ] B 大吉大利
    - [ ] C 年年有余
    - [ ] D 学业进步

2. 再听一遍健明和他外公外婆的这段对话，然后用中文回答下面的问题。

    ❶ 为什么健明的小姨不能亲自把红包给他？
    ❷ 健明的外公外婆做了什么给他吃？
    ❸ 为什么过年时要吃这个食品？
    ❹ 中国人过年的食品一般都讲究什么？

Unit Three 中国文化

二、Listen to the conversation and summarise the details given by Xiao Kang and her mum about the Lantern Festival. You are not required to write in full English sentences. You must give two details for question (a) and two details for question (b).

(a) Summarise the things Chinese people do during the Lantern Festival.

(b) Summarise what Xiao Kang says about nowadays things being better than before.

G 词语练习

根据英文，选字组词。

历　民　村

农（　）lunar calendar
农（　）countryside
农（　）peasant

日　半　深

（　）夜　day and night
（　）夜　late at night
（　）夜　midnight

佑　护　证

保（　）to protect
保（　）to bless
保（　）to guarantee

论　语　分

评（　）to give a mark
评（　）comment
评（　）to discuss

据　传　听

（　）说　legend has it
（　）说　it is said
（　）说　to hear of

跑　课　离

逃（　）to run away
逃（　）to escape
逃（　）to skip classes

肖　活　动

生（　）life
生（　）lively
生（　）zodiac

春　关　对

（　）联　couplet
（　）联　New Year scroll
（　）联　associated with

祈　幸　祝

（　）福　to pray for happiness
（　）福　happiness
（　）福　blessing

赶　逐　邪

驱（　）to drive away
驱（　）to expel, to banish
驱（　）to drive away the evil spirits

野　怪　医

兽（　）vet
（　）兽　monster
（　）兽　wild animal

响　大　人

巨（　）huge
巨（　）huge noise
巨（　）giant

G 选词填空

1. 的　得　地　在　着　了　过　都　对

过年时，中国到处是喜气洋洋（　　）气氛。妈妈准备好（　　）年夜饭，就兴高采烈（　　）说："开饭啦！"饭桌上放（　　）糖醋鱼、长命菜、炒年糕、蛋饺汤等，各种菜（　　）美味极了。我从来没吃（　　）这么好吃的鱼，每个人都吃（　　）津津有味。

2. 此起彼伏　辞旧迎新　喜气洋洋　驱邪祈福　各种各样　兴高采烈

在这（　　）的时候，爆竹声、锣鼓声（　　）。人们见了面都会互相说（　　）的祝贺语，表示（　　）的心愿。

T 翻译练习

1. Translate the following paragraph into English.

　　正月十五是元宵节，也叫花灯节，是中国的传统节日之一。这一天，南方人吃汤圆，北方人吃元宵。其实汤圆就是元宵。人们还放鞭炮、挂花灯、舞狮子等。

　　晚上，在公园里或者广场上，布置了各种各样的花灯，供大家欣赏。那里还有不少小摊卖小吃，也有些挂着花灯，让游人猜谜语。

　　这个节日虽然没有春节有名，但是我觉得它很热闹，也很有趣。

2. 把下面的一段文字翻译成中文。

　　Eating dumplings during Spring Festival is one of the festive customs widely practised among the Chinese wherever they live. People put different fillings inside the dumplings; meat, vegetables and prawns are very common ingredients used. Sometimes a coin is put into one of the dumplings. Whoever picks it up is thought to be lucky in money matters.

　　Another practice is to put sugar inside a dumpling. It is said to bring the picker a sweet life and luck in the coming year.

10 清明祭祖

短文一　Text One

主题：清明见面

丽莎表姐：

　　你好！告诉你一个最新消息：妈妈昨天说，我们今年三月底会回一次台北，要去祭祖。想到回去就能跟你再见面，真高兴。不过，我不明白什么是"祭祖"。

玛莉

玛莉：

　　你好！听到你要回来的消息，我也很高兴！

　　"祭祖"就是"祭拜祖先"。清明节在公历4月5日左右，人们一般会去先人的坟墓前，献上鲜花，摆上死者生前喜爱的食品等，表示对死者的感恩和悼念。

　　每年清明节我们都要去给外公和外婆扫墓。他们生前特别爱山茶花，我们去扫墓时，总是带一束山茶花去敬献。

　　我和父母已经说好了，祭拜完毕后，会跟你们和其他亲戚一同去附近的阳明山踏青。那里的风景优美，是游山玩水的好地方。你还记得我俩小时候一起在那座山上放过风筝吗？期待你回来！

丽莎

生词

消息	xiāoxi	news
祭祖	jìzǔ	to pay respect to ancestors
祭拜	jìbài	to worship
坟墓	fénmù	grave
献上	xiàn shang	to offer (such as flowers)
摆上	bǎishang	to put in front of
死者	sǐzhě	the dead
生前	shēng qián	before a person's death
感恩	gǎn'ēn	thanksgiving
悼念	dàoniàn	mourning
扫墓	sǎomù	to sweep the grave
山茶花	shānchá huā	camellia
束	shù	a bunch (of flowers)
敬献	jìngxiàn	to present (respectfully)
踏青	tàqīng	to do an outing

Chapter 10　清明祭祖

R　读完上面的短文，回答下面的问题。Answer the following questions in Chinese.

1. 玛莉告诉丽莎什么消息？
2. 清明节是什么时候？
3. 清明节时人们会做什么？
4. 丽莎和家人会带什么去祭拜外公外婆？为什么？
5. 今年扫墓后，他们计划做什么？
6. 玛莉和丽莎小时候喜爱做什么？

―― Snippet ――

清明节与复活节

　　清明节一般在农历二月中旬，公历4月5日前后（多为5日，有时为4日或者6日）。用农历的节气（solar terms）来计算，清明就在春分（Equinox）后的第15天。

　　西方的复活节（Easter Sunday）跟清明节一样，每年的日期也不同。复活节的计算方法是每年3月21日，或者过了3月21日月圆后的第一个星期日。

　　如果清明节刚巧跟复活节很接近，很多海外华人会利用复活节的假期回乡扫墓，也借此机会探亲和旅游。

短文二　Text Two

清明节的习俗

　　每年公历的4月5日或前后一天是清明节。这时候气温升高，雨量增多，"清明前后，种瓜种豆"，正是春耕春种、植树造林的好时节。古时候，人们忙完春种后，亲朋好友们会结伴去踏青、探春，亲近自然，放松自我，同时也可以增进人与人之间的亲情与友情。清明节还有插柳、荡秋千和放风筝的习俗，这是人们绿化环境、强身健体的好方法。

　　古时候，还有一个寒食节，在清明节前的一两天。这是一个禁止用火、只吃冷食以及扫墓的日子。由于两个节日接近，逐渐合二为一，清明节开始有了扫墓祭祖的风俗，而寒食节则被人们渐渐地忘记了。

　　总之，清明节有对祖先的悼念和感恩，也有对寒冬过去、春天回来、迎接新生的欢乐之情。

生词

种瓜 种豆	zhòngguā zhòngdòu	to grow melon and bean
春耕 春种	chūngēng chūnzhòng	to grow crops in spring
植树 造林	zhíshù zàolín	to plant trees to make a forest
结伴	jiébàn	to do something together with others
探春	tànchūn	to explore the spring scenery
插柳	chāliǔ	to plant willows
荡秋千	dàngqiūqiān	to play on a swing
寒食节	hánshíjié	Cold Food Festival
禁止	jìnzhǐ	to forbid

87

Unit Three 中国文化

R 读完上面的短文，回答下面的问题。Answer the following questions in Chinese.

1. 清明节在什么时候？
2. 清明时节适合做什么？
3. 亲朋好友一起踏青有什么好处？
4. 古代清明节有什么习俗？这些习俗对什么好？
5. 清明节怎么会有扫墓的风俗？
6. 扫墓有什么意义？

短文三 Text Three

《清明上河图》

《清明上河图》是中国古代十大名画之一，是北宋时一位名叫张择端（1085—1145）的画家所作。

这幅画描绘了当时的首都（今天的开封）以及汴河两岸的自然风光和繁华景象，还有百姓的日常生活。从这幅画上可以看到，路上、河边、树林里有赶去扫墓的或者踏青回来的人；街道上有"王家纸马店"，专门卖扫墓祭品。不过这幅画的主题是清明时节的活动，并不专门描绘清明的扫墓和祭祖。

在这幅宽约 0.25 米、长 5.28 米的画上，大概有 814 个人、60 只动物、170 棵树、28 艘船、30 座建筑、20 辆车和 8 顶轿子等。因为有人物和建筑，所以从这幅画也可以看到当时人们的服饰风格、他们的职业、商店的种类以及建筑的风格。

《清明上河图》是一幅世界闻名的风俗画，现收藏在北京故宫博物院。

生词

北宋	Běisòng	Northern Song Dynasty (960-1127AD)
描绘	miáohuì	to depict
汴河	biànhé	Bian River, a river within Kai Feng
繁华	fánhuá	bustling; prosperous
景象	jǐngxiàng	scene
百姓	bǎixìng	people; general public
纸马	zhǐmǎ	paper horse (horse made with paper and bamboo strips)
专门	zhuānmén	specialised
祭品	jìpǐn	offerings put in front of grave
宽	kuān	wide
艘	sōu	(measure word for ships)
辆	liàng	(measure word for vehicles)
顶	dǐng	(measure word for sedan chairs)
轿子	jiào	sedan chair
服饰	fúshì	costume
风格	fēnggé	style
收藏	shōucáng	be kept (as in a museum)

R 读完上面的短文，回答下面的问题。Answer the following questions in Chinese.

1. 这幅画是哪一个时代的作品？
2. 这幅画描绘了什么地方的景色和百姓的生活？
3. 哪些场景表现了清明习俗？
4. 画上有些什么交通工具？
5. 为什么说这是一幅风俗画？
6. 你现在在哪里可以看到这幅画？

S 在网上看看《清明上河图》，选出一个你喜欢的部分，在班上用中文详细地描述这部分的景象、人物和活动，并说说为什么你喜欢这部分。

W 用中文写一篇文章（150字左右），说说你去拜祭先人的经过。文章内容可以包括：

1. 你跟谁去扫墓？
2. 你去扫谁的墓？
3. 你们带了什么祭品去扫墓？为什么？
4. 扫墓的时候，你们都做了什么？
5. 你觉得还有什么其他方式可以悼念先人？

Snippet

Qing Ming frequently appears in Chinese literature. Among these, the most famous is probably Du Mu's poem, simply entitled Qing Ming:

清　明
杜牧

清明时节雨纷纷，
路上行人欲断魂。
借问酒家何处有，
牧童遥指杏花村。

释：清明前后阴雨绵绵，淋湿的行人伤心悲哀。请问："哪儿有喝酒的地方？"放牛的孩子指向远处的杏花村。

句式学习

1. "大约/大概"与"左右"的分别

They all mean "approximately" or "about", but the position of each in a phrase is different. 大约/大概 are placed before the number, while 左右 is placed after the number.

Unit Three 中国文化

例句：**1a** 清明节参加植树造林的人数<u>大约／大概</u>有五百人。
　　　1b 清明节参加植树造林的人数有五百人<u>左右</u>。
　　　2a 中国的很多传统节日，已经有<u>大约／大概</u>三千年的历史了。
　　　2b 中国的很多传统节日，已经有三千年<u>左右</u>的历史了。

2. **年／月初，年／月底**
Early in the year/early in the month, end of the year/end of the month
例句：❶ 春节有时候在公历的一月<u>底</u>，有时候在公历的二月<u>初</u>，每年都不一样。
　　　❷ 李海在年<u>初</u>的时候买了去健身房的年卡，可是到年<u>底</u>发现自己一年一共去了不到十次。

3. **动词 + 好了**
This structure indicates that action has completed.
例句：❶ 外祖母把鸡蛋煮 + <u>好了</u>，孩子们可以开始做"画蛋"的活动了。
　　　❷ 小红做 + <u>好了</u>作业就去帮助妈妈做家务。

4. **某些**
Used before a noun, means "certain". Together they mean certain things or certain objects.
例句：❶ 明天的春游活动，<u>某些</u>人不会去。
　　　❷ 故宫博物院的<u>某些</u>名画曾经到香港展览过。
　　　❸ 清明节的时候，中国南方的<u>某些</u>地区要吃青团。

练习
1. 请在三篇短文中找出用以上句式的句子。
2. 请用上面的句式造句。Make up sentences using the sentence patterns above.

S 口语练习

主题二 中国文化
次主题 传统
清明节

你必须思考以下几点：
- 清明节有哪些常见的活动？
- 什么人过清明节？
- 华人为什么觉得清明节很重要？

W 写作练习

请写一篇 150 字左右的短文，可以考虑以下几点。

题目 谈谈《惠安馆》中的宋妈

1. 宋妈的语言有什么特点？
2. 她几次提到妞儿的什么外貌特征？
3. 宋妈为什么要"在铁道旁边"把妞儿的两件衣服烧了？

L 听力练习

一、请听小红和丽丽的一段对话。

1. 听对话，在正确的答案前打 ☒。

    ❶ 清明节在什么时候？
    - ☐ A 下个星期
    - ☐ B 下个月
    - ☐ C 下星期三
    - ☐ D 下个周末

    ❷ 丽丽是哪个组织的会员？
    - ☐ A 树林之友
    - ☐ B 地球之友
    - ☐ C 植树团体
    - ☐ D 我爱地球

    ❸ 丽丽计划在星期日做什么活动？
    - ☐ A 扫墓
    - ☐ B 看电影
    - ☐ C 做蛋糕
    - ☐ D 植树

    ❹ 丽丽会带什么去祭祖？
    - ☐ A 食物
    - ☐ B 树
    - ☐ C 鲜花
    - ☐ D 水

2. 再听一遍小红和丽丽的这段对话，然后用中文回答下面的问题。

    ❶ 清明节是做什么的好时节？
    ❷ 丽丽所在地区的"地球之友"小组准备举办一个什么活动？
    ❸ 小红为什么要带蛋糕去扫墓？
    ❹ 小红和丽丽约定什么时候在哪里集合？

Unit Three 中国文化

二、Listen to the conversation and summarise the details given by Mingdong and his mum about kite-flying. You are not required to write in full English sentences. You must give two details for question (a) and two details for question (b).

(a) Summarise what Mingdong did when his mum reminded him about going kite-flying during the Qing Ming Festival.

(b) Summarise what Mingdong's mum said about who first flew kites and what they used to make kites with.

G 词语练习

根据英文，选字组词。

祖　拜　品

祭（　）to worship
祭（　）offerings
祭（　）to worship ancestors

恩　动　谢

感（　）gratitude
感（　）to feel moved
感（　）thanksgiving

悼　想　纪

（　）念 commemorate
（　）念 to mourn
（　）念 to miss (someone)

华　忙　重

繁（　）flourishing
繁（　）heavy; strenuous
繁（　）busy

礼　献　重

敬（　）to offer with respect
敬（　）to respect
敬（　）to salute

禁　停　终

（　）止 to prohibit
（　）止 to stop
（　）止 to terminate

食　冷　假

寒（　）cold food
寒（　）winter vacation
寒（　）chilly

戚　切　爱

亲（　）dear
亲（　）relative
亲（　）kind

坟　扫　公

（　）墓 cemetery
（　）墓 grave
（　）墓 sweep the grave

都　先　相

首（　）capital
首（　）the first
首（　）prime minister

藏　入　成

收（　）to collect and store up
收（　）income
收（　）harvest

G 选词填空

1. 个　艘　辆　棵　幅　只　座　架

清明节放假，马兰和朋友们乘坐一（　　）旅游车来到郊区踏青。河上有一（　　）小桥，桥下停着两（　　）木船。河边长着七八（　　）古树，树上还有几（　　）小鸟在欢乐地叫着。这么美丽的风景，就好像一（　　）画。

2. 锻炼身体　强身健体　合二为一　游山玩水　植树造林　绿化环境

清明前后，不但适合人们去（　　），这也是一个（　　）的好时节。在室外为（　　）出力，还可以（　　），真是一举两得的好事情。

T 翻译练习

1. Translate the following paragraph into English.

中国的每个传统节日，差不多都有特别的饮食。例如春节吃饺子和年糕，中秋节吃月饼等，清明节也一样。

在广东，民间习俗认为，清明节吃个鸡蛋，一整年都能有好身体。清明节吃鸡蛋的起源，是古代某些地区有禁火的习俗。禁火就是不能点火煮食物，只能吃生食或者冷食。在禁火前把一些鸡蛋煮熟了，可以吃几天。鸡蛋成了禁火期间最好的食品。

清明节这天，鸡蛋除了吃，还可以让孩子做"画蛋"的活动。鸡蛋画得五颜六色的，特别有趣，受到孩子们的欢迎。

2. 把下面的一段文字翻译成中文。

In recent years spring outings have become extremely popular in China. Workplaces such as factories, offices organise group outings to go outside towns and cities for leisure.

These outings usually cover sightseeing trips to well-known places of historic interest and scenic beauty. Activities like these provide opportunities for establishing closer friendships among colleagues. Families also take advantages of the holidays to go to parks or the seaside to have fun.

Glossary:
Spring outings 春游（chūnyóu）

11 漫谈端午

短文一 Text One

端午节与屈原的故事

很多华人相信，过端午节跟纪念爱国诗人屈原有关。

大约在2300年前，中国分成多个小国，其中有一个叫楚国。楚国有一位大臣叫屈原，他也是一位出色的诗人。他提出过很多好建议来帮助楚国强大，可是楚王不但不听，还把他驱赶出了京城。屈原来到南方，经常在汨罗江边作诗。后来，楚国被秦国打败，屈原伤心极了。于是，在五月初五那天，他抱着石头跳江自杀了。

老百姓听到这个消息，纷纷划着船来救他，可是连他的尸体也找不到了。于是人们就用竹叶把米包成一个个粽子扔进江里，把雄黄酒倒进江里，百姓们希望龙和鱼吃饱喝醉，就不会去吃屈原的尸体了。

此后每年的五月初五，人们都以划龙舟、包粽子的活动来纪念屈原。这些活动也逐渐成了端午节的传统习俗。

生词		
楚国	Chǔguó	the State of Chu
大臣	dàchén	minister
提出	tíchū	to suggest
驱赶	qūgǎn	to expel; to banish
汨罗江	Mìluó jiāng	Miluo River, situated in northern Hunan Province
秦国	Qínguó	the State of Qin
打败	dǎbài	to defeat
自杀	zìshā	to commit suicide
尸体	shītǐ	corpse
扔进	rēngjìn	to throw in
雄黄	xiónghuáng	realgar, a mineral
喝醉	hēzuì	be drunk

R 读完上面的短文，回答下面的问题。Answer the following questions in Chinese.

1. 屈原是谁？
2. 他为什么会离开京城？
3. 他为什么自杀？
4. 老百姓听到屈原自杀的消息后做了些什么？
5. 老百姓为什么这么做？
6. 现在人们怎么纪念屈原？

短文二 Text Two

端午节的风俗

农历的五月初五，也叫"端午"。这个时节，天气湿热，蚊子、苍蝇、害虫和蛇都出来了，病菌也繁殖得快，人很容易生病。

古人早就认识到清洁卫生的重要，所以到了五月，家家户户都会大扫除。人们还会戴香包，在门旁挂香草、大蒜等来驱赶蚊蝇。雄黄是一种能够杀菌的中药，古人会在院子里洒雄黄水消毒，有的人还喝雄黄酒。

由此可见，端午节原来是一个预防疾病的日子，后来因为楚国的爱国诗人屈原在这一天跳江自杀，从此端午节就与纪念屈原相关了。据说划龙舟可能起源于古代中国的南方，那里有祭水神或龙神的活动；粽子也是南方早就有的一种食品。后来，赛龙舟、吃粽子、大扫除、挂香草、戴香袋等习俗逐渐都成为了端午节的传统习俗。

生词

湿热	shīrè	hot and humid
蚊子	wénzi	mosquito
苍蝇	cāngying	fly
害虫	hàichóng	pest
病菌	bìngjūn	bacteria
繁殖	fánzhí	to breed
卫生	wèishēng	hygiene
香包	xiāngbāo	scented pouch
香草	xiāngcǎo	herb
大蒜	dàsuàn	garlic
杀菌	shājūn	to kill germs
洒	sǎ	to sprinkle
消毒	xiāodú	to sterilise
预防	yùfáng	to prevent
疾病	jíbìng	illness

R 读完上面的短文，回答下面的问题。Answer the following questions in Chinese.

1. 为什么端午时节人很容易生病？
2. 从哪里可以看出古人对清洁卫生的重视？
3. 雄黄是一种什么中药？
4. 雄黄水可以用来做什么？
5. 你知道划龙舟的起源吗？
6. 谈谈端午节有哪些传统习俗。

―――――― Snippet ――――――

粽子是一种什么食品？

粽子是一种用竹叶或苇叶包裹糯米的食品。从外形看，常见的有三角粽、四角粽或枕头粽等；从食材看，有鲜肉粽、蛋黄粽、豆沙粽、红枣粽或红豆粽等。粽子的起源据说与古代祭龙或后来祭屈原有关。

Unit Three 中国文化

Rice dumplings are usually eaten around the Dragon Boat Festival. They are made with glutinous rice or sticky rice and wrapped in bamboo or reed leaves. They can have three or four points or just be a flat parcel. The fillings for savoury dumplings may include meat, salted eggs and dried shrimps; while sweet ones may include bean paste, dates and nuts. According to legend, rice dumplings may have been used as offerings to worship dragons or to pay respect to Qu Yuan in ancient times.

短文三 Text Three

《白蛇传》的故事

《白蛇传》讲的是一个关于人和妖的爱情故事。

白素贞本来是一条白蛇，为了报答书生许仙前世的救命之恩，变成了人。她用了法力，跟许仙相爱并结了婚。

金山寺的和尚法海告诉许仙，他的妻子是一条蛇，许仙不太相信。法海说服他在端午节那天，让素贞喝下了雄黄酒。喝了酒的白素贞真的变回了一条蛇，还把许仙吓死了。

为了救丈夫，素贞到天上去偷了仙草。可是法海把许仙关在金山寺里，素贞见不到丈夫。她就和妹妹小青作法，发大水淹了金山寺。可是她们伤害了其他生灵，要受惩罚。素贞一生下孩子，法海就把她压在雷峰塔下。直到她的儿子长大做了官，到塔前祭母，才把母亲救出来。全家人才终于团聚。

《白蛇传》的故事很受欢迎，多次被拍成电影和电视剧。

生词

妖	yāo	evil spirit; demon
白素贞	Bái Sùzhēn	Bai Suzhen, name of the white snake
报答	bàodá	to repay a favour
书生	shūshēng	a scholar
许仙	Xǔ Xiān	Xu Xian, name of the scholar
前世	qiánshì	previous life
救命之恩	jiùmìng zhī'ēn	the kindness of saving a life
法力	fǎlì	supernatural power
金山寺	Jīnshān Sì	Golden Mountain Temple
和尚	héshang	monk
法海	Fǎ Hǎi	Fa Hai, name of the monk
说服	shuìfú	to convince by persuasion
吓死	xiàsǐ	to scare to death
仙草	xiāncǎo	celestial grass
作法	zuòfǎ	to use magic
淹	yān	to flood
伤害	shānghài	to harm
生灵	shēnglíng	creature; living things
惩罚	chéngfá	to punish
压	yā	to press down
雷峰塔	Léifēng Tǎ	Lei Feng Pagoda
官	guān	court official

R 读完上面的短文，回答下面的问题。Answer the following questions in Chinese.

1. 《白蛇传》讲的是什么故事？
2. 白蛇为什么要变成人？
3. 许仙是怎么死的？
4. 素贞为什么会被压在雷峰塔下？
5. 许仙一家人是怎么才团圆的？

S Compare the story of 白蛇传 with a similar story you know in which creatures of different species fall in love and become a couple. Tell the story in Chinese in the class. You can include the following points:

1. 这故事叫什么？是哪个国家／民族的传说？
2. 故事是怎么开始的？
3. 后来怎样了？
4. 结果呢？
5. 你喜欢这个故事吗？为什么？

句式学习

1. **来／去连接两个动词性词组，表示两个之间的关系**

   The word 来 or 去 can be used to connect two verb phrases to show that the purpose of the first verb is to achieve the second verb. It can be translated as "in order to…", and "… so that".

   例句：❶ 古人早就知道戴香包 + 来 + 驱赶蚊子了。

   ❷ 人们划着龙舟 + 去 + 寻找屈原的尸体。

   ❸ 中医用草药 + 来 + 医治疾病。

2. **跟／与……有关**

   This structure indicates that something has something to do with …; has a bearing on; relate to; be connected with.

   例句：❶ 据说，龙舟赛的习俗 + 跟 + 古代中国南部祭水神和祭龙神 + 有关。

   ❷ 中国的很多传统习俗 + 与 + 农耕社会的生活 + 有关。

3. **别 + 动词**

   This structure indicates negation for imperatives. It can be used in place of 不要.

   例句：❶ 妈妈说，别买这家店的肉粽，它不新鲜！

   ❷ 白素贞请许仙别相信法海的话。

Unit Three 中国文化

> **练习**
> 1. 请在三篇短文中找出用以上句式的句子。
> 2. 请用上面的句式造句。Make up sentences using the sentence patterns above.

S 口语练习

主题二 中国文化

次主题 传统

端午节

你必须思考以下几点：
- 常见的端午节食品。
- 端午节常见的活动。
- 现代华人需要保存端午节的传统习俗吗？

W 写作练习

请写一篇150字左右的短文，可以考虑以下几点。

题目 谈谈龙舟赛

1. 说说赛龙舟的起源。
2. 介绍一下你观看过或者参加过的龙舟赛。
3. 你对龙舟赛成为一个国际性的活动有什么看法？

L 听力练习

一、请听小马和大虎的一段对话。

1. 听对话，在正确的答案前打 ☒。

    ❶ 大虎在端午节做了什么？
    - ☐ A 划龙舟
    - ☐ B 看朋友划龙舟
    - ☐ C 给龙舟队打气
    - ☐ D 组织龙舟赛

    ❷ 那个龙舟赛有几条龙舟参加？
    - ☐ A 12条
    - ☐ B 16条
    - ☐ C 一百多条
    - ☐ D 两百多条

❸ 大虎的龙舟队赢了什么奖？
- [ ] A 男子组的第一名
- [ ] B 青少年组的第一名
- [ ] C 青少年组的第二名
- [ ] D 男子组的第二名

❹ 小马在哪里过端午节？
- [ ] A 在姨妈家
- [ ] B 在外婆家
- [ ] C 在学校里
- [ ] D 在家里

2. 再听一遍小马和大虎的这段对话，然后用中文回答下面的问题。
   ❶ 龙舟赛是在哪里举行的？
   ❷ 龙舟赛那天，除了划龙舟的参赛者以外，还有什么人到那里？
   ❸ 小马在端午节那天做了什么？
   ❹ 大虎可以跟谁学习包粽子？

二、Listen to the conversation and summarise the details given by Wenyue and her mum about a custom practised during the Dragon Boat Festival. You are not required to write in full English sentences. You must give two details for question (a) and two details for question (b).

(a) Summarise what this custom can do.
(b) Summarise what shapes of sachets Wenyue's mum is making and for whom.

G 词语练习

根据英文，选字组词。

怕　虫　处

害（　） demerit
害（　） be scared
害（　） pests

防　报　演

预（　） forecast
预（　） to prevent
预（　） to rehearse

热　度　润

湿（　） hot and humid
湿（　） humidity
湿（　） moist

心　害　风

伤（　） to hurt
伤（　） sad
伤（　） cold (an illness)

Unit Three 中国文化

意 望 志
愿（　） hope
愿（　） be willing
（　）愿 aspiration

毒 息 化
消（　） to digest
消（　） news
消（　） to disinfect

诗 法 文
作（　） to make magic
作（　） to compose poem
作（　） composition / to write

黄 英 伟
（　）雄 hero
雄（　） majestic
雄（　） realgar

牌 杯 状
奖（　） certificate of merit
奖（　） trophy
奖（　） medal

洁 楚 新
清（　） clear
清（　） clean
清（　） fresh

G 选词填空

1. 的　得　被　把　对　着　向

如今超市里也买（　　）到粽子，所以端午节自己包粽子（　　）人越来越少了。现在我正在看（　　）外婆用竹叶（　　）米和肉一起包成有趣的三角粽，希望能（　　）外婆学习包粽子。

2. 虽然……但（是）……　为了……　因为……所以……　既然……就…….

中国人戴香包已经有两千多年的历史了。这（　　）是一种民间的习俗，（　　）也是一个预防疾病的方法。用香草、中药做成香包能驱赶蚊子、苍蝇，古人（　　）保护孩子的健康，会把香包挂在他们的身上和床边。

T 翻译练习

1. Translate the following paragraph into English.

龙舟赛本来只是端午节的一个传统活动，不是正式的体育运动。自从 1976 年，香港第一次举办国际龙舟邀请赛以后，龙舟赛就逐渐演变成一项现代化和国际化的活动。在 1976 年的龙舟赛中，参加的大多是香港的龙舟队；从外国来的，只有日本一个代表队。

后来龙舟赛传入欧美，很多国家积极参与。近年参赛的队伍，每年都有几百支。因此，比赛是非常激烈的，也吸引了成千上万的人来参观。

2. 把下面的文字翻译成中文。

　　Last June I went to Hong Kong with my family to attend my brother's wedding, which happened to be a few days after the Dragon Boat Festival. There were a series of dragon boat races going on in different places. My brother took me to one of them.

　　When we arrived at the venue, there were a lot of people already. The rowers were doing warm-up exercises and getting ready to start. There were many stalls, selling food and drinks, and souvenirs. There were also entertainments and games for the whole family.

12 中秋佳节

短文一 Text One

欢度中秋

　　昨天是中秋节。我和父母带了一盒外公、外婆最爱吃的莲蓉月饼去看望他们。

　　外婆请我们吃河蟹，还告诉我，这个时节的河蟹是最鲜美的。我们一边吃，一边听外公讲关于中秋节的历史。

　　据说在唐朝时，中秋节就已经是汉民族的重要节日了。秋收后，人们要庆祝丰收，同时也要感谢天地。人类除了付出自己的劳动以外，还要有好的天气和肥沃的土地，才能获得丰收。

　　古代的中国人崇拜月亮，所以中秋之夜，用圆饼做祭品，向代表天的月亮表示感谢。圆圆的月饼也象征着全家人的团圆。孩子们点着蜡烛、提着灯笼的传统活动，据说跟古代秋收后祭土地神有关。

　　晚上我和家人一起欣赏月亮、品尝月饼，还想起了"嫦娥奔月"的故事。不知道太空人登陆月球的时候，有没有看到过嫦娥和玉兔？

生词

莲蓉	liánróng	lotus seed paste
河蟹	héxiè	river crab
鲜美	xiānměi	tasty; delicious
唐朝	tángcháo	Tang Dynasty (618AD-907AD)
秋收	qiūshōu	autumn harvest
象征	xiàngzhēng	to symbolise
蜡烛	làzhú	candle
提灯笼	tí dēnglóng	to carry a lantern
土地神	tǔdìshén	God of Earth
嫦娥奔月	cháng'é bēnyuè	Chang E running to the moon
登陆	dēnglù	to land
玉兔	yùtù	Jade Rabbit

R 读完上面的短文，回答下面的问题。Answer the following questions in Chinese.

1. 我和父母给外祖父母带了什么中秋礼物？
2. 外婆告诉我关于河蟹的什么知识？
3. 秋收后，人们会做什么？为什么？
4. 月饼为什么是圆的？
5. 中秋节孩子们可以做些什么活动？
6. 中秋之夜，我和家人做什么？

短文二 Text Two

中秋节的起源

秋季是农历的七、八、九三个月,而八月十五正好在中间,所以这天就叫中秋节。

对于农耕社会来讲,天气和土地影响着一年的收成。古代帝王要在秋天祭月,北京的月坛就是明清两代皇帝祭祀的地方。古人还有在收获后祭祀土地神的活动,以感恩养育人类的土地。古代的这两个秋祭,后来就变成了中秋节,不少活动与习俗也一直流传到今天。

圆圆的月饼最初是用来敬献给月神的祭品,后来人们逐渐把中秋赏月与品尝月饼,作为家人团圆的象征,月饼也就成了中秋的特别食品。因此中秋节也可以称作"团圆节"。

中国人认为月是阴、日是阳,月神嫦娥是女的,因此中秋节也可叫"女儿节"。

生词

农耕社会	nónggēng shèhuì	agricultural society
收成	shōuchéng	harvest
月坛	Yuètán	Temple of the Moon
感恩	gǎn'ēn	to be thankful
人类	rénlèi	human beings
秋祭	qiūjì	offering to gods and ancestors in autumn
流传	liúchuán	to hand down
团圆节	tuányuán jié	Reunion Festival
阴阳	yīnyáng	Yin and Yang, the two opposing principles in nature, with Yin representing the feminine and Yang the masculine

R 读完上面的短文,回答下面的问题。Answer the following questions in Chinese.

1. 中秋节是什么时候?
2. 北京的月坛在古代是什么地方?
3. 中秋节有哪些活动和习俗?
4. 月饼最早有什么用处?
5. 为什么中秋节也叫"团圆节"?
6. 中秋节也叫"女儿节"的原因是什么?

S **W** Discuss the following two scenarios in the class and choose one of them to write about.

1. 如果你是嫦娥,有一天看到太空人登上了你居住的月球,你会有什么样的反应?你会跟那些宇航员说什么?
2. 如果你是太空人,有一天你登上月球,看到了嫦娥和玉兔,你会有什么样的反应?你会跟他们说什么?

Unit Three 中国文化

短文三 Text Three

"嫦娥"的传说

中秋之夜，一家人一边吃着美味的月饼，一边赏月。这时，大人们往往会指着月亮上隐隐约约的影子，告诉孩子：那是美丽的嫦娥，她身边的玉兔正在捣药；那是吴刚在砍桂花树，可这棵树永远也砍不倒；那儿还有一只三脚蟾蜍……如果孩子好问，大人还会解释，嫦娥、吴刚和玉兔是怎么到月亮上去的。当然，这些只是古人的想象和传说。

"桂"与"贵"是同音字，桂花树是吉祥的树；蟾蜍不仅吃害虫，而且多子，是吉祥的动物。在古代，比赛得第一，或者考试出色，就被称作"蟾宫折桂"。兔子不但繁殖得快，而且在传说中，玉兔捣的是长生不老的药！

总而言之，无论是想象，还是传说，都表达了古人祈求富贵吉祥、健康长寿和多子多福的愿望。

生词

隐隐约约	yǐnyǐn yuēyuē	indistinct
捣药	dǎoyào	to pound medicine in a mortar
吴刚	Wú Gāng	Wu Gang, the woodcutter on the moon
砍	kǎn	to fell (a tree)
桂花树	guìhuā shù	osmanthus tree
蟾蜍	chánchú	toad
好问	hàowèn	inquisitive
不仅	bùjǐn	not only
蟾宫折桂	chángōng zhéguì	It literally means plucking osmanthus flowers in the Palace of the Moon. It is used to describe someone succeeding in the imperial examination.
长生不老	chángshēng bùlǎo	immortality
祈求	qíqiú	to pray for
富贵吉祥	fùguì jíxiáng	wealth, honour and luck
健康长寿	jiànkāng chángshòu	good health and longevity
愿望	yuànwàng	wishes

R 读完上面的短文，回答下面的问题。 Answer the following questions in Chinese.

1. 传说月亮上有什么？
2. 为什么月亮上有这些动植物？
3. 从传说中，我们可以了解古人的哪些心愿？
4. 你能介绍一个与中秋节有关的故事或传说吗？

Snippet
中秋节的习俗

中秋节除了有吃月饼、赏月和拜月的习俗以外，人们还看灯笼。尤其是小孩子，他们都喜欢提着灯笼到外面玩，也喜欢观看别人的灯笼。

Apart from eating moon cakes, appreciating the moonlight and offering food to the moon, there are other customs associated with the Mid-Autumn Festival. Adults enjoy the lanterns, and children would carry their lanterns outside to show each other.

据说中秋节这天也是土地公公的生日，他给了人类肥沃的土地，让他们获得丰收。为了感恩，那天孩子们会点蜡烛、提灯笼，为他庆祝生日。

According to legend, the Mid-Autumn Festival is also the birthday of the Earth God. People wanted to thank him for giving them fertile land so that they got good crops. To show their gratitude, children would light candles and carry lanterns to celebrate his birthday.

S 在电影《天水围的日与夜》里面，贵姐是怎样过中秋节的？你可以说说以下几点：
1. 她跟谁一起过节？
2. 他们吃了什么中秋食品？
3. 他们一起做什么？
4. 根据贵姐过中秋节的情况，你认为她是一个怎么样的人？

句式学习

1. **象征**

   If used as a verb, it means to symbolize; if used as a noun, it means symbol.

   例句： **1a** 因为桂花树的"桂"跟富贵的"贵"是一样的读音，所以古人认为桂花树<u>象征</u>富贵。

105

Unit Three 中国文化

1b 因为桂花树的"桂"跟富贵的"贵"是一样的读音，所以古人把桂花树当作是富贵的象征。

2a 在中国的传说中，月亮上住着嫦娥和玉兔。因此，人们常常用嫦娥或者玉兔来象征月亮。

2b 在中国的传说中，月亮上住着嫦娥和玉兔。因此，人们觉得嫦娥或者玉兔都是月亮的象征。

2. 形容词重叠

In Chinese certain types of adjectives may be duplicated. Repetition of an adjective gives more emphasis and, as it implies a high degree, such adjectives are usually not modified by adverbs of degree. The form of repetition is AA for monosyllabic adjectives and AABB for disyllabic ones.

例句：① 三角粽的米白白的，里面的豆沙甜甜的，好吃极了。
② 来观看龙舟赛的小女孩有一双大大的眼睛，一头长长的黑发，衣服也穿得漂漂亮亮的，十分可爱。

练习

1. 请在三篇短文中找出用以上句式的句子。
2. 请用上面的句式造句。Make up sentences using the sentence patterns above.

S 口语练习

主题二 中国文化
次主题 传统
中秋节

你必须思考以下几点：
- 中秋节有哪些常见的活动？
- 什么人会过中秋节？
- 华人为什么觉得中秋节很重要？

W 写作练习

请写一篇150字左右的短文，可以考虑以下几点。

题目 谈谈《请投我一票》中罗雷的家长是怎么帮他拉票的

1. 罗雷的父母是做什么工作的？
2. 他们建议罗雷利用中秋节做什么？
3. 做了以后有什么效果？
4. 你同意他们这样的做法吗？为什么？

L 听力练习

一、请听大明和小叶的一段对话，他们正在讨论买月饼送礼给亲戚。

1. 听对话，在正确的答案前打 ⊠。

   ❶ 大明和小叶去购物中心买什么？
   - [ ] A 冰淇淋
   - [ ] B 月饼
   - [ ] C 火腿
   - [ ] D 豆腐

   ❷ 他们的外公外婆喜欢吃什么？
   - [ ] A 莲蓉
   - [ ] B 绿豆
   - [ ] C 红豆
   - [ ] D 牛肉

   ❸ 他们的爷爷奶奶喜欢吃什么？
   - [ ] A 冰淇淋
   - [ ] B 火腿
   - [ ] C 红豆
   - [ ] D 水果

   ❹ 大明和小叶想试试什么中秋食品？
   - [ ] A 豆沙月饼
   - [ ] B 火腿月饼
   - [ ] C 冰皮月饼
   - [ ] D 莲蓉月饼

2. 再听一遍大明和小叶的这段对话，然后用中文回答下面的问题。

   ❶ 小叶说月饼的品种多，为什么？
   ❷ 大明和小叶去买什么种类的月饼？
   ❸ 他们买月饼送给谁？为什么？
   ❹ 他们还要买什么月饼尝尝？

二、Listen to an excerpt of an interview between a radio reporter and the owner of a shop selling lanterns. You are not required to write in full English sentences. You must give two details for question (a) and two details for question (b).

   (a) Summarise the reasons given by Mr Li about why his lanterns are so popular.
   (b) Summarise the designs of Mr Li's lanterns.

Unit Three 中国文化

G 词语练习   根据英文，选字组词。

沃　胖　料

肥（　）fat
肥（　）fertiliser
肥（　）fertile

月　花　讲

（　）坛　altar for moon
（　）坛　pulpit
（　）坛　flowerbed

殖　华　忙

繁（　）flourishing
繁（　）to breed, to reproduce
繁（　）busy

陆　山　报

登（　）to land
登（　）to publish in a newspaper
登（　）to climb a mountain

响　星　视

影（　）movie star
影（　）to influence
影（　）film and television

征　牙　棋

象（　）Chinese chess
象（　）ivory
象（　）symbol

传　行　动

流（　）to flow
流（　）to hand down
流（　）popular

收　满　富

丰（　）abundant
丰（　）plump
丰（　）bumper harvest

种　人　分

（　）类　mankind
（　）类　type, kind
（　）类　classification

蛋　动　药

捣（　）to stir up
捣（　）to make trouble
捣（　）to pound medicine in a mortar

拜　高　敬

崇（　）sublime
崇（　）respect
崇（　）to worship, to adore

跑　放　月

奔（　）to run
奔（　）unrestrained
奔（　）to run to the moon

G 选词填空

1. 肥沃　欣赏　品尝　丰收　感恩　收成

秋天是一个（　　）的季节。中国人会过中秋节，美国人会过（　　）节。没有（　　）的土地，就不会有美味的食品供我们（　　）。

108

2. 团团圆圆　隐隐约约　清清楚楚　高高兴兴

中秋之夜，我和朋友们（　　　）地去公园欣赏月亮。小云说她（　　　）地闻到桂花的香味，问我们闻到了没有，我们都说没有。

T 翻译练习

1. Translate the following paragraphs into English.

    王山和他太太陈月芬对园艺都很有兴趣。他们家的花园很小，所以就在家附近租了一小块土地种菜和水果。

    他们差不多每天下班后都到这个菜园来劳动。春天下种，夏天浇水、除草，秋天收割，冬天就休息。陈月芬说，秋天是他们最开心的季节，因为他们能收获很多不同的蔬菜和水果，例如：白菜、菠菜、苹果和梨等。不过，夏天也很好，草莓、蓝莓、李子等都是这个季节成熟的。

    去年中秋节刚好是周末，他们在菜园开了一个庆祝会，请了邻近的几家人去品尝他们用刚收获的蔬果做的食物。我们一家人也去了。大家坐在地上，一边赏月，一边吃美食，真有意思！

2. 把下面的文字翻译成中文。

    The Mid-Autumn Festival is one of the most important holidays celebrated by Chinese around the world. Traditionally, it is celebrated on the 15th day of the eighth lunar month to mark the autumn harvest.

    Although old ceremonies are no longer followed, families still gather for a day to relax and eat moon cakes.

    On this occasion, the legends of the Moon Goddess, Chang E and the Jade Rabbit, who live on the moon making herb medicine, are often told to children.

13 中国的传统习俗

短文一　Text One

吉祥的红色

生词		
火焰	huǒyàn	flame
熟食	shúshí	cooked food
万物	wànwù	all things
佳节	jiājié	festival
婚嫁	hūnjià	marriage
主色调	zhǔsè diào	main colour
步步高升	bùbù gāoshēng	rising step by step
上级领导	shàngjí lǐngdǎo	superior; leader
气色	qìsè	complexion
亮点	liàngdiǎn	highlight

中国人喜欢红色，这几乎是世界各国人民都知道的。可是中国人为什么喜欢红色呢？

古代中国人认为红色的火焰可以驱赶野兽，给人安全，还可以带给人温暖和熟食；日出时的太阳红红的，代表新的开始。古人早就知道，万物只有在阳光下，才有生命，才能生长。

因此，自古以来，红色代表着温暖、生命和热情等。在庆祝佳节、孩子出生或男女婚嫁的喜庆日子里，红色总是主色调。

在中文里，"红"经常是成功的象征。比如"走红"，意思是一个人开始受到欢迎，步步高升；"红人"是指得到上级领导赏识的人；"红光满面"是形容一个人看上去身体健康、气色好。现在，在网络媒体上走红的人被称为"网红"。

由此可见，"红色"是中国文化习俗中的一个亮点。

R 读完上面的短文，回答下面的问题。Answer the following questions in Chinese.

1. 世界人民都知道中国人喜欢红色吗？
2. 中国古人是从哪儿看到红色的？
3. 中国人为什么喜欢红色？
4. 谈谈在哪些场合常常看到红色？
5. 举两个中文中用"红"组成的词，并说说它们的意思。

短文二 Text Two

纯净的白色

在中国的丧礼习俗里，长辈去世了，晚辈都要穿白色的衣服，戴白花，束白腰带等。因为汉民族认为白色代表悲哀、痛苦和死亡。在3000多年前的《周礼》一书中就规定了用白色做丧服。

中国人很早就把五种主要颜色与五个方位对应：东—青、南—红、西—白、北—黑、中—黄。后来中国受到佛教的影响，古人相信人死了，会去西方极乐世界。佛教还有生死轮回的说法，人死了一切就要重新开始，而白色正好代表纯净与空白。

按照传统习俗，丧礼能反映人们对长辈是否孝顺。丧礼办得隆重，就表示晚辈对长辈感恩孝顺。因此晚辈按照《周礼》定的规矩，穿戴白色，认真地送别去往极乐世界的长辈，怀念他们的养育之恩。这既表现了下一代对长辈的孝，也表达了中国人对生命不息的追求。

生词

纯净	chúnjìng	pure; clean
丧礼	sànglǐ	funeral
束腰带	shùyāo dài	to tie a belt round one's waist
悲哀	bēi'āi	sorrow
痛苦	tòngkǔ	pain
死亡	sǐwáng	death
《周礼》	Zhōulǐ	The Rites of Zhou Dynasty
规定	guīdìng	to stipulate
丧服	sāngfú	mourning clothes
方位	fāngwèi	bearing
对应	duìyìng	correspond
青	qīng	blue green
佛教	fójiào	Buddhism
极乐世界	jílè shìjiè	paradise
轮回	lúnhuí	reincarnation
空白	kòngbái	blank
孝顺	xiàoshùn	filial obedience
隆重	lóngzhòng	grand; solemn
不息	bùxī	non-stop; incessant

R 读完上面的短文，回答下面的问题。Answer the following questions in Chinese.

1. 汉民族认为白色代表什么？
2. 中国丧服用白色有多久的历史了？
3. 说说中国古人是怎么把颜色与方位对应起来的？
4. 说说佛教对中国人的影响？
5. 为什么华人的传统丧礼办得那么隆重？

Unit Three 中国文化

短文三 Text Three

茶的文化

茶，在中国不仅是一种传统饮料，同时还在婚姻习俗中起着重要的作用。

古时候，茶是女子的嫁妆，后来成为男子向女方求婚的聘礼。到了元朝、明朝，"茶礼"几乎成为了婚姻的代名词。女家同意求婚，接受聘礼称作"吃茶"。

如今在华人的传统婚礼上，还有新婚夫妇向双方父母敬茶的习俗。这茶叫做"改口茶"，因为喝了这杯茶，他们彼此的称呼就改变了。

有些地区在婚礼上的敬茶仪式很有意思。首先新娘、新郎向亲朋好友敬花茶，感谢大家来参加婚礼；其次是新娘向新郎敬红茶，希望婚后的新生活红红火火；接着新郎向新娘敬铁观音茶，祈求观音送子；最后是新婚夫妇向双方父母敬普洱茶，感谢父母的哺育之恩。

中国的茶文化还反映在其他很多方面，"改口茶"只是其中之一。

生词		
嫁妆	jiàzhuang	dowry
聘礼	pìnlǐ	bride price
称作	chēngzuò	is called by
新婚	xīnhūn	newly wed
敬茶	jìngchá	to offer tea respectfully
彼此	bǐcǐ	one another
称呼	chēnghū	form of address
仪式	yíshì	ceremony
铁观音茶	tiěguān yīnchá	Tie Guan Yin tea
观音	Guānyīn	Guanyin (in Buddhism, it is called Avalokitesvara)
普洱茶	pǔerchá	Pu'er tea

R 读完上面的短文，回答下面的问题。Answer the following questions in Chinese.

1. 茶在什么习俗中有重要作用？
2. 请解释"茶礼"是什么。
3. 华人的传统婚礼上要喝什么茶？为什么？
4. 为什么新娘向新郎敬的是红茶？
5. 为什么新郎向新娘敬的是铁观音？

S 在班上用中文详细描述你参加过的一个婚礼，说说婚礼上的仪式，新人穿的衣服等。你觉得这个婚礼跟上面提到的有什么不同？

Snippet
筷子

筷子是中国古老又简单的一种餐具。最初可能只是用来取烫热的熟食，后来才慢慢演变成将食物夹起并送入口中的餐具。用筷子吃饭需要一些技巧，因此用筷子可以锻炼人的手眼协调能力。

筷子是成双的，结婚时可以作为定情之物。夫妻像两根筷子，永不分离，白头到老。筷子还有快生贵子，快快乐乐的意思。在吃年夜饭的时候，许多家庭会在饭桌上放新筷子以求好运；十双筷子在一起有十全十美的意思。

因为古人在祭祖或者扫墓的时候，是把筷子竖插在饭碗里的米饭上的，所以华人平时吃饭，禁止这样做，筷子得放在饭碗旁边。

Chopsticks, ancient yet simple eating utensils, have been used by the Chinese for centuries. Their original usage was probably to handle hot food after roasting or boiling. It gradually evolved into a form of cutlery for picking up food to put into the mouth. Using chopsticks requires some skill. Hence, it can train eye-hand coordination.

Chopsticks come as a pair. Because of that they are quite often used by lovers as a token of attachment to each other. Husband and wife are like the chopsticks: they don't separate, as the saying goes "till death us do part". People take advantage of the pronunciation of chopsticks and make it into auspicious blessings such as 快生贵子, wishing newly-wed couples a new baby soon, and 快快乐乐, wishing someone happiness. At the Chinese New Year's Eve dinner, many families like to use new chopsticks to pray for good luck. And having ten pairs of chopsticks can mean 十全十美, being perfect in every way.

In ancient times, people often left chopsticks standing up in a bowl of rice when they made offerings to their ancestors. As a result, when Chinese people eat, they must rest the chopsticks by the bowl at the dinner table.

Unit Three 中国文化

句式学习

1. "其他""其它"和"别的"的用法

They all mean "the other, others, else", but 其它 is used to refer to objects only while the other two can be used to refer to people and things.

例句：❶ 茶除了可以做饮料，还有其它／其他／别的用途吗？

❷ 我会和父母去参加表姐的婚礼，还有其他／别的亲友去吗？

Note that you can't say：我会和父母去参加表姐的婚礼，还有其它亲友去吗？

2. 是否

This structure is formed by affirmative and negative words, similar to 是不是, to express "whether or not".

例句：❶ 你学习中文已经多年，是否了解中国传统的四大节日？

❷ 在西方的婚礼上，是否有跟中国差不多的习俗？

3. 因此

因此 is a short way to say 因为这个, and has the meaning of "therefore", "for this reason" or "consequently".

例句：❶ 大概是中国的春节没有什么宗教背景，因此受到各国人民的欢迎。

❷ 布朗太太在英国大学教中文。她不但会说流利的中文，还十分了解中国的历史和文化，因此被人称作"汉学家"。

练习

1. 请在三篇短文中找出用以上句式的句子。
2. 请用上面的句式造句。Make up sentences using the sentence patterns above.

S 口语练习

主题二 中国文化

次主题 传统

习俗

你必须思考以下几点：

- 介绍一个中国的传统习俗。
- 中国人为什么现在还觉得这个习俗重要？
- 年轻人是怎么保存中国的传统习俗的？

W 写作练习

请写一篇 150 字左右的短文，可以考虑以下几点。

题目 谈谈《天水围的日与夜》中表现的传统文化习俗

1. 中秋节贵姐家吃什么？你知道他们为什么要吃这些食品吗？
2. 从贵姐参加的丧礼，你可以了解到中国人的什么习俗？
3. 繁华现代的香港在哪些地方还保持着传统习俗？

L 听力练习

一、请听学生马克跟李老师的一段对话。

1. 听对话，然后在正确的答案前打 ☒。

    ❶ 中国有龙吗？
    - ☐ A 很久以前有
    - ☐ B 只有中国有
    - ☐ C 现在没有龙
    - ☐ D 从来没有过

    ❷ 传说中的中国龙，身体像什么？
    - ☐ A 鱼
    - ☐ B 马
    - ☐ C 蛇
    - ☐ D 牛

    ❸ 马克参观过哪个博物馆？
    - ☐ A 故宫
    - ☐ B 古代
    - ☐ C 北京
    - ☐ D 习俗

    ❹ 皇帝衣服有几条龙？
    - ☐ A 8 条
    - ☐ B 6 条
    - ☐ C 9 条
    - ☐ D 10 条

2. 再听一遍学生马克跟李老师的这段对话，然后用中文回答下面的问题。

    ❶ 为什么中国人说自己是龙的传人？
    ❷ 龙为什么有很多不同动物的特征？
    ❸ 在哪儿可以看到龙的图案？
    ❹ 中国古人认为什么数字是吉祥的？为什么？

Unit Three 中国文化

二、Listen to a dialogue between a grandmother and her granddaughter. You are not required to write in full English sentences. You must give two details for question (a) and two details for question (b).

(a) Summarise the reasons given by grandmother why there is no cat in the Chinese Zodiac list and why the rat is in first place.

(b) Summarise the animals the Chinese Zodiac includes and the reason for having the Chinese Zodiac.

G 词语练习

根据英文，选字组词。

暖 和 习

温（　　）to revise
温（　　）warm
温（　　）gentle

色 声 查

（　　）调　tone
（　　）调　hue
调（　　）survey

络 红 页

网（　　）cyber star
网（　　）internet
网（　　）webpage

礼 服 失

丧（　　）to lose
丧（　　）funeral
丧（　　）mourning clothes

长 晚 半

（　　）辈　younger generation
（　　）辈子　half of one's life
（　　）辈　older generation

笨 严 隆

（　　）重　ceremonious
（　　）重　serious
（　　）重　bulky

顺 敬 心

孝（　　）filial sentiments
孝（　　）to show filial respect
孝（　　）filial obedience

定 矩 划

规（　　）plan
规（　　）rule, custom
规（　　）to stipulate

礼 服 姻

婚（　　）wedding dress
婚（　　）wedding
婚（　　）marriage

嫁 化 梳

（　　）妆　to make up
（　　）妆　dowry
（　　）妆　to dress up

礼 用 书

聘（　　）bride price
聘（　　）to hire
聘（　　）letter of appointment

仪 方 样

（　　）式　style
（　　）式　ceremony
（　　）式　the way

116

G 选词填空

1. 几乎　是否　其他　之一　一些

   学习中文的学生（　　）都知道，中国人在喜庆的日子里爱穿红衣服。这只是中国的传统习俗（　　），你还知道（　　）的吗？

2. 被　把　了　向　在

   （　　）古代中国，茶不仅可以是男子（　　）女方求婚的聘礼，还可以（　　）当作女孩子出嫁时的嫁妆之一。

T 翻译练习

1. Translate the following paragraph into English.

   重阳节也是中国的一个传统节日，时间是农历九月初九。古时候，人们在这一天会有很多活动，其中最主要的是秋游、登高、吃重阳糕。古人认为"九"是一个吉祥的数字，重阳节有两个"九"，有长寿的意思。1989年，中国政府把农历九月初九定为"老人节"，希望成年子女能够在这一天回家看望父母。

   Glossary:
   重阳节（Chóngyángjié）Chong Yang Festival

2. 把下面的一段文字翻译成中文。

   According to legends, the Chinese dragon is a far different beast from the Western one. The Western dragon is usually an evil beast. It is fierce and can hurt people. By contrast, the Chinese dragon is a nice creature, symbolizing strength, wisdom and good luck. Therefore, Chinese parents like to give their male babies names with the character "dragon".

第四单元　中国文化——文化活动

这个单元覆盖了与中国文化有关的阅读、电影、电视和音乐这四个方面。

• 电影

1905 年中国自己拍摄了京剧舞台片《定军山》，中国电影以这部戏曲纪录片为开端，已经有 100 多年的历史了。电影的内容和主题随着中国历史的进程，一直发生着变化。在 1949 年后的 30 年里，中国拍摄的电影数量很少，电影院也主要以放映国产的故事片为主。不过自从改革开放以来，中外电影业的交流增加了。中国每年进口不少外国影片，美国好莱坞的大片以及韩国的情感片特别受年轻人的欢迎。中国的武侠片也打开了国外的市场，成龙、李连杰等成了世界闻名的武侠明星。近十年来，中国电影业快速发展，在全球化的影响下，出现了中外电影公司合拍和中外演员合演的影片。

• 电视

1958 年 5 月 1 日北京电视台（1978 年 5 月 1 日改名为中央电视台）第一次试播。那个时候拥有电视机的人很少，但现在电视机在中国已经很普及。全国目前有 300 多个省、市，甚至县级电视台。中国自己制作的电视节目非常多样，近年来还向英国、法国等国家购买了有创意的节目专利，加入中国元素，推出"中国超人秀""中国好声音""谁想成为百万富翁"等节目，获得了极大的成功。与此同时，欧美及韩国、日本的电视节目也在中国获得很高的收视率。电视彻底改变并丰富了人们的文化生活。

• 音乐

中国的音乐有 8000 年左右的历史了，考古发现用骨头做的笛子也有大约 7000 年的历史了。中国的传统乐器很独特，有鼓、锣、笛子、古筝、月琴、编钟、葫芦丝等不计其数。现在很多中国小孩学的乐器是钢琴、提琴等西方乐器。中国的传统民歌的体裁有小调、号子和山歌；传统戏剧，除了京剧，还有越剧、粤剧、豫剧、黄梅戏、评弹等，地方色彩浓郁的民歌与戏曲一直得到人们的喜爱。现在网络音乐正在逐渐取代传统的黑胶唱片和光盘，一些免费的中西方的古典音乐、民歌民谣、流行音乐等都很容易下载，人们有了更多的选择。年轻人尤其爱听韩国、日本和欧美流行音乐，因此，国外的音乐也影响着中国音乐的发展。

• 阅读

中国最早的书籍出现在商代，是刻在竹子和木片上的，最早的印刷书籍是公元 868 年印的《金刚经》。中国的书籍承载着几千年的中华文化，流传至今。华人素来重视教育，不少孩子从小读唐诗，背《三字经》等，要懂得"好读书，读书好，读好书"的道理。近年来中国已经成为全球书籍出版量最大的国家；今天的互联网时代，高科技也为人们提供了更多的阅读途径。手机、电脑上可下载电子书、有声书，要看什么有什么，但是中国人均阅读量却很低。社会为了鼓励人们，尤其是年轻人多看书，还举办了"世界读书日""最受读者欢迎的100本书"等活动。

Unit 4　Chinese Cultural Activities

Unit 4 focuses on the topics of film, television, music and reading which relate to Chinese culture.

• Film

The film industry in China has been developing rapidly in recent years. As a result, the choice of films has certainly increased to satisfy the taste of the audience. However, the industry didn't really develop until its open-door policy began in the 1980s. In the 30 years after 1949, not many films were made, and cinema-going was not a known pastime in China. Things are different in Taiwan and Hong Kong though, where domestically produced films, foreign films from America and Britain have always been popular. The cinemas were usually well-attended, especially in the evenings and at weekends. Over the last two decades, Korean and Japanese films have also become in demand, particularly among young people. Chinese films which have made it to market overseas are usually of the martial art genre. Some of the action film stars have indeed achieved worldwide fame.

• Television

In 1958 China's Central TV Channel (formerly known as Beijing TV Channel) broadcast for the first time. Very few people had access to a TV set then. Nowadays owning a TV set is very common in China. There are currently over 300 regional TV channels in the whole country. Apart from making their own programmes, Chinese TV channels have also bought the rights of foreign programme ideas from Britain and France to make their own "X Factor", "Voice of China", "Who Wants to Be a Millionaire" and achieved big success. There are many American, European, Korean and Japanese TV programmes being shown in China and most receive high ratings. Television has indeed changed people's cultural life completely.

Unit Four 中国文化——文化活动

• Music

Chinese music has about 8,000 years of history. Chinese traditional instruments include drums, cymbals, flutes, zithers, lutes, bells, pipes etc. However, nowadays Chinese children mostly learn to play Western instruments such as piano and violin. Although there is a rich culture of traditional Chinese music which ranges from folk songs to operas, it is pop music which is dominant in the music scene. There is still a sizeable fan base for traditional operas including Beijing opera and Cantonese opera which are still very popular today. With technological advances, music is easily accessible via the Internet. All kinds of music can be downloaded, giving people lots of choices to listen to. Young people in China love Korean, Japanese and Western pop music, which in turn has influenced the development of music in China.

• Reading

The earliest book found in China was probably in the Shang Dynasty. It was made from bamboo and wood strips, with the words inscribed rather than written. The earliest printed book – the Diamond Sutra - was produced in 868AD. Chinese people have always put much emphasis on education and young children had to learn and recite the Tang poems, and the *Three Character Classic* etc. to develop their literacy. Parents also believed that this would help them to understand the motto of "love to read, reading is good". In recent years China has become the leading publisher in the world, producing books mainly for domestic consumption. The Internet, coupled with digital technology and has also provided people with choices of different ways to read. One can download e-books and audio books of all kinds on mobile phones and computers. However, the number of books Chinese people read on average is quite low. In order to encourage the reading habit, especially among the younger generation, events like World Book Day and the Top 100 Books, are held to attract readers.

14 好读书 读书好 读好书

短文一 Text One

"阅"读越爱读

今天我们全家人坐高铁去广州看望外婆。在车上我们通常都喜欢阅读。

我今天读的是一本从图书馆借来的书，叫《科学故事》。作者用简单的文字解释了一些难懂的科学理论，对我的学习很有帮助。

妈妈正津津有味地看《红楼梦》电子书。她说自己年轻时，从来没读过这本古典小说，因为她以为这本书讲的只不过是一个爱情故事，没有什么特别的。现在才发现，这本书真是现代人了解明清历史的一本百科全书。

爸爸在平板电脑上看一本武侠小说《天龙八部》。他说他小时候爱看武侠小说，工作以后就再也没有时间看了，他觉得生活因此都变得枯燥了。现在他只能利用碎片时间来阅读他的最爱。

妈妈告诉我，外婆也很喜欢看书，可是她的眼睛不太好，所以这次买了一些有声书送给她。

生词

高铁	gāotiě	high speed rail in China
广州	Guǎngzhōu	Guang Zhou, also known as Canton
理论	lǐlùn	theory
《红楼梦》	Hónglóumèng	The Story of the Stone, a classic Chinese novel
明清	míngqīng	the era of the Ming Dynasty and Qing Dynasty
百科全书	bǎikē quánshū	encyclopaedia
武侠小说	wǔxiá xiǎoshuō	martial art novel
《天龙八部》	Tiānlóng bābù	Tian Long Ba Bu, the title of one of the well-known martial art novels written by Jin Yong
枯燥	kūzào	dull and dry
碎片时间	suìpiàn shíjiān	small breaks in time
有声书	yǒushēng shū	audio book

Unit Four 中国文化——文化活动

R 读完上面的短文，回答下面的问题。Answer the following questions in Chinese.

1. "我"读的书是从哪儿来的？
2. 为什么《科学故事》对"我"的学习有帮助？
3. 妈妈在哪儿阅读《红楼梦》？这是一本什么样的书？
4. 爸爸在哪儿阅读《天龙八部》？他工作后在什么时候可以阅读武侠小说？

S / W 跟你的同学在课上讨论上面的短文，然后写一篇 100—150 字的短文，说说你喜欢看电子书还是纸质书。

Snippet
唐诗宋词

中国诗歌的成就在唐朝和宋朝达到高峰。唐诗基本是格律诗和古体诗。李白的诗歌想象力丰富，非常浪漫；而杜甫的诗歌则注重反映社会现实和人民的苦难。

宋词也叫长短句，便于歌唱。苏轼是豪放派的代表人物，而李清照是婉约派的代表人物。

Chinese poetry reached its literary height during the Tang and Song Dynasties. Tang poems essentially follow two styles. The first is the classical poetic composition, usually having five or seven characters to each line; and the second adheres more closely to tonal pattern, rhyme scheme, etc. Famous poets such as Li Bai and Du Fu are both from the Tang Dynasty. Li's poems are more imaginative and romantic while Du's poems tend to reflect the society and the hardship of the people.

Song poetry is written to certain tunes with strict tonal patterns and rhyme schemes. It has long and short lines, and is thus designed for singing. Song poetry is generally represented by the well-known poets Su Shi and Li Qingzhao. Su's style is bold uninhibited while Li's is graceful and restrained.

短文二　Text Two

咖啡书店

去年暑假我去台北探亲、旅游。表妹知道我喜欢看书，很乐意当导游，带我去了一间很特别的咖啡书店。

一踏进那间店，我就喜欢上了那幽雅的环境。靠墙是放满图书的书架，靠窗的地方有精致的盆栽。店里没有太多的顾客，可能是因为咖啡店在郊外，吸引不了很多上班族或游客。

两位店主都很年轻。听表妹说，他们大学毕业后，在商界工作了好几年，觉得没有成就感。他俩都喜欢阅读和收藏书籍，于是决定把咖啡店和书店结合起来，开了这家店。

在饮品送来之前，我在书架前浏览。图书的种类真多，有古典小说，也有现代小说，还有非小说类的书。我随手拿起一本介绍台湾茶的书。我们一边喝咖啡，一边看书，不知不觉天就黑了。

离开之前，我把那本书买下了。

生词

台北	Táiběi	Taipei, provincial capital of Taiwan
踏进	tàjìn	to step into
幽雅	yōuyǎ	quiet and tastefully decorated
靠窗	kào chuāng	by the window
精致	jīngzhì	delicate; exquisite
盆栽	pénzāi	pot plant
郊外	jiāowài	outskirts of a city
商界	shāngjiè	the commercial world
收藏	shōucáng	to collect
浏览	liúlǎn	to browse
非	fēi	not
随手	suíshǒu	not purposefully
不知不觉	bùzhī bùjué	without knowing

R 读完上面的短文，回答下面的问题。Answer the following questions in Chinese.

1. 表妹为什么带"我"去咖啡书店？
2. 请介绍一下这家书店的环境。
3. 咖啡书店店主原来是做什么的？
4. "我"在咖啡书店做了些什么？
5. "我"买了一本什么书？

W/S When you choose a book to read for leisure, which factors would you consider the most important? Discuss this in the class in Chinese. You can write down the factors first.

Unit Four 中国文化——文化活动

短文三 Text Three

▍自助图书馆

生词		
路边	lùbiān	roadside
共享	gòngxiǎng	sharing
自动售货机	zìdòng shòuhuò jī	automatic sales machine
放置	fàngzhì	to place
柜子	guìzi	cabinet
零食	língshí	snack
登记	dēngjì	to register
凭	píng	using something as proof of
随时	suíshí	anytime
读者	dúzhě	reader
影视娱乐	yǐngshì yúlè	film / TV entertainment
重视	zhòngshì	to see as important
平均	píngjūn	on average
俄罗斯	Éluósī	Russia

　　近年来，在中国有些大城市的路边，出现了一种"大书柜"，提供免费图书共享服务。这些书柜被叫做"自助图书馆"。

　　"自助图书馆"其实跟自动售货机差不多，就是在路边放置一个大柜子，里面放的全是图书。人们从那里借书，就像在自动售货机买饮料或零食一样。不过他们必须先登记成为会员，然后才可以凭会员证借书。

　　这个新服务一出现就得到很多人的支持。虽然"自助图书馆"提供的书籍不太多，可是你随时都可以借书，方便了那些没有时间去图书馆借书的读者。

　　根据调查，不少人在网络影视娱乐方面花了太多时间，阅读书籍已经越来越不被重视。近年来，中国人一年平均读的书比美国、俄罗斯和日本的都少。"自助图书馆"主要是为了鼓励大家多看书，尤其是中国的年轻人。

R 读完上面的短文，回答下面的问题。Answer the following questions in Chinese.

1. 图书共享服务出现在哪儿？
2. 什么是"自助图书馆"？
3. 怎样才可以从"自助图书馆"借到书？
4. 为什么很多人支持这项新服务？
5. 出现这项新服务的目的是什么？

Snippet

中国古典四大名著

中国明清时期的小说《水浒传》《三国演义》《西游记》《红楼梦》都有很高的文学水平和艺术成就。小说不但人物刻画细致，而且每部都有着深刻的思想，影响了一代又一代中国人的道德观念。

The four great classical Chinese novels: *Water Margin* (also translated as *Outlaws of the Marsh*), *Romance of the Three Kingdoms*, *Journey to the West* (better known as the *Monkey King*), *The Story of the Stone*, were written during the Ming and Qing Dynasties.

Each of these four books depicts numerous characters in their respective story and the portrayal of each character is lively and lifelike, showing the high level of literary standard as well as artistic achievement.

In each of these books is a profound philosophy, which has influenced the morality of generations of Chinese people.

S 口语练习

主题二 中国文化
次主题 文化活动

阅读

你必须思考以下几点：
- 介绍一本与中国文化有关的书。
- 阅读与中国文化有关的书的好处。
- 中国年轻人喜欢通过新媒体学中国文化的原因。

W 写作练习

请写一篇 150 字左右的短文，可以考虑以下几点。

题目 谈谈你的阅读习惯

1. 你有哪些阅读习惯？
2. 你喜欢读哪类书？为什么？
3. 请简单介绍其中一本书。
4. 你认为每个人都应该多阅读吗？为什么？

Unit Four 中国文化——文化活动

L 听力练习

一、请听一段对话，小兰和大明正在聊他们喜欢的书籍。

1. 听对话，然后在正确的答案前打 ☒。

   ❶ 小兰和大明的学校举行了什么投票活动？
   - ☐ A 最出色的学生
   - ☐ B 最努力的班长
   - ☐ C 中学生最爱读的书籍
   - ☐ D 最有趣的杂志

   ❷ 大明在今年的投票中选了哪本书？
   - ☐ A《哈利·波特》
   - ☐ B《城南旧事》
   - ☐ C《龙的传说》
   - ☐ D《猴子大王》

   ❸ 小兰在今年的投票中选了哪本书？
   - ☐ A《中文字的故事》
   - ☐ B《猴子大王》
   - ☐ C《城南旧事》
   - ☐ D《哈利·波特》

   ❹ 小兰在去年的投票中赢得了什么？
   - ☐ A 一本书
   - ☐ B 一张购书券
   - ☐ C《西游记》的原著
   - ☐ D 整套《哈利·波特》

2. 再听一遍小兰和大明的这段对话，然后用中文回答下面的问题。

   ❶ 说说大明在前后三次投票中选择了哪些书籍？
   ❷ 小兰去年选的书得奖了吗？
   ❸ 大明觉得《猴子大王》这本书怎么样？
   ❹ 小兰觉得《城南旧事》这本书怎么样？

二、Listen to the following podcast made by Ms. Wang, an educational psychologist. Summarise the details given by Ms Wang about helping children to develop a reading habit at home. You are not required to write in full English sentences. You must give two details for question (a) and two details for question (b).

   (a) Summarise the way Ms Wang got her son interested in reading.
   (b) Summarise the methods Ms Wang suggests for helping a child develop a good reading habit.

G 词语练习

根据英文，选字组词。

论 解 想
理（　）understanding
理（　）theory
理（　）ideal

术 器 力
武（　）weapon
武（　）force
武（　）martial arts

枯 干 烦
（　）燥 irritability
（　）燥 dry
（　）燥 boring

片 心 粉
（　）碎 to smash
（　）碎 broken heart
碎（　）shard

浏 阅 展
（　）览 to browse
（　）览 exhibition
（　）览 to read

会员 身份 学生
（　）证 student card
（　）证 membership card
（　）证 ID card

亲 望 险
探（　）to visit
探（　）adventure
探（　）to visit relatives

雅 默 静
幽（　）quiet and secluded
幽（　）humour
幽（　）quiet and tastefully decorated

藏 成 入
收（　）income
收（　）harvest
收（　）collection

手 时 地
随（　）conveniently (when doing something)
随（　）at any time
随（　）anywhere, everywhere

致 神 力
精（　）energy
精（　）spirit
精（　）exquisite

安 放 布
（　）置 to place
（　）置 to help to settle down
（　）置 to decorate

业 场 员
职（　）staff
职（　）occupation
职（　）world of employment

挥 现 展
发（　）to discover
发（　）to unleash
发（　）to develop

127

Unit Four 中国文化——文化活动

G 选词填空

1. 百科全书　古典小说　武侠小说　参考书籍　童话小说　现代小说

爸爸除了爱看《红楼梦》《西游记》等（　　），还常去电影院看从（　　）改编的电影，《天龙八部》就是他最爱看的一部。爸爸还喜欢看各类（　　）。因为爸爸知道的东西多，大家说他像（　　）。

2. 的　得　地　着　了

我真希望能在一间幽雅（　　）书房里，手里拿（　　）一本武侠小说，安安静静（　　）看半天。

G 名词综合练习

1. Common noun suffix:

师　员　子　者　手　家

孩（　）　演（　）　探险（　）　设计（　）
歌（　）　专（　）　教（　）　售货（　）
桌（　）　成（　）　艺术（　）　建筑（　）
帮（　）　作（　）　厨（　）　运动（　）

2. Noun phrases with 的:

火红的　枯燥的　有声的　收藏的　碎片的

❶ 今天招待客人的茶是爷爷（　　）。
❷ 那正在升起的太阳是（　　）。
❸ 外婆的眼睛不太好，妈妈买给她的书都是（　　）。

3. Collective nouns:

子女　师生　男女　风雪　道路　国家

❶ 在现代文明（　　），（　　）都是平等的。
❷ 虽然今夜有（　　），可是（　　）都回家过年来了。

T 翻译练习

1. Translate the following paragraphs into English.

我们学校的图书馆最近变了。它比以前大得多，而且更整齐，要找想要的书籍也更容易了。图书馆分成三个大房间：一个放可以借出的书籍，一个放不能借出的参考书，一个放影视光盘。学生可以在图书馆里上网找资料，或者用自己的笔记本电脑做作业。

我最高兴的是，现在图书馆里有很多外语书籍。英文的以前就已经有了，但现在增加了法文、日文、德文和西班牙文的故事书，还有杂志和报纸，方便了学外语的学生。

2. 把下面的文字翻译成中文。

Our local library underwent a complete refurbishment recently. I went there with my friend after it reopened last week. We were pleasantly surprised as soon as we stepped into the library.

First, we saw a nice café in the corner for people to have tea or coffee and even a little cake. It was all very nice and peaceful. People talked very quietly and looked relaxed.

Then we saw the books arranged in a very neat way. I went to look for a book about films and found it very easily. After that we passed an area where lots of students were working on their laptops, probably doing their homework.

15 电影

短文一　Text One

中国的电影业

中国现代电影的商业化开始得比较晚。欧美电影较早进入了中国市场，这些外语片通常会配上中文对话，或者打上中文字幕。然而多年来，能打入国际市场的中国电影大多还只是动作片。

近40年来，中国的影片在各类国际电影节上获过奖的已经超过100部。如何让中国影片不但能在国际上得奖，并且能有广大的观众，是当代电影界要解决的问题。根据调查发现，无论是早期的获奖影片《大闹天宫》《红高粱》，还是后来中美合拍的《卧虎藏龙》，以及近年得奖的《天注定》，这些电影要么有着鲜明的中华文化元素，要么讲述着中国今天的故事。

这是一个多元文化的世界，中华文化跟其他民族的文化一样，独特而丰富。相信中国的电影会走向世界，并成为让世界了解中国的窗口。

生词		
商业化	shāngyèhuà	commercialisation
字幕	zìmù	subtitled
获奖	huòjiǎng	to win a prize
如何	rúhé	how
当代	dāngdài	contemporary
无论	wúlùn	regardless of
《大闹天宫》	Dànào tiāngōng	Havoc in Heaven
《红高粱》	Hónggāo liang	Red Sorghum
《卧虎藏龙》	Wòhǔ cánglóng	Crouching Tiger, Hidden Dragon
《天注定》	Tiānzhùdìng	A Touch of Sin
鲜明的	xiānmíngde	distinctive
元素	yuánsù	element
独特	dútè	unique

R 读完上面的短文，回答下面的问题。Answer the following questions in Chinese.

1. 中国观众为什么能看懂欧美电影？
2. 进入国际市场的中国影片大多是哪一类？
3. 当代中国的电影界需要解决什么问题？
4. 能在国际上获奖的中国电影有什么特点？
5. 我们生活在一个什么样的世界？
6. 什么可以成为让世界了解中国的窗口？

Snippet

华人演员在好莱坞

提起华人演员在欧美电影界中成功出名,很多人都会提到李小龙。其实早在20世纪20年代,好莱坞就已经出现了一位美籍华人(Chinese American)电影演员,她叫黄柳霜 Anna May Wong。

她 1905 年出生在美国,父母是第二代移民。黄柳霜从小就热爱电影。在那个默片时代,她凭着第一部彩色电影《海逝》走红。之后还跟当时有名的男演员拍了好几部电影。

后来她回到祖辈的故乡学习中国语言与文化,并且跟随梅兰芳学习京剧。再次回到美国后,她继续拍电影。在 50 年代,她开始在一个电视连续剧中担任主角。本来还计划参演其他电影的她,不幸于 1961 年逝世了。

在她离世后的数十年里,黄柳霜留给人的记忆主要是西方人眼中典型的东方女性形象。

短文二 Text Two

年轻人爱看的电影

《中国电影报》最近做了一项调查,了解到现在的年轻人喜爱看的电影类型。

生词

类型	lèixíng	genre
科幻片	kēhuàn piàn	science fiction movies
场景	chǎngjǐng	scene
真实	zhēnshí	realistic
穿越片	chuānyuè piàn	time-travel movies
矛盾	máodùn	conflict
侦探片	zhēntàn piàn	detective movies
猜	cāi	to guess
古装片	gǔzhuāng piàn	costume / period drama
朝代	cháodài	dynasty

小陈:我爱看科幻片。今天的科技发达,电影里的场景都很真实,特别刺激。

王生:我也看科幻片,现在有不少穿越片,让现代人穿越到古代,挺有趣的。我喜欢想象自己带着现代的思想,穿着古代的服装,过起那时的生活,那一定很有挑战性。

小雨:我喜欢看跟现代生活有关的电影,例如家庭矛盾、情侣关系等。我可以向电影里的人物学习怎样解决感情问题。

丽红:我看的多是侦探片。中文的、英文的我都看,尤其是那些要你边看边猜的,让人有一种自己做侦探的感觉!

林芬:我从小就喜欢看古装片,其中不少电影讲的是不同朝代的故事,看了也可以学一点历史。

Unit Four 中国文化——文化活动

R 读完上面的短文，回答下面的问题。Answer the following questions in Chinese.

1. 《中国电影报》最近调查了什么？
2. 小陈爱看哪一类影片？为什么？
3. 王生为什么喜欢看穿越剧？
4. 小雨喜欢看跟什么有关的电影？为什么？
5. 丽红特别爱看什么样的侦探片？
6. 林芬觉得看什么影片可以学点儿历史？

S / W 跟你的同学在课上讨论上面的短文，然后写一篇 100—150 字的短文，说说你喜欢看什么类型的电影，并且解释原因。

短文三 Text Three

国际性影展

台北金马影展创办于1962年，至今已有半个多世纪的历史了。

今天的金马奖已经成为华语以及华人电影创作的最高荣誉之一。只要是华语片或华人制作的影片都可以报名参赛，很多默默无闻的影片都是因为这个奖项而被大家了解的。组织者为发现和培养新人，以及推广中华文化，做出了巨大的贡献。中国的不少导演和演员，甚至今天世界闻名的李安导演，都曾经得益于这个奖。

金马影展还给了华人一个了解各国好电影的平台，并且让电影创作者与投资发行公司有了更多的合作机会。参加2017年第54届金马影展的影片一共有576部，包括历史片、动画片、纪录片和侦探片等，数量和质量都再次得到了提高。

生词

金马影展	Jīnmǎ Yǐngzhǎn	Golden Horse Film Festival
创办	chuàngbàn	to found
金马奖	Jīnmǎjiǎng	Golden Horse Awards
创作	chuàngzuò	making
荣誉	róngyù	honour
默默无闻	mòmò wúwén	little known
组织者	zǔzhīzhě	organiser
推广	tuīguǎng	to promote
导演	dǎoyǎn	film director
李安	Lǐ Ān	Ang Lee
得益于	deyìyú	benefited
平台	píngtái	platform
投资	tóuzī	investment
发行公司	fāxíng gōngsī	distributor
动画片	dònghuàpiàn	cartoon movies
纪录片	jìlùpiàn	documentaries
数量	shùliàng	quantity

R 读完上面的短文，回答下面的问题。Answer the following questions in Chinese.

1. 台北金马影展有多长的历史？
2. 金马奖有什么样的地位？
3. 哪些影片可以报名参加金马奖比赛？
4. 金马影展有哪些贡献？
5. 金马影展给华人提供了什么样的平台和机会？
6. 在 2017 年的金马影展上，什么再次得到了提高？

S

在国外放映的中国电影大多是动作片，而演员都要会武术，西方人眼中的典型东方人形象好像就是这样的。因此，要参演西方电影的华人演员，几乎都要演同一类型的角色。对此你怎么看？

你可以说说以下几点：

1. 说说你看过有华人演员的西方电影。
2. 他们演的是什么角色？
3. 你认为他们演的角色都属同一类型吗？
4. 你觉得有什么方法可以改变情况？

S 口语练习

主题二 中国文化
次主题 文化活动
中国电影

你必须思考以下几点：

- 说说你喜欢什么类型的电影。
- 你觉得这类型的电影吸引哪些观众？为什么？
- 你觉得中国电影怎样才可以吸引到更多外国观众？

W 写作练习

请写一篇 150 字左右的短文，可以考虑以下几点。

题目 谈谈你看电影的习惯

1. 你看电影有些什么习惯？
2. 你喜欢看哪类电影？为什么？
3. 请简单介绍其中一部电影。
4. 你认为在电影院看电影好吗？为什么？

Unit Four 中国文化——文化活动

L 听力练习

一、大山和小路在讨论怎么过周末的晚上。

1. 听对话，然后在正确的答案前打 ⊠。

   ❶ 他们准备去看什么电影？
   - [ ] A 宽屏
   - [ ] B 立体
   - [ ] C 激光
   - [ ] D 全景

   ❷ 看一场电影要多少钱？
   - [ ] A 160 元
   - [ ] B 350 元
   - [ ] C 300 元
   - [ ] D 免费

   ❸ 凭借什么可以借毛毯？
   - [ ] A 学生证
   - [ ] B 工作证
   - [ ] C 身份证
   - [ ] D 居民证

   ❹ 他们决定看多长的电影？
   - [ ] A 一小时
   - [ ] B 小半天
   - [ ] C 一晚上
   - [ ] D 一整天

2. 再听一遍小路和大山的这段对话，然后用中文回答下面的问题。

   ❶ 小路原来打算周末做什么？
   ❷ 她觉得在家里电视上看电影有什么好处？
   ❸ 特色电影院的座位有些什么特点？
   ❹ 在特色电影院连着看三场电影，可以得到哪些服务？

二、Listen to the following conversation. You are not required to write in full English sentences. You must give two details for question (a) and two details for question (b).

   (a) Summarise what Wan Li says about the Chinese Film Club in Berlin.
   (b) Summarise how Dr. Lehman became a fan of Chinese culture.

Chapter 15 电影

G 词语练习
根据英文，选字组词。

字 银 屏
( ) 幕 screen
( ) 幕 subtitle
( ) 幕 screen in cinema

产 农 商
( ) 业 commerce
( ) 业 business
( ) 业 agriculture

奖 得 收
获( ) obtained
获( ) have won
( )获 harvest

明 美 新
鲜( ) tasty
( )鲜 fresh
鲜( ) bright-coloured

素 旦 首
元( ) New Year's Day
元( ) element
元( ) head of state

述 台 师
讲( ) podium
讲( ) lecturer
讲( ) to tell

种 肉 别
( )类 type, variety
( )类 meat
类( ) classification

激 刀 身
刺( ) bayonet
刺( ) exciting
刺( ) sashimi

越 针 戴
穿( ) to thread a needle
穿( ) to wear
穿( ) to pass through

古 服 西
( )装 clothing
( )装 ancient clothing
( )装 western clothing

盾 头 长
矛( ) contradiction
矛( ) spearhead
( )矛 long spear

尤 他 实
( )其 specially
其( ) actually, in fact
其( ) other

135

Unit Four 中国文化——文化活动

G 选词填空

1. 挑战性　竞争性　刺激性　严重性

　　不少年轻人觉得看穿越片（　　）很强。如果真的现代人穿越到古代去生活，一定非常有（　　）。

2. 自己　其他　别的　哪些　那些　有些

　　老师问："（　　）同学希望周末活动去看历史片？"（　　）同学愿意去，她（　　）也想去看，（　　）同学愿意去看侦探片。

G 语法综合练习

There are two types of commonly used adverbs in Chinese: one is called referential adverb, which is used before a verb; the other shows degree, which is used before an adjective.

1. Translate the following sentences into Chinese. You must use the referential adverb given in the brackets for each sentence.

    ❶ The Documentary *Please Vote for Me* is one of the films to watch for the exam. It is important that we watch it again.（再）

    ❷ We'll watch the new movie this weekend then!（就）

    ❸ I have no time to watch a movie until this weekend.（才）

    ❹ Ma Ming loves watching movies but has no time.（却）

    ❺ This is also a winning movie.（也）

    ❻ Many young people like to watch American movies.（都）

    ❼ The detective film I watched yesterday is very exciting, and I still want to watch it again.（还）

    ❽ I only watch foreign movies with Chinese subtitles.（只）

2. Translate the following sentences into English.

    ❶ 哥哥周末特别喜欢和朋友们去看午夜电影。

    ❷ 我觉得这部电影比那部得奖的电影更好看。

    ❸ 很多中国制作的卡通片非常棒。

    ❹ 中国的功夫片十分受欢迎。

T 翻译练习

1. Translate the following advertisement into English.

临时演员招聘广告

熊猫制片公司现正招聘 20 名临时演员。拍摄的场景包括城市广场和街道。详情如下：

电影类别：现代爱情片

角色详情：

中国男性：18—55 岁，会讲中文，扮演中国游客。

中国女性：18—55 岁，会讲中文，扮演中国游客及导游。

被选中者，必须在 9 月第一个星期内有 4 天参加拍摄。

试镜日期：5 月 17 日

报酬：一天 200 块人民币

报名方式：

请将简历及照片用邮件发给我们。有或没有演出经验的都欢迎报名。如有演出经验的，请将有关电影名字、照片与海报，连同简历一起发到我们的邮箱。

XMgongsi@vip.com

Glossary:
临时演员（línshí yǎnyuán）extras
试镜（shìjìng）screen test
报酬（bàochou）wage

2. 把下面的邮件翻译成中文。

Dear Mark,

I have good news to tell you. I went for an audition yesterday and got selected! I will be an extra in a new martial art film produced by Panda Film Company.

My role will be the owner of a small town restaurant. I will even be able to say one line! The film will start shooting in July this year and will last for five days. That will suit me very well as my summer holidays will start in mid-June.

The pay is not bad for working five days. I can use that money to go travelling afterwards! I have already planned to visit you in Taiwan. You can show me your hometown.

David

Glossary:
audition（miànshì）
面试

16 电视

短文一 Text One

受欢迎的烹饪节目

俗语说"民以食为天",各大电视台最近似乎都在热播不同形式的烹饪节目,例如《大厨讲座》《烹饪比赛》等,都很受欢迎。还有些节目是以电视纪录片的形式出现的,比如《舌尖上的中国》,它在中国的收视率十分高,还吸引了海外片商购买。

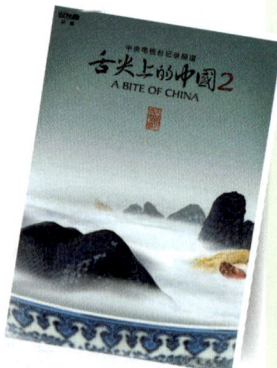

这个节目专拍家常菜,着重介绍中国各地的特色菜,讲述人和食物之间的故事,展示传统的农耕中国,以及不同民族的饮食,同时也反映出中国的很多传统正在改变。

在有些片子中出现的人很有可能是最后一代传承手艺的人了。例如,在拍摄香港一个很受欢迎的虾酱时,导演把做虾酱的老奶奶和她去世的丈夫怎么做了一辈子虾酱的感人故事,也记录在这部电视片里。

这些节目让世界更了解中国的饮食文化,以及中国人对美食的追求。

生词

俗语	súyǔ	common saying
民以食为天	mínyǐshí wéitiān	food is everything to the common people
热播	rèbō	to broadcast frequently
烹饪节目	pēngrèn jiémù	cookery programme
《舌尖上的中国》	Shéjiān shang de Zhōngguó	A Bite of China
片商	piān shāng	film company
着重	zhuózhòng	with emphasis on
反映	fǎnyìng	to reflect
传承	chuán chéng	to passed down and to inherit
手艺	shǒuyì	craft
虾酱	xiājiàng	shrimp paste
记录	jìlù	to record
追求	zhuīqiú	pursuit

R 读完上面的短文,回答下面的问题。Answer the following questions in Chinese.

1. 电视台播放的烹饪节目有哪些形式?
2. 为什么烹饪节目能在各大电视台热播?
3. 怎么可以看出《舌尖上的中国》是一个成功的节目?
4. 它拍摄的内容与其他烹饪节目的有什么不同?
5. 《舌尖上的中国》记录的什么内容特别有价值?

> 看一集《中国达人秀》或《中国好声音》，说说你对这些电视节目的看法。
> Discuss what you think of either of these programmes in the class in Chinese. Do you think the TV formula works in China?

短文二 Text Two

制作电视节目的方向

最近，中国传媒界做了一项调查：年轻人希望看到什么样的电视节目？结果发现，"新"是出现最多的词，年轻人期待节目的内容和形式都能推陈出新。在15—39岁的人群中，收看电视的四大主要原因是放松心情、了解社会、掌握时尚和打发时间。

在高科技快速发展的今天，坐在电视机前看节目的年轻人越来越少。一部手机连上网，基本上什么电视节目都能收看了。

不少电视台把传统的电视节目和网络结合起来。有些节目在正式开播前，先在新闻网和微博上播放，网友可以拨打热线电话，或者通过微博发表看法；有些节目在播放后有观众点赞和投票活动，在线上、线下同时展开互动。

另外，因为不少年轻人有自我表现的欲望，电视台在制作节目的时候，不但会考虑怎样吸引观众的关注，还会考虑增加观众的参与机会。

生词

传媒界	chuánméi jiè	the media
推陈出新	tuīchén chūxīn	out with the old, in with the new
人群	rénqún	cohort
掌握时尚	zhǎngwò shíshàng	follow the new trend
打发	dǎfā	to while away (one's time)
开播	kāibō	to begin broadcasting
微博	wēibó	Weibo (China's version of Twitter)
拨打	bōdǎ	to dial
点赞	diǎnzàn	"like it", it is an online network phrase, used to express "praise"
互动	hùdòng	to interact
欲望	yùwàng	desire

R 读完上面的短文，回答下面的问题。Answer the following questions in Chinese.

1. 中国传媒界最近做了什么调查？
2. 年轻人看电视的主要原因是什么？
3. 为什么坐在电视机前看节目的年轻人变少了？
4. 谈谈电视台怎样增加观众的参与机会。
5. 电视节目制作的时候要考虑什么？为什么？

Unit Four 中国文化——文化活动

W S Talk to your friends about the types of TV programmes you like to watch and why. Which factors would you consider the most important when choosing your favourite programme? Discuss this in the class in Chinese. You can write down the types of programmes and the factors first.

短文三 Text Three

看电视的利与弊

随着电视机的普及、电视频道的增加和电视节目的多样化，电视打开了人们的视野，丰富了大家的文化生活。

然而，当人们花大量的时间观看电视节目的同时，就不得不减少与家人交流和沟通的时间，也不得不放弃一些阅读和户外活动的时间，甚至我们安静思考的时间。

不少中小学生能流利地背诵广告词，却说不出诗词佳句或名人格言；他们能专心地观看电视节目，却无法集中注意听老师讲课；有些甚至成了"沙发上的土豆"，而不是运动场上的健儿。

有教育工作者说，如果青少年一周内看电视的时间超过10个小时，就会影响他们跟人的交流和语言能力，限制他们的思维范围，使得他们缺乏创意。如何指导青少年有选择地、有节制地看有意义的电视节目，是社会、学校和家长都要关心的事情。

生词

普及	pǔjí	becoming common
频道	píndào	channel
视野	shìyě	horizon
丰富	fēngfù	to enrich
放弃	fàngqì	to give up
佳句	jiājù	well-turned phrase or saying
格言	géyán	maxim; motto
沙发上的土豆	shāfā shang de tǔdòu	couch potato
健儿	jiàn'ér	athlete
限制	xiànzhì	to limit
思维范围	sīwéi fànwéi	the scope in thinking
指导	zhǐdǎo	to guide
有节制地	yǒujié zhìde	controlled; disciplined
有意义的	yǒuyì yì de	meaningful

R 读完上面的短文，回答下面的问题。Answer the following questions in Chinese.

1. 为什么电视能丰富大家的文化生活？
2. 如果看电视的时间多了，会产生哪些不好的影响？
3. 谈谈电视对中小学生的影响。
4. 根据教育专家的说法，什么使得青少年缺乏创意？
5. 社会、学校和家长应该关心什么事情？

W 请写一篇 150 字左右的短文，可以考虑以下几点。

题目 再谈《天水围的日与夜》中的张家安

1. 你觉得电影上半场中的张家安是"沙发上的土豆"吗？为什么？
2. 他后来有了什么变化？为什么会有这些变化？
3. 请概括他的性格特征。

S 口语练习

主题二 中国文化
次主题 文化活动
电视

你必须思考以下几点：
- 介绍一个与中国文化有关的电视节目。
- 你喜欢这个节目吗？为什么？
- 你认为这类电视节目能吸引外国观众吗？为什么？

W 写作练习　　　　　　　　请写一篇 150 字左右的短文，可以考虑以下几点。

题目 谈谈你看电视的习惯

1. 你平常什么时候、怎样看电视？
2. 你喜欢看什么类型的节目？为什么？
3. 你认为人们现在每天看电视的时间多不多？为什么？

L 听力练习

一、明东和他爸爸正在谈做饭的事情。
　　1. 听对话，然后在正确的答案前打 ☒。
　　　　❶ 明东家平常谁做饭？
　　　　　　☐ A 明东
　　　　　　☐ B 他妈妈
　　　　　　☐ C 他爸爸
　　　　　　☐ D 他爸爸和妈妈
　　　　❷ 明东的妈妈今晚要做什么？
　　　　　　☐ A 做饭
　　　　　　☐ B 出外吃饭
　　　　　　☐ C 出外买菜
　　　　　　☐ D 看电视

141

Unit Four 中国文化——文化活动

❸ 妈妈刚看完了一本什么书？
- ☐ A 爱情小说
- ☐ B 烹饪书籍
- ☐ C 武侠小说
- ☐ D 动物书籍

❹ 妈妈要看的电视剧一共有多少集？
- ☐ A 3 集
- ☐ B 4 集
- ☐ C 12 集
- ☐ D 24 集

2. 再听一遍明东和他爸爸的这段对话，然后用中文回答下面的问题。

❶ 为什么明东的爸爸今晚要做饭？
❷ 明东的妈妈今晚要看什么电视节目？
❸ 这个节目什么时候播放？
❹ 明东向他爸爸建议什么？

二、Listen to the following conversation between Chen Shan, a high school student, and his friend Qiu Yu. Summarise the details given by Chen Shan about the travel programme he watched on TV. You are not required to write in full English sentences. You must give two details for question (a) and two details for question (b).

(a) Summarise the contents of the travel programme Chen Shan watched last night.

(b) Summarise the reason why Chen Shan had to wait before planning for his visit to Hong Kong.

G 词语练习

根据英文，选字组词。

本 础 层

基（　）basic
基（　）foundation
基（　）base level

打 正 款

拨（　）to dial
拨（　）to allocate funds
拨（　）to set right

欲 希 展

（　）望 hope
（　）望 outlook
（　）望 desire

作 造 度

制（　）system
制（　）manufacture
制（　）to produce

动 换 相

互（　）each other
互（　）to exchange
互（　）interactive

博 笑 小

微（　）China's version of Twitter
微（　）tiny
微（　）to smile

赞 头 火

点（　）to give the thumbs up
点（　）to light a fire
点（　）to nod

票 球 降

投（　）to pitch (a ball)
投（　）to vote
投（　）to surrender

及 通 选

普（　）common
普（　）widespread
普（　）general election

频 道 率

频（　）channel
频（　）frequency
频（　）repeatedly

野 力 察

视（　）vision
视（　）field of vision
视（　）to inspect

制 省 目

节（　）to save
节（　）to control
节（　）programme

范 包 巾

（　）围 to surround
（　）围 range
围（　）scarf

播 线 心

热（　）hotline
热（　）to broadcast a lot of similar popular programmes
热（　）warm-hearted

G 选词填空

1. 在　从　到　给　为了

　　中国不少电视台（　　）吸引年轻的观众，近年来（　　）国外引进了不少有创意的节目。《中国好声音》《中国达人秀》等节目（　　）大家带来了新鲜的感觉。

2. 用　坐　跟　比　离

　　现在看电影，不一定要去电影院。如果家里有一台宽屏立体声电视，（　　）坐在电影院看差不多。有些人觉得坐在客厅的沙发上看（　　）去电影院看舒服。有时候，可以躺在床上，（　　）手机也可以看电影。

Unit Four 中国文化——文化活动

G 语法综合练习

In Chinese grammar, verbs are not conjugated to show tenses like in English. Instead aspect markers are used. The aspect markers below are commonly used:

① 在 to show continuation;
② 着 to show progression;
③ 了 to show completion;
④ 过 to show past experience.

All these aspect markers must be directly preceded by the verb.

1. Translate the following sentences into English.
   ① 奶奶在看烹饪节目。
   ② 我班的同学几乎都看过《中国好声音》。
   ③ 妹妹正专心地看着卡通片《小猫钓鱼》。
   ④ 昨天英国电视台播放了一个关于中国地理的节目。

2. Translate the following sentences into Chinese.
   ① We are discussing this variety show.（在）
   ② Xiao Yu is reading quietly in the library.（着）
   ③ I have watched this TV show once already.（过）
   ④ I just watched a gardening programme on TV.（了）

There are also structural markers which are used frequently in Chinese sentences. They are:

① attributives with 的;
② descriptive adverbials with 地;
③ complement with 得.

3. Translate the following sentences into Chinese.
   ① The TV programme broadcast yesterday was very funny.
   ② In the weekend cookery show, the chef taught the audience how to make a cake step-by-step.
   ③ That Chinese actress speaks English fluently.
   ④ Jackie Chan performed outstandingly in that film.

T 翻译练习

1. Translate the following paragraphs into English.

   叔叔做饺子做得非常好，最近他参加了电视节目《家常菜巧手》举办的做饺子比赛。比赛昨晚进入了决赛阶段，在电视上播放。

我们一家人坐在电视前，一边看，一边大喊"加油"，虽然我们都知道他听不到。比赛很紧张，参赛者的水平都很高，而且很有创意。最终，叔叔得了第二名，我们都很高兴。

> Glossary
> 巧手（qiǎoshǒu）
> a dab hand

2. 把下面的文字翻译成中文。

　　My parents tell me that I watch too much TV. But I don't agree.

　　I watch TV for half an hour after school every day. In the evening I watch for an hour when I finish my homework. I tell them that I must watch news so that I get to know what's going on in the world. At the weekends I watch more programmes, especially if there is an important football match on.

　　I am really not a "couch potato" as my parents think I am.

17 怡人的音乐

短文一　Text One

▍K 歌串烧

今年暑假,我跟父母去香港参加表哥的婚礼。传统的婚礼仪式在早上举行,婚宴在晚上,之后是卡拉OK娱乐活动。

我在英国参加过这类活动,唱的都是西方流行歌曲。这是我第一次体验中西合璧的K歌串烧!出席婚礼的宾客男女老少都有,年轻人主要唱外国和香港本地的流行歌,长辈则唱粤剧小曲。虽然他们唱的从内容到形式都很不相同,但是每个人都唱得兴高采烈,气氛很和谐。

最让我感到惊奇的是,当长辈唱粤剧的时候,年轻人也一起唱,似乎他们平时也唱粤剧。表姐说,祖父母在家听粤剧小曲,很多时候晚辈也会听到,听得多了,他们也就会唱了。

粤剧在香港和广东有数量庞大的粉丝,同时,粤剧艺人一直在很热心地推广这种传统音乐。

回英国前,我买了一张粤剧光盘作为香港之行的纪念品。

生词

婚宴	hūnyàn	wedding banquet
卡拉OK	kǎlā OK	karaoke
体验	tǐyàn	to experience for oneself
中西合璧	zhōngxī hébì	Chinese and Western combined together
K歌串烧	K gē chuàn shāo	singing a variety of songs
出席	chūxí	attending
宾客	bīnkè	guest
粤剧	yuèjù	Cantonese opera
小曲	xiǎoqǔ	arias
和谐	héxié	harmonious
惊奇	jīngqí	surprised
数量庞大	shùliàng pángdà	great number
粉丝	fěnsī	fans
艺人	yìrén	artist
光盘	guāngpán	CD

R **读完上面的短文，回答下面的问题。** Answer the following questions in Chinese.

1. "我"和家人去香港的目的是什么？
2. 在那里"我"有了什么新体验？
3. 香港的年轻人喜欢唱什么？
4. 年纪比较大的人喜欢唱什么？
5. 他们喜欢唱的歌受欢迎吗？为什么？

Snippet
戏曲艺术

中国古代戏剧因以"戏"和"曲"为主要因素，所以称做"戏曲"。戏曲跟诗、词、文、赋一样，在中华文化中占着很重要的地位。戏曲主要有唱、念、做、打四种艺术手段，综合了对白、音乐、歌唱、舞蹈、武术和杂技等多种表演方式。

戏曲种类繁多，最为人熟悉的是京剧。但是在全球华人社会里，除了京剧以外，粤剧、昆曲都很受欢迎。这三类剧种已经被列入联合国《人类非物质文化遗产代表作名录》。

Ancient Chinese opera's main elements were drama and song, hence the name "xiqu". Xiqu, like poetry and prose, is a very important art in Chinese culture. It incorporates various art forms such as songs, dialogues, acting, martial arts, dance, acrobatics, as well as literature to become the traditional Chinese opera we know nowadays.

There are many regional varieties of traditional Chinese opera. Beijing opera is well known around the world. Among the overseas Chinese communities, Cantonese opera and Kun opera are also very popular. These three operas have been included in the *UNESCO Intangible Cultural Heritage Lists*.

W S Talk to your friends about the types of music you like to listen to and why. Which factors would you consider the most important when choosing your music? Discuss this in the class in Chinese. You can write down the types of music and the factors first.

短文二 Text Two

音乐会后记

生词

效果	xiàoguǒ	result; effect
出奇	chūqí	surprisingly
管弦乐团	guǎnxián yuètuán	orchestra
《梁祝》协奏曲	Liáng Zhù Xiézòuqǔ	Butterfly Lovers In italics
幽怨	yōuyuàn	resentment; bitterness
联想	liánxiǎng	to associate; to imagine
梁山伯	Liáng Shānbó	Liang Shanbo
祝英台	Zhù Yīngtái	Zhu Yingtai
娶	qǔ	to marry (a woman)
悲剧	bēijù	tragedy
二胡	èrhú	a two-stringed bowed instrument
琵琶	pípa	a plucked string instrument with a fretted fingerboard
笛子	dízi	bamboo flute
贝多芬	Bèiduōfēn	Beethoven
《命运交响曲》	Mìngyùn Jiāoxiǎngqǔ	Symphony No.5
惊喜	jīngxǐ	nice surprise
音色	yīnsè	timbre

　　我们学校最近举办了一场音乐会。因为学乐器的学生多，有学西方乐器的，也有一些学中国乐器的，所以当晚的节目学生要么用西方乐器演奏中国音乐，要么用中国乐器演奏西方乐曲。演出效果出奇地好，观众被深深地吸引了。音乐会结束时，全体观众站起来热烈地鼓掌。

　　音乐会给我印象最深的是管弦乐团演奏的《梁祝》协奏曲。听着那小提琴幽怨的声音，我就联想到梁山伯因为娶不到祝英台而病倒，最后死去的悲剧。中乐团的学生用二胡、琵琶、笛子等民族乐器演奏了一段贝多芬的《命运交响曲》，给了观众很大的惊喜。

　　音乐会最后的项目是介绍当晚表演用过的中国乐器。每种乐器都由学生演奏一小段，让观众了解每种乐器的不同音色。

　　我打算以后也去参加一个乐器班，希望将来有机会表演。

R 读完上面的短文，回答下面的问题。Answer the following questions in Chinese.

1. 学校最近举办了什么活动？
2. 这个活动有什么特别之处？
3. 说说这次表演给"我"最深刻的印象是什么？
4. 活动结束前的一个项目是什么？目的是什么？
5. 这个活动对"我"有什么影响？

Find out the story of *Liang Shanbo and Zhu Yingtai* and listen to *Butterfly Lovers* in italics afterwards. Discuss how you feel about the story and the music in the class in Chinese. Do you think the two match well? If so, how and where do they match?

短文三　Text Three

对音乐有兴趣

生词

戴	dài	to wear
耳机	ěrjī	earphone
连	lián	even
天赋	tiānfù	natural gift
嗓音	sǎngyīn	voice
缺	quē	to lack; be short of
摇滚乐	yáogǔnyuè	rock music

　　马明正一边做功课，一边戴着耳机听音乐，连他妈妈走进房间也不知道。妈妈并不反对马明这么一心二用，但要他能学好一种乐器，她认为这对马明将来申请大学会有好处。

　　马明常常跟她解释，他只喜欢听音乐，但不想学什么乐器，因为那需要花很多时间练习，况且自己也没有这个天赋。不过，他对唱歌则有很大兴趣，同学们也都说他的嗓音很好听。

　　班上有几位同学想组织一个乐队。他们有些会弹吉他，有一个会弹钢琴，有一个会打鼓，就缺一个歌手，问马明要不要参加。马明很想参加，因为这些同学跟自己一样，不只是喜欢流行音乐，民歌、摇滚乐等都爱。马明告诉妈妈，说参加了乐队，既可以合作演出，又可以用音乐来放松自己，一举两得。

　　马明的妈妈说，再考虑考虑。

R 读完上面的短文，回答下面的问题。Answer the following questions in Chinese.

1. 马明做功课时喜欢做什么？
2. 他妈妈对这有意见吗？
3. 为什么妈妈希望他学好一种乐器？
4. 为什么马明不要学乐器？
5. 他对什么更有兴趣？

Unit Four 中国文化——文化活动

6. 他想参加什么团队活动?
7. 他觉得参加这个活动有什么好处?

Snippet
中国的民族乐器

从周朝起,中国已经有了根据乐器制作材料进行分类的方法,主要分成金、石、丝、竹、土、革、木、匏八类,统称"八音"。如以用法分类,则分为吹奏乐器、弹拨乐器、打击乐器、拉弦乐器四大类。

常见的吹奏乐器有笛子、箫、唢呐,常见的弹拨乐器有古筝、琵琶、柳琴,常见的打击乐器有锣、鼓、钟、木鱼,常见的拉弦乐器有二胡、京胡等。上面提到的大多是汉族的乐器,其实少数民族都有他们自己的民族乐器。

As early as the Zhou Dynasty, Chinese musical instruments were grouped into 8 categories according to the material used to make them, that is metal, stone, silk, bamboo, clay, skin, wood and gourd. Together they were called "the eight tones". The instruments were also classified into four families according to how they were played, such as "blown", "plucked", "beat" and "bowed".

The "blown" family includes dizi, xiao, suona. The "plucked" family includes guzheng, pipa and liuqin. The "beat" family includes luo, gu, zhong and muyu. The "bowed" family includes erhu and jinghu. Most of these mentioned above are Han instruments. Ethnic minorities have their own instruments.

S / W 跟你的同学在课上谈谈你们知道的中国乐器,然后写一篇 100—150 字的短文,介绍其中一种,并说说为什么你选择这种乐器。

S 口语练习

主题二 中国文化
次主题 文化活动：
音乐

你必须思考以下几点：
- 介绍一个你喜欢的中国传统音乐作品。
- 这作品的背景与你认识的中国文化的关系。
- 年轻的华人更喜欢外国音乐的原因。

W 写作练习

请写一篇 150 字左右的短文，可以考虑以下几点。

题目 谈谈你听音乐的习惯

1. 你平常什么时候、怎样听音乐？
2. 你喜欢听哪类音乐？为什么？
3. 请简单介绍一个你喜欢的歌手或乐队。
4. 你认为听音乐对人的生活重要吗？为什么？

L 听力练习

一、王明在接受电台记者采访时谈他学乐器的经过。
  1. 听对话，然后在正确的答案前打 ☒。

❶ 王明是从什么时候开始学小提琴的？
- ☐ A 他姐姐六岁时
- ☐ B 他五岁时
- ☐ C 他六岁时
- ☐ D 他十一岁时

❷ 王明开始学小提琴时，她姐姐在学什么乐器？
- ☐ A 大提琴
- ☐ B 笛子
- ☐ C 钢琴
- ☐ D 小提琴

❸ 谁第一个教王明弹钢琴？
- ☐ A 他的小提琴老师
- ☐ B 一个钢琴老师
- ☐ C 他姐姐
- ☐ D 他妈妈

Unit Four 中国文化——文化活动

❹ 王明在今天的演奏会上演奏什么音乐？（可以多选）
- [ ] A 日本的流行歌曲
- [ ] B 中国的乐曲
- [ ] C 韩国的流行歌曲
- [ ] D 莫扎特的音乐

2. 再听一遍记者和王明的这段对话，然后用中文回答下面的问题。
   ❶ 王明为什么选择学小提琴？
   ❷ 为什么后来他又学钢琴？
   ❸ 为什么他的朋友们都觉得他更喜欢拉小提琴？
   ❹ 在今天的演奏会上，谁给他伴奏？

二、Listen to the following introduction made by Mr Chen, a music teacher at North Hill School. Summarise the details given by Mr Chen about helping children to develop an interest in music. You are not required to write in full English sentences. You must give two details for question (a) and two details for question (b).

(a) Summarise the interest groups for music they have at North Hill School.

(b) Summarise the performances there were at the Chinese New Year celebration.

G 词语练习

根据英文，选字组词。

仪　形　样
(　　) 式　type
(　　) 式　ceremony
(　　) 式　form

婚　国　晚
(　　) 宴　state banquet
(　　) 宴　wedding banquet
(　　) 宴　evening banquet

体　实　测
(　　) 验　test
(　　) 验　to experience for oneself
(　　) 验　experiment

似　几　在
(　　) 乎　almost
(　　) 乎　to seem
(　　) 乎　to mind

庞　巨　广
(　　) 大　vast
(　　) 大　great number
(　　) 大　enormous

奏　出　员
演 (　　)　to play a musical instrument in front of an audience
演 (　　)　to perform
演 (　　)　actor / actress

出　惊　好

(　) 奇　surprisingly
(　) 奇　curious
(　) 奇　surprise

鼓　手　握

(　) 掌　palm
(　) 掌　to applaud
掌 (　)　to grasp

虑　试　场

考 (　)　examination
考 (　)　to consider
考 (　)　venue for examination

效　结　水

(　) 果　fruit
(　) 果　result
(　) 果　effect

悲　喜　戏

(　) 剧　drama
(　) 剧　tragedy
(　) 剧　comedy

想　系　合

联 (　)　association of ideas
联 (　)　contact
联 (　)　to combine

G 选词填空

1. 中西合璧　兴高采烈　一举两得　和谐幸福

   李安的电影能够取得巨大的成功，首先得益于他（　　）的电影风格。多年的美国生活，使他比一些长期在中国大陆或台湾生活的导演，对西方社会的人情世故了解得多。另外，他的成功跟他（　　）的家庭生活，以及妻子对他的支持也是分不开的。

2. 幽怨　摇滚　流行　惊奇

   1986 年 5 月 9 日，崔健在北京工人体育馆举行的百名歌星演唱会上演唱了《一无所有》，从此宣告了中国（　　）乐的诞生。虽然一个人什么也没有，但是却没有给我们（　　）的感觉，因为他的内心有追求。

G 语法综合练习

Numerals: fractions, percentages, decimals, indeterminate, approximation, multiples and juxtapositions are often used in Chinese texts.

1. Translate the following sentences into Chinese, using one of the numerals mentioned above.

   ❶ One-eighth of our students study Chinese, three-eighths learn French, three-eighths learn Spanish, and one-eighth learn German.

   ❷ According to the survey, nearly 75% of young people in China like to listen to pop music.

Unit Four 中国文化——文化活动

❸ Today Grandpa's body temperature is 38.9 degrees. He has a high fever.

❹ His collection of rock music CDs has tripled in number from three years ago.

❺ China's oldest musical instrument has a history of about 7,000 years.

❻ My brother has been learning to play the flute for two or three years.

❼ More than 90 students in our school learn to play different instruments.

❽ This band has fewer than ten members.

翻译练习

1. Translate the following message into English.

文生：

　　明天晚上，红绿合唱队在我们市内的音乐厅开演奏会。我哥哥买了两张票，本来准备跟他女朋友去的，可是他感冒了，咳嗽咳得很厉害，不能去了。他把门票都给我了。

　　我知道你很喜欢红绿合唱队，你要和我一起去这个演奏会吗？如果你有空可以去的话，请在今天晚上前给我回复。

小清

2. 把下面的留言翻译成中文。

Xiaoqing,

　　I have heard about this concert and wanted to go. However, you know the rock band I joined last year? We are going to perform in a secondary school in west London tomorrow evening. Therefore I am afraid I won't be able to go with you. Thank you for thinking of me. I hope your brother will get better soon.

　　Our band has been invited to perform in the town hall on Saturday, the 10th June. The tickets are just £2 for students. I would really like you to come and see us perform. Let me know if you can come.

Wensheng

Unit Five 文学与电影 如何分析文学作品与电影

Chapter 18 《一只叫凤的鸽子》（作者：曹文轩，2014）
Chapter 19 《城南旧事》〈惠安馆〉（作者：林海音，1960）
Chapter 20 《城南旧事》〈爸爸的花儿落了〉（作者：林海音，1960）
Chapter 21 《请投我一票》（导演：陈伟军，2007）
Chapter 22 《天水围的日与夜》（导演：许鞍华，2008）

文学作品与电影

THREE

第五单元　文学与电影
如何分析文学作品与电影

分析文学作品和电影非常复杂，取决于其类型、形式和其他许多因素。这个单元只是集中在AS考试大纲所选取的作品上。它们是：

- **文学作品**
  1. 曹文轩的短篇小说《一只叫凤的鸽子》
  2. 林海音的自传体短篇小说集《城南旧事》中的《惠安馆》和《爸爸的花儿落了》

- **电影作品**
  1. 陈为军导演的纪录片《请投我一票》
  2. 许鞍华导演的故事片《天水围的日与夜》

上面列出的每个作品我们将从第18课到第22课分别来具体分析。下面段落提供的是关于如何分析这些作品的一般指导，以及关于在阅读故事或观看电影时的注意点。

分析电影与分析文学作品没有太大差别。有一点可以肯定的是，它们都需要在开始分析文字或影像之前熟悉这些作品。在任何分析中，如果要提出一个观点或论点，就必须给出证据。因此，重要的是要记住，这些作品需要全部阅读或观看，以便首先对作品有一个整体的了解，然后再重新仔细研读。你对作品的最初反应可以告诉你，它们带给读者或观众什么样的触动。稍后重新审视作品时，就需要你去寻找细节。因此，记下任何有用的东西，例如对话、叙述、场景、拍摄技巧等，来作为支持你的某一观点或论点的有用论据。

《惠安馆》和《爸爸的花儿落了》是作者林海音的两个自传体的短篇小说。她通过想象和虚构故事，创作了这些基于她个人经历的故事。《一只叫凤的鸽子》是作者曹文轩的一个虚构的创作。

- **分析文学作品**

在阅读分析短篇小说时，要把握好故事的背景、人物、情节、主题以及风格。

背景

思考一个故事的背景就是要搞清故事的时间和地点，当故事发生在一个特定的时代时，这一点尤其重要。生活在跟我们不同的时间或地点的人物，表现出来的态度和行为会带着那个时代的印记。例如，在《惠安馆》中，你会发现秀贞在生下宝宝后变"疯"的原因；或者在《爸爸的花儿落了》中，你会明白为什么英子即使在小时候被父亲殴打得很厉害，却仍然跟父亲非常亲近。

人物

"文学是人学"，只有通过人物刻画，无论是主要人物还是次要人物，小说的情节才可以发展，主题才得以表现。要注意作者是怎么通过对人物的形态、动作、语言、细节、心理等的描写来塑造人物的。例如，在《一只叫凤的鸽子》中，你自己会怎么来描绘秋虎这个人物？并思考：作者为什么塑造他成为那样一个形象？再想想：在同一个故事中，次要人物夏望是怎么样一个人？为什么作者赋予他这些性格特征？夏望的这些性格特征如何凸显出主要人物秋虎？小说的次要人物往往是为了刻画主要人物而设计的，分析人物，还需要分析人物之间的关系，比如在《一只叫凤的鸽子》中的夏望与秋虎；《惠安馆》中的秀贞与英子。

情节

故事情节通常有开端、发展/冲突、高潮、结局组成。冲突可以是人物之间的冲突，也可能是必须克服的障碍。例如，在《一只叫凤的鸽子》里，在哪里发生了冲突？故事的高潮是什么？冲突在最后如何解决？你需要找到必要的情节来帮助你分析和解释故事。

主题

一个故事通常有一个主题，无论是一个长篇、中篇还是短篇小说。作者通过故事内容、时代背景、人物形象来表现一些主旨。这些主题围绕着人性、战争、教育、性、爱情、友谊、青少年问题、社会结构等等。有些故事会涉及多个主题，有些主题很容易被发现，其它的可能需要深入挖掘故事才能找到它。例如，在《一只叫凤的鸽子》中，秋虎克服了所有困难，以实现他在鸽子飞行大赛中获胜的目标。作者是否想说这个成就可能只是因为秋虎强大的毅力和不懈的努力？

风格

写作是一门艺术，分析作者使用的各种文学手法非常重要，因为它们是用来表达作者意图或创造情绪的工具。当重新阅读故事时，尝试寻找这些写作手法，确认其最主要的是什么，思考这些手法是如何为表现作者的整体意思服务的。常见的文学手段包括隐喻、衬托、铺垫、反讽、象征等手法。问你自己这样的问题：作者创造了什么样的形象？作者在叙述中是否使用了倒叙或者插叙？作者是否突出对比？这些手法对塑造人物形象和表现主题起到了什么作用？例如：在《惠安馆》中，秀贞没有朋友，跟她父母的话也不多，作者用什么方式揭示秀贞的内心思想？在《一只叫凤的鸽子》中，"凤"有什么特别的作用？

• 分析电影作品

电影和文学共享类似的元素，如情节、人物、对话、场景、细节和主题等。因此，在分析一部电影时，也可以用分析文学作品相同的方式，来分析这些元素的使用及其效果。然而，与文学不同，电影是一种音响和视觉的艺术形式，它使用直接和特定的图像和声音来投射影像，所以就多了一个方面来分析电影作品。在本单元所涉及的两部影片中，《请投我一票》是一部纪录片，记录所发生的事情；《天水围的日与夜》是一部故事作品。

在分析电影时，我们可以从人物、场景、叙事结构和拍摄技巧方面入手。

Unit Five
文学与电影
如何分析文学作品与电影

人物

电影中的人物是影片造型的基础，是叙事的核心，是矛盾冲突的主体。影片中人物的塑造方法跟文学作品不一样，是通过演员的表演来实现的。因此演员的形体语言跟对白台词一样重要，我们在分析时不能忽视。对白是人物表达思想感情的重要手段，是影片中推动情节发展的重要元素。影片中真实而富有表现力的细节能凸显人物的性格，揭示人物的心理，并且为后面的情节做铺垫等。例如，在《请投我一票》中，导演如何表现三名参选学生的个性？另外，导演为什么要拍摄三位候选人的家人？有时候角色之间互动的细节，不但可以突出他们的个性，也可以为剧情的发展做准备。

场景

场景是影片重要的造型元素，它实质上是与文学作品最明显不同的部分。视听元素包括道具、服饰、设置、灯光、音乐、特效、舞蹈的编排等。要分析它们，重新观看电影很重要，因为注意某些场景可以帮助详细深入地分析，看出这些场景是如何共同促成情节的叙述结构和发展。例如，在《天水围的日与夜》中，导演为什么重复使用贵姐和张家安共进晚餐的场景？或者在外婆的生日聚会上，张家安看他的表兄弟姐妹在他们的手机上玩游戏的场景有什么意义？导演想要在这些场景中展示什么？另外，在《请投我一票》中，导演为什么要拍摄三位候选人的家庭场景？

叙事结构

在考虑叙事结构时，你应该思考影片中不同元素的构成和排列，包括角色及其动机、动作和情节线索。影片的创作者如何创造戏剧性结构，例如怎么设置情节？怎么推动情节发展？结局是什么？他或她这样组织和安排的意图是什么？例如，在《天水围的日与夜》中，为什么贵姐陪着梁婆婆去看她的孙子的情节很重要？尝试解答以上的问题，有助于你进一步深入地分析人物和主题。

摄制技巧

跟写作一样，电影摄制也是一门艺术。电影制作人在他们的作品中尝试不同的艺术手法。导演如何运用远景、近景、全景或者特写？例如，在《请投我一票》中，三位班长候选人在全班面前才艺表演时或后，为什么导演用特写镜头拍摄他们的哭泣？在《天水围的日与夜》中，导演如何运用了蒙太奇？尝试回答这些问题可能有助于加深你对电影的理解。

Unit 5 Literature and Film Analysis of Literary Works and Films

Analysing literary works and films can be very complex, depending on the genre, form and many other factors in play. Unit 5 focuses only on the works chosen in the AS specification. These are:

• Literature

1. *A Pigeon called Feng*, a short story by Cao Wenxuan;
2. *Hui An Guan* and *Father's Flowers Fell*, two autobiographical short stories from the collection *Tales of the Old City* by Lin Haiyin;

• Film

1. *Please Vote for Me*, directed by Chen Wenjun;
2. *The Way We Are*, directed by Ann Hui.

Each one of the works listed above will be dealt with in separate chapters from 18 to 22 in the Unit. The following passages give general guidance on how to analyse these specific works, in terms of what to look out for when reading the story or watching the film.

Analysing film is not so different from analysing literature. One thing for sure is that they both require careful study of the works to start with before going into the analysis of the texts and images. As in any analysis, if a point or argument is to be made, supporting evidence must be given. Therefore, it is important to remember that these works may need to be read or watched in their entirety once first to get a general feel of the works and then revisited later. Your initial reaction to the works can show you what sort of impact they have on you as a reader or audience. When revisiting the works later, you are looking for details. Therefore, it is useful to note down anything, such as dialogue, narration, scene, filming technique, etc. for use as evidence to support a point or argument.

The two stories *Hui An Guan* and *Father's Flowers Fell* are autobiographies of the author Lin Haiyin（林海音）who, through imagination and fictionalisation, created these stories based on her personal experience. *A Pigeon called Feng* is a fictional creation by Cao Wenxuan（曹文轩）.

Unit Five

文学与电影
如何分析文学作品与电影

• Analysing literature

When analysing a short story, we might consider the background, characters, plot, theme and writing style of the story.

Background

Thinking about the background of a story means asking when and where the story is set, and this is particularly important when the narrative takes place in a specific era. Characters living in a time or place different from our own will exhibit attitudes and behaviours that reflect their everyday world. For example, in *Hui An Guan* you might find out the reason why Xiu Zhen （秀贞）becomes 'mad' after giving birth to her baby; or in *Father's Flowers Fell* you might understand why Ying Zi （英子）remains close to her father even though she was beaten up by him when she was younger.

Character

The study of literature is the study of humankind. Characters, both major and minor ones, convey the plot, and through them central themes emerge. Pay attention to how characters are depicted, through their forms, actions, language and psychology. For example, in *A Pigeon Called Feng*, look at the character Qiu Hu（秋虎）. Describe him for yourself and ask why he is portrayed in that way. Consider supporting characters too. In the same story, describe Xia Wang （夏望）for yourself and ask why the author gives him these personality traits and how these traits make the main character stand out. You also need to find out how the different characters in the story form relationships with one another, such as Qiu Hu and Xia Wang in *A Pigeon called Feng* and Ying Zi and Xiu Zhen in *Hui An Guan*.

Plot

The storyline of a story usually follows the pattern of 'conflict', 'climax', and 'resolution'. Conflict can be a conflict between characters, or an obstacle that must be overcome. For example, in *A Pigeon called Feng*, where is the conflict? How is the climax reached in the story? And finally, how is the conflict resolved? Finding essential plot points will help you to analyse and explain the story.

Theme

A story usually has a central theme, be it a big novel or a short story. The author uses the context, setting, and characters to comment on an idea or ideas. These themes commonly revolve around human nature, social structure, coming-of-age, war, education, sex, love, friendship, to name just a few. Some stories deal with multiple themes. Some are easy to detect, while others may be hidden deep within the story. So, for example, in *A Pigeon called Feng*, Qiu Hu overcomes all hardship to achieve his goal of winning the pigeon flying competition. Does the author want to say that this achievement is possible only because of Qiu Hu's strong willpower and hard work?

Style

Writing is a craft and it is important to analyse the various literary devices that the author uses, as they are the very tools used to convey meaning or create a mood. When re-reading the story, try to look for these devices to identify the key points and their contribution to the author's overall meaning.

Common literary devices include allusion, foil, foreshadowing, irony, symbolism, etc. Ask yourself questions: What imagery does the author create? Does the author use flashbacks, or play with time in any other way in the narrative? Does the author highlight contrasts? How do these techniques work to shape the characters and to present the theme? For example, in *Hui An Guan*, how does the author reveal Xiu Zhen's inner thoughts as she doesn't really have any friend, or talk much to her parents? In *A Pigeon called Feng*, what is so special about the pigeon *Feng*?

• Analysing film

Film and literature share similar elements such as plot, characters, dialogue, settings, symbolism, and theme. So, when analysing a film, these elements can also be analysed for their intent and effect in the same way as literature. However, unlike literature, film is an audio and visual art form which uses direct and specific pictures and sounds to project images. So, there is an added dimension to analyse. Of the two films covered in this Unit, *Please Vote for Me* is a documentary which records what happens while *The Way We Are* is a feature film which is a work of fiction.

When analysing a film, we might consider characters, scenes, narrative structures and filming techniques.

Characters

Characters shape a film. They are the core of the narration, and the subject of conflict. The shaping of character in a film is different from shaping those in literature. In film, the development of character relies importantly on an actor to achieve this purpose. Dialogue is important, but so too is physical expression, such as body language, and this shouldn't be ignored when studying a film as it can reveal a significant part of a character's thoughts and feelings. For example, in *Please Vote for Me*, how does the director depict the personality of the three pupils standing for election? Also, why does the director film the home scenes of the three candidates? Sometimes focusing on the details of interactions between characters can highlight their individual personality and may also serve to prepare for the development of the plot.

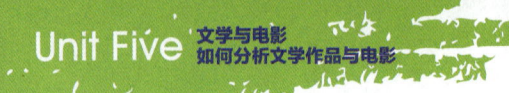

Scene (audiovisual elements)

This is basically the arrangement of compositional elements in a film. It is the part which is most distinct from literary works. Audiovisual elements include props and costumes, setting, lighting, music, special effects, choreography, etc. To analyse them, re-visiting the film is important as noting down certain scenes can help with detailed analysis of music, positioning of actors, placement of objects, etc., which together may contribute to the narrative structure and development of the plot. For example, in *The Way We Are*, why does the director use the scene of 贵姐 and 张家安 eating dinner together repeatedly? Or what is the significance of the scene of 张家安 watching his cousins playing games on their mobile phones at the birthday party? What does the director want to show with these scenes?

Narrative structures

When considering narrative structures, you should think about the composition and arrangement of the different elements, including characters and their motivations, actions and plot. How has the film's creator gone about creating the dramatic structure like the setting up of the plot, the progression of the story, and finally the ending? What is his or her intent? For example, in *The Way We Are*, why is the storyline of 贵姐 accompanying 梁婆婆 to see her grandson important? Trying to answer these questions will hopefully give you further insight into the character and the theme.

Filming techniques

Just as with writing, film-making is a craft, and film-makers experiment with different artistic techniques in their work. How has the director used long-distance, close-up or panoramic shots to achieve the effects he wants? For example, In *Please Vote for Me*, why does the director use close-up shots of the three candidates crying when they put on a performance in front of the class? In *The Way We Are*, how has montage been used? Trying to answer questions like these may help to deepen your understanding of the film.

18 《一只叫凤的鸽子》

一、作者简介

曹文轩，1954年1月生于中国江苏盐城的农村，1974年进北京大学中文系学习，现在是北京大学中文系教授，同时也是著名的当代儿童文学家。他的作品获得过中国多项大奖以及2016年国际安徒生奖（Hans Christian Andersen Award）。

曹文轩的作品多数以真实的农村生活为题材，人物以善良的男孩子为主。故事中的主人翁一般都遭遇曲折，形象独特鲜明。作者的语言简洁流畅，情节跌宕起伏。读者在他的故事中可以领悟到人与人之间要互相关爱与帮助，要善待一切生灵的道理，同时故事也会唤起人们对真善美的追求。

二、内容简介

《一只叫凤的鸽子》介绍了两个爱鸽子的小男孩：秋虎和夏望。两个人是同学，都喜欢鸽子。可是，夏望家富，养的都是好鸽子；秋虎家穷，只能养一些土鸽子。一次意想不到的机会，秋虎得到了一只很好的鸽子。他给鸽子取了一个跟妹妹一样的名字"凤"。可秋虎那赌输了钱的爸爸把"凤"卖给了夏望家，秋虎伤心极了。之后，他不停地打鱼，卖鱼，一心攒钱要赎回自己的"凤"。不久，夏望的爸爸坐了牢，虽然家里被债主一抢而空，变穷了，但夏望把"凤"藏了起来。在一次放鸽比赛中，两个人都拿着自己的鸽子参赛。惊奇的是，第一个飞回来的"凤"飞回了秋虎家。最后，秋虎带着"凤"，叫上夏望，两个孩子肩并肩地跑去领奖了。

三、写作特点

1. 对比手法

这篇小说的一个显著的写作特点就是运用对比手法。这是文学创作中常用的一种表现手法，把对立的意思或事物、或把事物的两个方面放在一起作比较，让读者在比较中分清好坏、辨别是非。运用这种手法，有利于充分展示事物的矛盾，突出事物的本质特征，加强文章的艺术效果和感染力。

The novelette uses antithesis as an important writing technique. This device is commonly used in creative writing to express

---

思考题

❶ 秋虎和夏望的家境有什么不同？

❷ 请介绍一下夏望家与秋虎家的鸽子，以及人们对待两家鸽子的态度有什么变化。

❸ 秋虎在有了"凤"以后，心理发生了怎样的转变？

❹ 从语言、动作、神情与穿着等方面，分析夏望在他家发生变故前后有什么不一样。

contrasting ideas and things, or to compare the two aspects of the same idea or thing. It reflects more prominently the conflict in the storyline, and also highlights the personality of the characters or the characteristics of things.

2. 映衬手法

　　映衬，不是零碎、个别的对比手法，而是全文总体构思上的对比，可以增添文章的深度和广度。作者以"凤"来映衬秋虎，它和他都遭遇了坎坷，但都有着顽强的生命力和坚韧的毅力。

　　映衬 is not a piecemeal or individual comparing technique. Rather it is the contrasting of the whole concept of the story. It can increase the breadth and depth of the whole piece of writing. The author uses this technique to set off "the phoenix" against Qiuhu to show the bitter experiences and hardship they both encountered; despite that, both of them still held on to their vitality and strong willpower.

> **思考题**
> ❶ 请概括介绍秋虎的遭遇。
> ❷ 请概括介绍"凤"的遭遇。
> ❸ 简单分析秋虎与"凤"的遭遇有什么相同的地方。

四、综合思考理解

　　请先分组讨论下面的问题，然后在下面的思考题中选择一题，用中文回答，字数为 225—300 字。

1. 探讨在夏望和秋虎的关系变化中，鸽子"凤"起了什么作用。
   ❶ 秋虎是怎么得到"凤"的？
   ❷ "凤"怎么到夏望的家了？
   ❸ 夏望和秋虎如何因为"凤"成为了朋友？

2. 探讨夏望家的变故如何改变了夏望。
   ❶ 夏望的家庭情况如何？
   ❷ 夏望的家庭发生了什么变故？
   ❸ 在发生家庭变故后，夏望有了什么变化？

3. 从秋虎与"凤"的关系，谈谈秋虎的性格。
   ❶ 秋虎为什么给鸽子起名为"凤"？
   ❷ 秋虎是怎么失去"凤"的？
   ❸ 秋虎为什么到了夏望家，却没有拿回"凤"？

4. 探讨在秋虎得到"凤"的过程中，邱叔起了什么作用。
   ❶ 简单介绍一下邱叔。
   ❷ 秋虎是怎么得到那只折了翅膀的台湾鸽子的？
   ❸ 邱叔的什么建议与帮助让秋虎得到了"凤"？

19 《惠安馆》

一、作者简介

林海音（1918—2001）出生于日本，成长于北京，1948 年起定居台湾，是一位多产的作家、编辑和出版人。1960 年出版的小说集《城南旧事》获奖无数，奠定了她在世界华语文坛的地位。

林海音的作品具有观察仔细、刻画细腻的特点。她尤其善于运用节奏轻快的短句，语言很幽默。她的小说创作往往通过描写自己在故土的生活经历，选取大量琐碎而真实的、日常生活中的女性素材，叙说她们的生命轨迹。她大多数作品的主题是在浓浓的乡愁中，表达对中国女性命运的关心和思考。

二、内容简介

英子来到北京不久就认识了惠安馆里的"疯女人"秀贞，还有胡同口的妞儿，并且跟她们成了朋友。

英子经常去惠安馆玩耍，于是了解到秀贞曾与一个借住在她家的大学生思康相爱了，后来大学生说是回家请求父母答应他们的婚事，却再也没有回来。当时秀贞已经怀了孩子，后来生下的小桂子又被家人抱走，下落不明，秀贞由于受到双重打击而变疯了。

英子在跟小伙伴妞儿的来往中发现，妞儿的身世很像小桂子。又发现她脖颈后面有一块胎记，跟秀贞提到的小桂子的身体特征一模一样。原来她的母亲就是秀贞！英子偷了自己母亲的金镯子，帮助秀贞与离散多年的女儿相认、团聚、出逃去找思康，谁料结果却是秀贞与妞儿死在火车的轮子下。英子悲痛极了。

三、写作特点

语言描写是塑造人物形象的重要手法，包括人物对话和内心独白。

Using speech to shape the image of a character is an important technique in literature. It includes the use of dialogues between characters, as well as the inner monologues of a character.

1. 人物对话

人物对话应该要能显示其身份、职业、地位和经历。"言为心声"，对话要能表现出人物的思想、感情和性格。

Dialogues should be able to show the speaker's identity, occupation, status and experience. It should also show the thinking, emotion and personality of a character.

Unit Five
文学与电影
如何分析文学作品与电影

思考题
1. 作者是怎么运用对话，塑造出一个天真善良并有着好奇心的英子的？
2. 从宋妈和"换洋火"的婆子之间的对话，分析秀贞变"疯"的原因。
3. 从秀贞与英子的对话中，分析秀贞对"小桂子"和思康的思念。
4. 从与妞儿的对话，英子了解到妞儿身世的什么秘密？
5. 哪些对话表现出秀贞母亲因女儿未婚生子而感到羞耻愤恨？
6. 从哪些对话可以看出英子母亲对英子的关爱？

2. 内心独白

如果把一个人自言自语或想说却未说出来的话，用文学语言记录下来，这就是内心独白。

一个人的内心世界有时候是很隐秘的。在小说、戏剧或电影中运用内心独白手法，可以把人物形象塑造得更有血有肉，让读者或观众可以了解、理解、并把握人物的真实思想和性格。

If a person is speaking aloud, or wants to say something but has not quite uttered the words, their "speech" becomes inner monologues when it is written down in a literary work.

A person's inner world can be very private. When monologue is used in a play or film, the image of a character is made more realistic, allowing the reader or audience to know and understand that character, and grasp his / her real thinking and personality.

思考题
1. 找出秀贞内心独白的部分，并谈谈她是怎么与思康相爱的。
2. 找出英子内心独白的部分，并谈谈她的性格特点。

四、综合思考理解

请在课堂上分组讨论下面的综合思考题，然后在其中选择一题，用中文回答，字数为225—300字。

1. 探讨作品是如何通过语言描写来表现英子和妞儿的友谊的。可以考虑以下几点：
   1. 英子和妞儿是怎么认识的？
   2. 两个人的家庭背景和性格。
   3. 她们的友谊是怎么发展的？

2. 探讨思康在作品中的作用。可以考虑以下几点：
   1. 思康的家庭情况。
   2. 他与秀贞是怎么认识的？
   3. 秀贞的"疯"与他有什么关系？

3. 探讨秀贞父母在女儿变"疯"中的责任。可以考虑以下几点：
   ❶ 秀贞父母的背景和性格。
   ❷ "小桂子"出生后他们做了什么？
   ❸ 他们是怎么对待变成"疯子"的女儿的？

4. 探讨妞儿这个人物在全文中的作用。可以考虑以下几点：
   ❶ 妞儿现在的父母是谁？
   ❷ 她为什么要寻找亲生父母？
   ❸ 她与亲生父母团圆了吗？

5. 探讨是哪些因素让英子认为妞儿是秀贞失去的女儿的？可以考虑以下几点：
   ❶ 妞儿的身世是怎样的？
   ❷ 妞儿身上有什么特征？
   ❸ 这些都跟小桂子有什么关系？

20 《爸爸的花儿落了》

一、内容简介

《爸爸的花儿落了》是《城南旧事》中的最后一篇。英子小学毕业了，而且实现了爸爸对她的期望，要作为学生代表上台领取毕业证书并致答谢辞。可是爸爸病重，卧床不起，于是妈妈在英子衣襟上别了一朵夹竹桃，代表爸爸出席英子的毕业典礼。

英子坐在礼堂里，往事一一再现：前一天爸爸在医院对自己的嘱咐；六年前曾因为赖床想逃学被爸爸严惩；礼堂的钟声响起时，英子又想到爸爸爱花，以及因病而不能料理的花儿；当学生们唱起骊歌时，英子想到很多人盼望自己长大，还想到爸爸要她闯练，让她到银行汇款给在日本的陈叔叔的经过。

等英子毕业典礼结束后回家，看着院子里垂落的花儿，听到老高的话，她意识到爸爸的花儿落了，自己也已经长大了。

二、写作手法

1. 象征手法

象征手法包括象征体和本体两个方面，象征体和本体之间必须要有内在联系，这种联系就是从一事物想到另一事物的相通点，也就是从本体想到象征体的相似点和相近点，它可以使抽象的思想、意义和概念形象化、具体化。

In literature, symbolism can be used when one thing（本体）is meant to represent something else（象征体）. However, there must be a built-in link between 本体 and 象征体. This link will connect one to the other through a word, action, or event which has a deeper meaning in the context of the whole story. It is like through the similarity or closeness of the 象征体, which is linked to the 本体, abstract ideas, meanings and concepts are made to materialise and be visualised.

2. 插叙手法

插叙是指在叙述中心事件的过程中，暂时中断原来的情节，而插入另外的叙述，交代一些必要的人物或有关事情后，再接着原来的叙述写下去。

插叙可以起到丰富情节、扩展内容、交代人物和说明因果等深化主题的作用。

思考题

❶ 为什么在英子去参加毕业典礼前，母亲要在她的衣襟上别上一朵夹竹桃？

❷ 从哪儿可以看出英子的爸爸爱花？

❸ 这篇文章的本体和象征体各是什么？

❹ 你怎么理解这篇文章的题目？

❺ 谈谈本文运用象征手法所起的作用。

This technique is a narration interspersed with flashbacks. It is used when the narration of the main story is replaced temporarily by the narration of something else to clarify a point or a character, before reverting back to the main story.

The technique can enrich the plot, explain the characters, and account for the storyline.

> **思考题**
> ❶ 前天在医院爸爸对英子嘱咐了什么？
> ❷ 六年前发生了什么事儿，以致从此英子上学不再迟到？
> ❸ 为什么爸爸要英子去银行给日本的叔叔汇款？
> ❹ 哪些人盼望着英子长大？

三、综合思考理解

请在课堂上分组讨论下面的综合思考题，然后在其中选择一题，用中文回答，字数为 225—300 字。

1. 探讨《爸爸的花儿落了》是如何运用插叙的写作手法表现父亲在英子成长中所起的作用的。可以考虑以下几点：
   ❶ 父亲在医院里对英子叮嘱了什么？
   ❷ 六年前父亲打英子的原因是什么？其结果怎么样？
   ❸ 父亲为什么要英子去银行给她在日本的叔叔汇款？

2. 探讨在《爸爸的花儿落了》中，英子与父亲的深厚感情。可以考虑以下几点：
   ❶ 为什么英子希望病重的父亲能去参加自己的毕业典礼？
   ❷ 为什么有一天父亲让英子坐车去学校，后来还去学校给她送衣、送钱？
   ❸ 在整个毕业典礼的过程中，英子为什么一次次想起爸爸和他的花？

3. 探讨《爸爸的花儿落了》是如何运用"花儿"来象征爸爸的。可以考虑以下几点：
   ❶ 为什么在英子去参加毕业典礼前，母亲在她的衣襟上别上一朵夹竹桃？
   ❷ 你是怎么理解本文题目的？
   ❸ "爸爸的花儿落了"，"我也不再是小孩子"，这是文章的最后两句话，它们之间有什么关系？

21 《请投我一票》

一、导演介绍

陈为军，1969 年 11 月 30 日出生于北京，1992 年从四川大学新闻系毕业后，到武汉电视台工作，现任纪录片导演。

他说："拍纪录片需要深入一个人的生活。只要足够真诚，肯定会触摸到最真实的东西。"他以真诚之心，在 2004 年拍摄了反映河南艾滋病家庭的《好死不如赖活着》，获得美国广播电视文化成就奖。2007 年讲述小学生班长选举的《请投我一票》入围 2008 奥斯卡最佳纪录片，还获得了英国国家纪录片奖。他参与了全球纪录片《为什么贫穷》，拍摄了关于中国教育的《出路》，赢得了极大的反响。他的影片大多"记录难以接受的真实"。

二、剧情简介

《请投我一票》记录的是武汉市常青第一小学三年级一班选班长的过程。罗雷、成成和许晓菲这三个候选人是老师们商定的，每位候选人可自选两名同学做帮手。班主任张老师解释了民主选举的规则——谁当选班长由得票多少决定。

第一轮是才艺表演，三个候选人在各自家长的指导下做准备。晓菲首个上台，还没表演，成成就串通同学们起哄；成成表演时虽然唱歌跑调，但是大家一齐叫好；罗雷吹长笛时，成成按照父母所教，再次带头起哄。

第二轮是辩论，三个候选人收集了对手的缺点并进行质问。在成成觉得自己已经赢得多数同学支持的时候，罗雷做警察的父亲请孩子全班同学免费坐轻轨观光，之后罗雷人气上升。成成按照家长的指导，针对罗雷经常打同学的问题，提出班长应该是管理者，而不是统治者；而罗雷则揭发成成背后说会选他，这会儿又说选自己，是个"骗子"。

最后一轮是演讲与投票，家长都倾全力帮助自己的孩子做准备。罗雷演讲后，把父亲准备好的中秋小礼物和贺卡分送给了同学与老师。最后，投票结果是罗雷以 25 票当选班长。

思考题

1. 影片名字出现前，导演为什么要给两位学生以特写镜头？
2. 新学期开学典礼上，镜头特写了哪几位学生？为什么？
3. 在才艺表演环节，特写镜头下三位候选人哭泣的原因分别是什么？
4. 在投票结束后，镜头为什么要特写其他两位哭泣的普通同学？

三、影片特点

1. 特写镜头

特写镜头是电影艺术里的一种拍摄手法。近距离拍摄，把人或物的局部加以放大、强调，以造成强烈的艺术效果。

Close-up is a method used in filming. It shows great detail as it is taken very near to the subject being filmed, thus creating a strong effect through enlargement and focus.

2. 对白

对白是影片或戏剧中角色之间的对话，它可以起到塑造人物和推动情节发展的主要作用。

Dialogue is the conversation between characters in a film or play. Its main function is to shape a character and to help with the plot development.

> **思考题**
> ❶ 找出三位候选人家长与孩子的对白，谈谈家长对孩子教育上的相同点与不同点。
> ❷ 从三位候选人跟自己的帮手以及其他同学的对白，分析他们各自用了什么方法来拉票？
> ❸ 通过三位候选人在辩论时的对白，分析家长在这场选举中起了什么作用？
> ❹ 从班主任张老师与学生们的对白，分析她在这场选举中所起的作用。

3. 重复辞格

重复辞格，是影视表达的一种方式，指相同或者相似的场景、音乐、诗词、动作、物件等在影视中重复出现。运用这种手法可以突出创作者希望表达的用意。

Repetition of expressions is a technique used in the process of visual presentation. Basically, it is the repetition of the same or similar scenes, music, poetry, actions and objects in the film. The function of this technique is to emphasise the creator's intended theme.

> **思考题**
> ❶ 请记下影片开始，学生从操场回到教室以及结尾时一起大声背诵的相同口号。
> ❷ 为什么这段口号在影片中多次出现？
> ❸ 在这次民主选举班长的过程中，三位候选人做到"诚实勇敢"了吗？
> ❹ 通过这场选举，你认为小学生们可能会学做怎样的人？为什么？

四、综合思考理解

请在课堂上分组讨论下面的综合思考题，然后必须在其中选答一题，用中文回答，字数为 225—300 字。

1. 探讨罗雷成功当选班长的原因。可以考虑以下几点：
   ❶ 从罗雷当选班长的经过，可以看出他的什么个性？
   ❷ 他的父母是怎样影响班长选举的？
   ❸ 罗雷当选班长是民主选举的胜利吗？为什么？

2. 探讨成成的性格特点。可以考虑以下几点：
   ❶ 成成为什么要做班长？
   ❷ 他用了哪些方法来拉票？
   ❸ 他对待父母的态度怎么样？

3. 探讨许晓菲败选的原因。可以考虑以下几点：
   ❶ 晓菲的性格和家庭背景。
   ❷ 晓菲在班长选举中表现如何？
   ❸ 你觉得她没能当选班长的主要原因是什么？

4. 探讨班主任张老师在电影中的作用。可以考虑以下几点：
   ❶ 张老师是怎么解释民主选举班长的？
   ❷ 候选人是怎么产生的？
   ❸ 她是怎样引导这场选举的？

5. 探讨候选人家长在电影中的作用。可以考虑以下几点：
   ❶ 一个记录班长选举过程的影片，为什么要拍摄候选人的家庭及其家长？
   ❷ 哪位家长给你留下的印象最深刻？为什么？
   ❸ 你对家长们在这场选举中的表现有什么看法？

6. 探讨影片如何通过三位候选人的家庭场景来表现主题。可以考虑以下几点：
   ❶ 从影片的名字谈谈该片记录的应该是什么？
   ❷ 影片同时还记录了候选人的哪些家庭场景？
   ❸ 你从影片可以看到这个社会的哪些真实面？

22 《天水围的日与夜》

一、导演简介

许鞍华，1947 年 5 月 23 日出生于中国辽宁鞍山。毕业于香港大学，后去伦敦进修电影。她是香港新浪潮电影制作人之一，曾任香港导演会会长，获得了六届香港电影金像奖、三次金马奖以及亚洲电影大奖颁发的终生成就奖。

她的电影作品题材广泛，内容有着深厚的人文（humanity）价值。这除了体现在她的电影中那浓郁的香港本土气息外，还体现在（embodied in）质朴的表现形式和真实的细节运用上。在她的影片中，无论底层人物的生活多么平凡或者无奈，但从他们身上，我们看到的总是勤奋、善良、宽容、温情以及生存的力量。

由于对电影事业以及社会的贡献杰出，她还荣获英女皇颁发的英帝国员佐勋章和香港政府颁发的铜紫荆星章。

二、剧情简介

在香港天水围的一幢公屋里，住着贵姐和她的独生子张家安。早年守寡的贵姐在一家超市的水果档做售货员。她十四岁就做徒工，赚钱供两个弟弟到国外读书。如今弟弟们事业有成，生活富足。家安是应届会考生，正值暑假等放榜，大多时间是待在家里睡懒觉、看电视。家安舅舅说如果家安考不上中六，就会资助他出国留学。

梁欢（梁婆婆）新近搬入贵姐所住的楼，还在贵姐工作的超市里找到一份工作。贵姐在工作上、生活上都很照顾这位孤独的老妇人。贵姐除了教家安要买有赠品的报纸，以及如何剥榴莲，还让他帮梁婆婆搬电视机，换电灯泡等。贵姐在自己母亲生病住院时，却优先陪梁婆婆去看望她的外孙，结果两人白跑了一趟。梁婆婆对外孙没有前来见面吃饭很失望，就把买给外孙、前女婿和他新妻子的首饰都给了贵姐。

后来，家安开始帮助母亲做家务，并考上了中六。贵姐母子邀请梁婆婆一起过中秋节，三人相处得如同一家人。

三、影片特点

1. 真实的细节

细节，是表现对象的细微之处。人物、景物和事件等细节必须真实典型，并且符合生活的逻辑，这样的细节能起到烘托环境气氛、刻画人物性格和表现主题思想的作用。

Detail is used to present all the fine points about the subject. The details of characters, scenes and events must be realistic and typical, as well as logical in life. Such details can make the atmosphere of a situation, the portrayal of a character, and the expression of the central theme stand out.

Unit Five
文学与电影
如何分析文学作品与电影

思考题
1. 贵姐为什么总是要买有赠品的报纸？
2. 梁婆婆买 10 块钱的牛肉后是怎么吃的？影片要表现什么？
3. 你从梁婆婆吃了饭后一个人发呆的这个细节，体会到了什么？
4. 贵姐帮弟媳打麻将时，她是怎么处理自己赢钱和输钱的？
5. 贵姐如何解决了梁婆婆既想买便宜的油，但又不需要一下子买三瓶的问题？
6. 请描述一下贵姐在丢弃丈夫裤子时的细节，说说她此刻的心理活动。
7. 为什么贵姐吃饭时把冬菇夹到家安的饭碗里？
8. 家安参加团契活动时，画了一幅什么画？这画表现了他与母亲怎样的关系？

2. 运用蒙太奇手法的作用

在影视艺术作品中，经常运用蒙太奇手法。简单地说，这手法就是将不同镜头剪接、穿插、拼贴在一起，产生出新的意义。蒙太奇手法使得影片在时间和空间上更自由，可以起到充实故事情节，表现完整的思想内容的作用。

Montage is often used in the visual arts. It puts different shots and cuts into a collage to produce a new picture and meaning. This method enables the free use of time and space to support the plot and to show the full meaning of the contents.

思考题
1. 当贵姐母亲在医院感慨贵姐 14 岁就当女工时，导演是怎么运用蒙太奇手法，呈现了那个时代香港女工的劳动与生活的？
2. 导演在什么时候，怎么运用蒙太奇手法交代了贵姐当年的丧夫之痛？

四、综合思考理解

请在课堂上结对或分组讨论下面的综合思考题，然后必须在其中选答一题，用中文回答，字数为 225—300 字。

1. 探讨影片如何通过细节来表现贵姐与家安之间的母子亲情。可以考虑以下几点：
   1. 贵姐是怎么照顾和关心家安的？
   2. 家安在团契活动时画的树表达了他与母亲怎样的关系？
   3. 家安后来有了什么变化？

2. 探讨影片如何通过细节来表现贵姐对家安成长的影响。可以考虑以下几点：
   1. 贵姐让家安帮助梁婆婆做了些什么？
   2. 家安为什么每天去医院看望外婆？
   3. 贵姐是怎么对待亲朋好友的？

3. 探讨影片中梁婆婆的性格及其人物意义。可以考虑以下几点：
   ❶ 梁婆婆平时生活是怎么精打细算的？
   ❷ 她为什么要把冬菇和首饰送给贵姐母子？
   ❸ 你觉得她的生活孤独、单调吗？为什么？

4. 探讨影片是如何通过细节表现贵姐和梁婆婆的友情的。可以考虑以下几点：
   ❶ 贵姐和梁婆婆是怎么认识的？
   ❷ 她们的背景与性格有什么相同之处？
   ❸ 她们后来怎么会相处得亲如一家？

5. 探讨影片是如何塑造贵姐的性格的。可以考虑以下几点。
   ❶ 她是怎么帮助新邻居新同事梁婆婆的？
   ❷ 代替弟媳打麻将时，她是怎么处理自己赢钱和输钱的？
   ❸ 在医院，当母亲感叹"做人真是很难"时，贵姐反问"有多难啊？"可见贵姐是怎样的性格？

6. 探讨贵姐赢得亲戚朋友尊敬的原因。可以考虑以下几点：
   ❶ 为什么贵姐母子与两个弟弟去参加亲戚的丧礼时，她买了大家要送的花牌？
   ❷ 当弟媳犹豫女儿应该去什么学校的时候，为什么要向贵姐征求看法？
   ❸ 梁婆婆为什么说她即便死了也会保佑家安？

Appendix I: Transcripts of listening exercises

第一课 Transcript

马克：这个星期六你有空吗？我想去看电影。
小英：不行。下星期三是我妈妈的生日，我答应了请她星期六去看电影，然后去饭馆吃饭。
马克：你爸爸和哥哥不去吗？
小英：哥哥跟学校去法国了，他说回来以后再请妈妈吃饭。我们是单亲家庭，爸爸现在住在美国，我们很少见面的。
马克：你们一家只有三口人，我家可热闹呢！我家有六口人：爸爸、妈妈、妹妹和我，还有爷爷、奶奶。
小英：那你每年都要买五份生日礼物，要很多钱的。
马克：没关系，中国新年的时候，我和妹妹都会收到很大的红包。

第二课 Transcript

妈妈：这个星期六你爷爷过生日，我们一起出去吃饭。你一定要参加哦！
小英：不行。我们公司这个周末要在一家酒店开会，星期六晚上还有舞会，非常重要。
妈妈：你总是忙！跟我们一起活动的时间，你都说没空，你觉得工作比家人重要吗？
小英：家人当然重要，可是我的工作真的很忙。我每天都要外出跟客户见面，帮他们设计产品，然后给公司写报告，每星期还要做工作总结。有时候我还要到国外去出席会议，参加训练班，我的难处你们知道吗？
妈妈：别说了，你不去就算了！
小英：妈妈，庆祝爷爷生日的活动，能改到下个周末吗？

第三课 Transcript

陈明亮：我叫陈明亮。我是独生子，爸爸妈妈很疼爱我，虽然他们赚的钱不多，但是他们总是把最好的吃的、喝的、穿的都给我。不过，他们对我的期望很高、很高，甚至把他们所有的希望都放在我身上，所以我感觉压力太大了。
王小玲：我是王小玲。我没有兄弟姐妹，学习不太好。妈妈担心我将来找不到好工作，赚钱不多，等她老了的时候，我不能照顾她。
李大山：我叫李大山。我爸爸妈妈也是这样，他们很疼爱我。他们给我最好的学习环境，在家里我什么家务都不用做，爸爸妈妈认为我的学业比其他一切都重要。我的生活就是学习，但有时候我觉得生活真的没有什么乐趣。
张 莉：我叫张莉。你们不要这样说，做独生子女有什么不好？我挺喜欢的。在家里我想吃什么、喝什么，爷爷奶奶就马上给我做或者买回来。如果我的考试成绩好，爸爸妈妈就带我去国外旅游。如果有兄弟姐妹，也许我就不能享受这些了。

第四课　Transcript

大海：妈妈，您好！
母亲：大海，你工作这么忙，今天怎么来看我了？
大海：今天是重阳节，也是老人节。我祝妈妈身体健康！
母亲：谢谢！我最近身体很好。
大海：养老院的生活怎么样？
母亲：我对这儿的生活非常满意。服务员很友好，做的菜也很好吃，最高兴的是我有了新朋友。
大海：你的新朋友是谁啊？
母亲：她过去跟我一样，也是教师。她有一个女儿，现在在英国工作、生活，所以她和丈夫都住进了这个养老院。我们都爱好书法，每天都要写毛笔字。
大海：您新朋友丈夫的爱好是什么？
母亲：他喜欢摄影，常常给我们照相。你看，这是他给我们拍的照片。
大海：真好看！妈妈，我下个周末带您孙女一起来看您。
母亲：好，我的新朋友可以帮我们拍照！

第五课　Transcript 1

丽丽：欢迎你来参加我们东海中学的开放日活动！
马文：谢谢！这所学校真大啊！
丽丽：是啊！我们学校不但很大，而且教学很好。
马文：我很喜欢英语，你们的英语老师怎么样？
丽丽：我的英语老师姓林，也是我的班主任。学生们都爱上他的课。他很热情，他的学生每年考试都考得特别好。
马文：希望我也会有一位好老师。
丽丽：这儿是实验室。左边的是化学实验室，右边的是物理实验室，物理实验室对面是生物实验室。
马文：实验室的设备都很先进。
丽丽：对！
马文：下课以后你常常做什么？
丽丽：我常常去体育馆锻炼身体。有时候去游泳，有时候去健身房跑步。
马文：希望明年我也能成为这所学校的学生。
丽丽：欢迎！

Appendix 1

Transcript 2

小田： 奶奶，您好！新学期开始了，我现在是高中生了！
奶奶： 小田，你喜欢你的新学校吗？
小田： 喜欢得不得了。大家都说我们的校服很好看。
奶奶： 你的学校有校车吗？
小田： 有，但是我家离学校近，不可以坐校车，我骑自行车去学校。如果下雨，妈妈就开车送我去。
奶奶： 你在学校吃午饭吗？
小田： 除了星期五以外，我每天都在学校的餐厅吃午饭。星期五的中午，我只有35分钟的休息时间，所以我就带三明治、水果和饮料当午饭。
奶奶： 你上些什么课呢？
小田： 除了数学、科学、英文、中文、地理和历史等必修课外，我还选修了戏剧呢。
奶奶： 你应该多多参加体育锻炼啊！
小田： 我每周有两节体育课，另外，我还是学校网球队的运动员呢，常常参加比赛。
奶奶： 好！好！希望你好好学习，天天快乐啊。
小田： 谢谢奶奶！

第六课　Transcript 1

爱玛： 小红，你的暑假过得怎么样？
小红： 马马虎虎。你呢？
爱玛： 很好啊！暑假一开始我就去快餐店打工，然后用自己赚的钱去法国度假了。
小红： 你家的条件这么好，为什么还要打工？
爱玛： 我17岁了，应该自己赚零用钱。再说打工很有意思，可以认识很多新朋友。你暑假做什么了呢？
小红： 我每天去英语和数学补习班。
爱玛： 你的成绩常常是全班第一名，为什么还要补习？
小红： 我父母希望我上名牌大学，所以我一定要非常努力。
爱玛： 你自己想不想上名牌大学？
小红： 我父母的希望就是我的希望。
爱玛： 你希望暑假天天学习吗？
小红： 不希望。你知道我喜欢历史，我想去丝绸之路旅游。
爱玛： 那你为什么不去？
小红： 我父母说……
爱玛： 你17岁了，自己的事应该自己决定。

Transcript 2

记者：玛丽小姐，欢迎您来我们东方电视台做客！
玛丽：谢谢，很高兴见到您。
记者：您的中文讲得真好！
玛丽：哪里！哪里！我还要努力学习，希望自己的中文能和您的一样好。
记者：您是从什么时候开始学中文的呢？
玛丽：中学毕业以后，我报考了爱丁堡大学的中文系。因为我小学时住在香港，学过一点儿中文，我觉得中文非常有意思。大学毕业以后我来山东中医学院留学。现在为了学好中医，我得把中文学得更好。
记者：您的学习一定很忙吧？
玛丽：还可以，我还有时间做兼职工作呢。
记者：什么工作？
玛丽：每个周末我都做英语家庭教师。通过做家教，我不仅可以赚零用钱，还可以了解中国家庭。
记者：您觉得中国的中学生和英国的有什么不同？
玛丽：英国的中学生在放学后，有很多时间做各种体育运动，看自己爱看的书，做自己爱做的事。中国的中学生每天要花太多的时间做功课。除了学校的功课以外，还有家长或者家庭教师给的功课，哪里还有时间运动啊？
记者：谢谢你的介绍。
玛丽：不客气！

第七课　Transcript 1

小雨：你准备申请那个服装厂的工作吗？
兰兰：我考虑过了，决定不申请。我想自己做生意，开一家商店。这样我就可以自己做老板，自由一些。
小雨：你想开什么商店？
兰兰：我要开一家网上毛衣店。
小雨：你卖什么毛衣呢？
兰兰：我在大学是读时装设计的，我特别喜欢研究不同国家的毛衣设计。我先自己设计样式，然后请退休工人织毛衣。
小雨：你去哪儿找工人呢？
兰兰：早上去公园找呀！有很多退休女工的爱好是织毛衣。还有，她们一般都有很多空闲时间。
小雨：你卖的毛衣贵吗？
兰兰：我毛衣的价格和市中心商店里的差不多，但是式样会不一样。
小雨：好主意啊！那我一定要做你的第一个顾客。
兰兰：谢谢你的支持！

Appendix 1

Transcript 2

小李：小王，你在超市的工作怎么样？

小王：谢谢你帮我找到这份工作。在超市打工比以前在工厂做杂工好。

小李：辛苦吗？

小王：辛苦！但是工资比以前高。而且因为我在这儿打工，所以在这里买东西可以便宜一些。

小李：你每天工作几个小时？

小王：每天我从早上8点工作到下午4点，星期六上午工作4个小时，星期天可以休息。

小李：你在超市做什么工作呢？

小王：我负责把蔬菜、水果放到架子上去。

小李：你工作得快不快乐？

小王：很开心，经理说我将来可以接受培训，然后试着做别的工作。还有，因为我们在一起打工的有几个是同乡，我们可以一起聊聊家乡的事。

小李：很好。继续努力，希望你将来有机会升职。

小王：谢谢！

第八课　Transcript 1

小花：叔叔，好久不见，您的肚子快要跟我爸爸以前的一样了！

叔叔：快要怎么样？

小花：快要有一个啤酒肚子了！

叔叔：哈哈！叔叔胖了。

小花：叔叔，太胖了就不健康了。

叔叔：是啊！人人都说我太胖了。

小花：叔叔，您还喝酒吗？

叔叔：我常常喝酒，但是不会喝醉。不过，我发胖不是因为我喝酒，而是因为我的工作。以前在鞋店工作，不觉得怎样；可是，现在在办公室里工作，我整天坐在电脑面前，午饭也是坐在电脑前吃饭，一天就这样坐大约十个小时；下班回家还要坐下来帮孩子辅导功课，根本没有时间做其他的活动。

小花：这样的生活方式对健康不太好吧。爸爸常说工作当然重要，可是休息和休闲活动也同样重要。爸爸现在除了每天要做半小时的运动以外，还经常跟我们一起做一些休闲活动。周末我们一家人会外出游玩，有时候去游泳，有时候去逛公园，总之就是做一些跟工作没有关系的活动。

叔叔：这个建议挺好，我一定要试试。

Transcript 2

记者：李医生，很多人常常觉得时间不够用，你觉得是不是这样呢？

顾问：每个人在一生中，都会在某些阶段觉得时间不够用。例如：当你要照顾小孩或者年老的亲人时，或者要应付一个非常重要的考试时，又或者刚开始做生意时，在这些阶段，你会觉得一天 24 小时都不够用。

记者：那怎么办呢？

顾问：这种情况，很可能是你没有办法改变，也不容易改变的。很多专业人士认为如果你学会接受现状，反而会帮助你减少压力。

记者：有什么方法可以帮助人们应付工作和生活两方面的压力？

顾问：在工作方面，有困难可以跟老板和同事讨论，不要放在心里；要做的事情按照重要性排序；下班后就把手机及电脑等关掉，不要再想工作。在生活方面，要照顾好自己，有健康的身体才能好好工作，然后才能去照顾别人；有什么自己不能解决的问题，不要怕向人求助；给自己时间做工作以外的活动；不论做什么，如果时间不够，就不要太要求完美。

第九课   Transcript 1

健明：外婆、外公，新年好！恭喜发财！

外婆：健明啊，新年快乐！这是我们给你的红包。你不是想要一个手机吗？用这钱去买吧！那个红包是你小姨让我给你的，这个春节她去欧洲旅游了。她还说回来以后请你吃她亲手做的饺子。

健明：谢谢！祝外公、外婆身体健康，永远年轻。

外公：我今年 83，你外婆也快 80 岁了。年轻啊，发财啊，我们都不想了，只希望身体好。来，小健，来吃青菜炒年糕！你最喜欢吃的。

健明：为什么过年要吃年糕啊？

外婆：年糕的"糕"和"高兴"的"高"读音一样。吃了年糕啊，希望孩子长得高，考试的分数高，天天高高兴兴。

健明：中国的节日习俗真好玩。

外公：中国人过年的时候，说的、吃的都要表示吉利。

健明：我知道，年夜饭吃鱼是希望"年年有余"，对吗？

外公、外婆：对！对！

Transcript 2

妈妈：元宵煮好了，快来吃吧！

小康：这不是汤圆吗？我记得我们平常也吃的。

妈妈：汤圆也叫元宵。今天是元宵节，华人除了吃元宵，还有看花灯、猜灯谜的习俗。

小康：元宵节是几月几号？

妈妈：农历的一月十五日。过完了元宵节，春节的庆祝活动也就结束了。有人说元宵节是中国的情人节。

小康：为什么呢？

Appendix 1

妈妈：因为在古代，女孩子平时是不可以随便到外面去的，只有元宵节晚上才能出去游玩，才有机会看到喜欢的男孩子。

小康：还是现在好，我可以天天出去玩，也可以常常跟我喜欢的男孩子见面。

第十课　Transcript 1

小红：丽丽，下个周末就是清明节了，现在正是播种和植树的好时节。爸爸妈妈说我们可以安排一个植树的活动。你有兴趣吗？

丽丽：很有意思啊，小红！你知道我参加了"地球之友"，我们地区的小组准备举办一个活动，就是去我们附近的小山上植树。会员的亲友都可以参加。你和你父母有兴趣吗？

小红：有啊！这个活动是安排在星期六还是星期日？

丽丽：星期日。星期六我们会去扫墓，去祭拜祖先。我们每年都去的。

小红：很好啊！我们星期六也去扫墓，给我爷爷扫墓。妈妈说爷爷生前最喜欢吃蛋糕，星期五我会做一个苹果蛋糕，星期六带去，放在爷爷的坟墓前拜祭。

丽丽：我们只带些鲜花去祭祖，比较简单。

小红：星期日的安排是怎样的？

丽丽：大家约定了在星期日早上八点，在南山公园大门口集合。你们要自己带食物和水，植树活动从八点开始，到下午三点结束。

小红：好！我们到时候见。

Transcript 2

妈妈：明东，明天我们去给爷爷扫墓，扫完后，我们会去附近的小山放风筝，别忘了把你和妹妹的风筝都带去。

明东：知道了，我昨天把风筝拿出来的时候，发现妹妹的风筝破了。不过，我已经用纸和竹片帮她做了一个新的，是一个蝴蝶风筝，她很高兴呢！对了，妹妹问我为什么清明节要放风筝，平时不能放吗？

妈妈：平时也可以放风筝，不过放风筝是清明节的习俗。古代人认为，把风筝放走了，也就把疾病、烦恼和坏运气都带走了。另外，大概跟天气有关。这个时候天气晴朗，有风，但风力不太大，是放风筝的好季节。

明东：妈妈，哪个国家的人最先放风筝？

妈妈：中国是风筝的故乡。很久很久以前，中国人已经会用竹片、纸或者木条做风筝了。风筝的形状各式各样，有蝴蝶、龙、鱼和熊猫等。明年我们去台湾看你叔叔的时候，可以去那里的风筝店买你们喜欢的风筝。

第十一课　Transcript 1

小马：大虎，端午节假期你过得怎么样？

大虎：好极了！我参加了我们地区举行的龙舟赛。

小马：真的！那天有很多人吗？一共有多少条龙舟参加比赛？

大虎：有 12 条龙舟参加，每条龙舟上有 16 个人，参赛者的亲友们都来给他们加油了，另外还有很多人来观看比赛。

小马：你们赢了吗？

大虎：我们得了青少年组的第一名，每个队员都得到了一个奖牌。

小马：恭喜！恭喜！

大虎：谢谢！那你呢，小马？端午节你过得好吗？

小马：上午我帮父母大扫除，下午妈妈和外婆在家教我包粽子。

大虎：包粽子难学吗？粽子好吃吗？

小马：包粽子不难学。外婆是一个好老师，她教我包肉粽，妈妈教我包红豆粽，因为我喜欢吃素的。下次我们再包粽子的时候，你可以来我家，我妈妈一定愿意教你。

Transcript 2

文月：妈妈，这是什么？很好看啊！

妈妈：这是香包。端午节快到了，我要做几个香包给你们。

文月：香包是什么？用来做什么的？

妈妈：端午节有戴香包的习俗。古人相信戴香包能驱赶蚊子和苍蝇。这里没有苍蝇，但有蚊子。你可以把香包挂在房间里或者放在床上，这样，房间里会有香气，蚊子就不会来叮你了。

文月：真的？那太好了。香包里面装着什么？

妈妈：以前人们喜欢在里面放中草药，现在我放的是薰衣草，就是我们花园里的 lavender，我知道你喜欢这种香味。据说放在床上，可以帮助你睡觉。

文月：妈妈，这个心形的香包是给谁的？

妈妈：是给你妹妹的。做完这个，我会做一个鱼形的给你，你喜欢吗？然后我还要做一个给你外婆，她喜欢苹果形的。

文月：谢谢，妈妈。

第十二课　Transcript 1

大明：小叶，你知道我们今天来购物中心买什么吗？

小叶：你说要买月饼，是吧？

大明：我们要买各种各样的月饼，送给不同的人。

小叶：这儿的月饼品种真多！中国很大，每个地方都有自己独特风味的月饼。

大明：外公外婆喜欢红豆沙，我们可以买豆沙月饼给他们；爷爷奶奶喜欢吃肉，买火腿月

183

Appendix 1

饼给他们最合适；爸爸妈妈什么都喜欢，我们可以买莲蓉月饼给他们。你觉得好吗？

小叶：好啊！其实买月饼送给他们，他们总是请我们一块儿吃，所以我们也吃得到。

大明：小叶，你看，这里还有一种新鲜的月饼，叫冰皮月饼，你吃过没有？

小叶：没有，但是我听叔叔说过。冰皮月饼跟传统月饼不一样，它的外表是白色的，传统的是金黄色的，而且制作方法不同。

大明：我也没吃过，我们可以买一盒试试。

小叶：好主意！

Transcript 2

记　者：先生，你们灯笼店的生意很红火，很多人都来买中秋灯笼，为什么呢？

李先生：因为我们保存了手工制作灯笼的传统方式，其他店卖的大多是在工厂大量制作的，不如我们做的独特。这里每个灯笼都是经过我们精心设计，并且用传统材料制作的。所以每年中秋节，都吸引了非常多的人来看或者买灯笼。他们当中，有本地人，也有外国游客。

记　者：你们设计的灯笼有些什么形状？

李先生：什么形状的都有，水果的、动物的，尤其是十二生肖的更受欢迎。不少游客专门来买灯笼，还要在这里拍照。

第十三课　Transcript 1

马克：李老师，中国春节要舞龙，端午节要划龙舟，那是不是中国古代有过龙？

老师：现在没有龙，古代也没有。

马克：那么中国人为什么说自己是龙的传人呢？

老师：中国龙是中国文化的象征。

马克：怎么会呢？

老师：中国龙看上去像什么？

马克：我觉得它的身体像蛇、头像马、尾巴像金鱼……

老师：那是因为在很久以前，中国各个地方崇拜不同的动物，这些被崇拜的动物叫图腾。后来各地统一了，就把很多不同的图腾合起来，就变成了现在的龙。

马克：真有意思！我去参观故宫博物院时，看到建筑上、家具上、皇帝穿的衣服上，都有龙的图案。

老师：因为龙也是权力的象征，只有皇帝的衣服上可以有九条龙。

马克：为什么不可以是八条？中国人不是喜欢数字"八"吗？

老师：在古代，中国人认为"九"是最大的数字，是一个吉祥的数字。

Transcript 2:

孙女：奶奶，狗年快到了。你是狗，我也是狗。

奶奶：我们不是狗，我们只是在狗年出生。

孙女：奶奶，今年是什么年呢？

奶奶：今年是鸡年。我来考考你，你知道中国的生肖有多少种动物？

孙女：我知道，有十二种动物。

奶奶：真聪明！那你能告诉我，是哪十二种动物吗？

孙女：我知道爸爸是猪，妈妈是牛。对了，还有兔子、猴子、马、羊……

奶奶：你知道十二生肖的第一个是什么动物吗？

孙女：是老鼠。我不喜欢老鼠，我喜欢猫。

奶奶：为什么十二生肖里没有猫呢？

孙女：不知道。

奶奶：因为安排十二生肖的时候，中国还没有猫。

孙女：为什么老鼠是十二生肖的第一名呢？

奶奶：老鼠什么时候出来偷吃东西？

孙女：半夜里。

奶奶：对啊！中国古代用十二种动物代表十二个时间段。而生肖先后是按照动物的活动时间来安排的。第一个时间段是半夜十一点到一点，这是老鼠活动的时间。

孙女：那么，狗代表什么时间段？

奶奶：狗代表晚上七点到九点。那个时间人们要休息睡觉了，狗就要去看门，保护主人。

第十四课　Transcript 1

小兰：大明，学校为了选出在校中学生最爱读的书，要举行投票，校长星期五就宣布结果。你投票了吗？

大明：当然投了！你呢，小兰？

小兰：投票一开始，我就去投了。你觉得你投的书会不会得第一？

大明：很难说，前年我投的是《哈利·波特》的最后一部书，它被选为第一名。去年，我投了《龙的传说》，它只得到第十六名。今年我投了《城南旧事》，不知道会不会胜出。小兰，你投了哪本书？

小兰：今年我投了《猴子大王》，这是专门为中学生编写的版本，不像原著《西游记》那么长、那么难。去年我投了《汉字的故事》，它被选为第二名，我挺高兴的！我还得到了一张购书礼券。

大明：我看过《猴子大王》，我也很喜欢这本书，文字简单，图画有趣，实在是一本好书。

小兰：我也看过了《城南旧事》，里面的故事很感人，读到最后那个故事，我差点哭了出来。我希望我们选的书都能胜出。

Appendix 1

Transcript 2:

　　我收到很多家长的邮件，问我怎样鼓励孩子养成良好的读书习惯。我在这里跟大家分享一下我的经验。当我的孩子还在年幼的时候，我就已经开始跟他一起读书了。当然那时候，我们看的都是图画书，我们只是说说书里面的图画。不久，他就对书产生兴趣了。

　　要孩子爱读书，我觉得最重要的是让他们先对书产生兴趣。多带他们去图书馆、书店，让他们浏览各类图书，自己选择喜欢看的书。慢慢地你再开始给他们介绍其他的书，扩大他们的读书面。在家里，定下每天读书的时间，十分钟、十五分钟都可以，在那段时间里，大家都安静地读书。看完以后，再说说自己的感受。最后一点，我觉得挺重要的，就是让他们看到你对阅读的热爱。

第十五课　Transcript 1

大山：小路，这个周末的晚上你打算怎么过？
小路：在家阅读。
大山：那多无聊啊！我请你看电影，好吗？
小路：我在家里的大屏幕电视机上看电影，跟在电影院看差不多，而且更放松。
大山：那不一样。我请你去北京的特色电影院看3D电影。
小路：我在家也可以看3D电影。
大山：那个特色电影院的沙发座位又宽大又舒服。3D电影票160块一张。凭身份证，还可以免费借两条毛毯。
小路：要借毛毯做什么？
大山：我准备请你看通宵电影，三场电影只要350元，还提供小蛋糕、爆米花和一瓶饮料，不要另外付钱。
小路：看一个晚上的电影，太累了！
大山：没关系，第二天是星期天，可以回家睡觉。再说，如果你看电影看累了，可以把沙发靠背放低，盖上毛毯，睡一会儿。
小路：好吧，我们去看通宵电影。

Transcript 2

李莉：我刚从中国来德国留学，请问，周末可以去哪儿玩？
万里：我介绍你去柏林的中国电影俱乐部，有意思极了。
李莉：是中国留学生俱乐部吗？
万里：不是，这个俱乐部现在成了开展中国文化活动的场所，除了看电影，还可以打乒乓球，下象棋，打牌，打台球等。
李莉：谁是这个中国电影俱乐部的负责人？
万里：负责人是德国人，雷曼博士，他是一个中国文化迷。
李莉：他怎么会成为中国文化迷呢？

万里：30年前，他被派到中国同济大学教德语，在上海住了五年。一边教德语，一边学中文，还和一位中医结婚了。

李莉：我真想认识他。

万里：他回到德国以后，热心推广中国的传统医学。他最喜欢到中国度假，一去中国就买很多新电影的光盘带回德国。2001年，他在自己的家里成立了中国电影俱乐部。

李莉：这个俱乐部的成员都是中国人吗？

万里：不！中国人和德国人大约各占一半。经常来参加活动的既有去过中国的德国人、学汉语的外国学生，也有华人留学生和中国移民。

李莉：太好了，我不但可以看中国电影，还可以交德国朋友。

第十六课　Transcript 1

明东：爸爸，平常都是妈妈做饭的，怎么今晚你来做饭？

爸爸：因为你妈妈要看电视。她说今晚由我来做饭。她还说有什么问题，我们要自己解决，不要问她。

明东：看电视？什么节目这么重要？连饭也不做？

爸爸：她说有一部武侠连续剧，叫什么《天龙八部》，今晚开始播放。她刚看完了这部武侠小说，觉得太好了，她一定要看这个电视剧，不能错过。

明东：爸爸，只是今晚吗？还是好几晚？

爸爸：听说这个连续剧一共有24集，只在周末两晚播放。你说要几个周末才能放完？

明东：天啊！要12个周末才播完，那不是要三个月的时间吗？

爸爸：是啊，我做饭需要助手，你就做我的助手吧！

明东：可以的。不过，爸爸，我们能不能看看电视上的烹饪节目，学一些基本技术？也学一些不同的菜式，否则每个星期我们都要吃同样的菜了。

爸爸：好的！从明天开始，我们就多看电视上的烹饪节目。

Transcript 2

陈山：秋雨，昨天晚上你有没有看《经济旅游》那个电视节目？

秋雨：没有。很好看吗？昨晚的节目带你去哪里？

陈山：去香港。这个旅游节目跟一般的旅游节目不同，它不介绍香港闻名世界的旅游景点，而是带你去一些很少人知道的地方。在昨晚的节目中，主持人带观众去了一个古老的渔村，这可能是香港现在唯一留存下来的渔村。那里的风土人情跟城市里的很不一样。村里有一个简单的展览室，展览很多当地的照片，都是关于渔村发展过程的。

秋雨：为什么你喜欢看这些？

陈山：你知道我对历史和地理很有兴趣，我还喜欢旅游。这类旅游节目包括了我的三个兴趣爱好。

Appendix 1

秋雨：那你准备去香港旅游吗？
陈山：会。不过，我要考完试以后才能计划这个旅行。还有，我要工作两三个月，等我赚到足够的钱才能去。

第十七课　Transcript 1

记者：王明先生今天在城市音乐厅开演奏会。很高兴他接受了我们电台的采访。王先生，大家都知道您在音乐方面的成就。您是从什么时候开始学乐器的？
王明：我六岁开始学小提琴。当时我姐姐在学钢琴，我不想跟她一样弹钢琴，我要学不同的乐器。当时我在电视里看到别人拉小提琴，好像很有趣，所以就选择了小提琴。
记者：我知道您也会弹钢琴。那您什么时候开始学的？
王明：我拉小提琴拉了五年以后，老师觉得我拉得不错。他问我对钢琴有没有兴趣，其实平常看姐姐弹钢琴，我挺喜欢的。我也跟着姐姐学，不过只是玩玩而已。老师就介绍我去一位钢琴老师那里学习。
记者：那两种乐器，您更喜欢哪种？
王明：两种乐器各有各的好，我都喜欢。如果出外旅游，我只可以带着我的小提琴，所以很多朋友以为我更喜欢小提琴。
记者：今天您准备演奏什么乐曲？
王明：我会演奏两首中国的乐曲，还有三首莫扎特的音乐曲目，其中两首是由我姐姐伴奏的。
记者：好。谢谢您接受访问。祝您的音乐会成功！

Transcript 2

北山学校很注重音乐。我们相信培养孩子们对音乐的兴趣，能帮助他们学习其他的科目。所以学校里有各种各样的课外音乐小组，让学生自由选择参加。

我们除了有合唱团、各类乐器班、流行歌曲班、古典歌曲班以外，还有一个京剧班。这是一个很特别的兴趣小组，刚开始的时候，很少有学生参加。后来他们看到京剧不只是唱歌，还包括其他方面，例如武术、舞蹈等，慢慢地参加的学生就多了起来。

在今年学校庆祝农历新年的晚会上，我们安排学生表演了不同的节目，有演奏乐器的，也有唱歌的，最后京剧班表演了京剧《花木兰》，精彩极了，节目结束时观众热烈地鼓掌。

Appendix II: Keys to the listening exercises

Chapter 1

1. ❶ 下星期三。
   ❷ 她星期六会请她妈妈去看电影和吃饭。
   ❸ 她家有三口人。
   ❹ 美国。
2. Summaries
   (a) There are 6 people in Mark's family. They are his mum and dad, his grandparents, his younger sister and himself.
   (b) He and his sister get big "red packets" during Chinese New Year. They can use that money to buy birthday presents for the whole family.

Chapter 2

1. ❶ 这个星期六。
   ❷ 他们要一起出去吃饭。
   ❸ 小英说她不能参加，因为她公司在周末有活动。
   ❹ 她建议把庆祝爷爷生日的活动改到下个周末。
2. Summaries
   (a) She has to go out to meet with her clients and help them to design products; she has to write reports to her company.
   (b) In addition to the above, she has to write weekly work summaries. Sometimes she has to go abroad to attend meetings; take part in training courses.

Chapter 3

1. ❶ 因为父母对他的期望非常高，还把他们所有的希望都放在他身上。
   ❷ 小玲将来没有好工作，赚钱不多，就不能照顾年老的自己。
   ❸ 他的学业比其他一切都重要。
   ❹ 她想吃什么、喝什么，爷爷奶奶就马上给她做或者买回来。
2. Summaries
   (a) They all think that their parents have very high expectation of them. So they feel a lot of pressure.
   (b) She enjoys the pampering from her grandparents at home; and she enjoys the parents' praises and rewards when she does well at school.

189

Appendix II

Chapter 4

1. ❶ 因为今天是重阳节，也是老人节。
   ❷ 她说那里的服务员很友好，做的菜也很好吃，最高兴的是她有了新朋友。
   ❸ 书法。
   ❹ 他会跟他女儿去看望他母亲。
2. Summaries
   (a) She said the staff there were very friendly, and the food was very good too.
   (b) She and her new friend both liked calligraphy. They practised writing with a brush everyday. The hobby of her new friend's husband was photography.

Chapter 5

一、1. ❶ B ❷ B, C ❸ B, C ❹ A, D
   2. ❶ 英文。
      ❷ 东海中学的英文老师。
      ❸ 因为他很热情，他的学生每年考试都考得特别好。
      ❹ 设备很先进。
二、Summaries
   (a) He cycles to school. If it rains, his mum takes him to school by car.
   (b) He has lunch in the school canteen every day except Friday when he brings sandwiches, fruit and drink to school.

Chapter 6

一、1. ❶ B ❷ C ❸ C ❹ D
   2. ❶ 她觉得自己 17 岁了，应该自己赚零用钱。她还觉得打工有意思，可以认识新朋友。
      ❷ 去旅游。
      ❸ 是她父母要她去的。
      ❹ 她不喜欢。她想去丝绸之路旅游。
二、Summaries
   (a) Mary lived in Hong Kong when she was small and learned some Chinese there. She studied Chinese at Edinburgh University.
   (b) She is studying Chinese medicine in Shan Dong now and tries to improve her Chinese at the same time. She also works part-time as an English tutor.

Chapter 7

一、1. ❶ C ❷ C ❸ C, D ❹ C
   2. ❶ 她可以自由一些，还可以做老板。

❷ 读时装设计。

❸ 她喜欢研究不同国家的毛衣设计。

❹ 很多退休女工的爱好是织毛衣，她们一般都有很多空闲时间。

二、Summaries

(a) Xiao Wang's salary is higher now. He gets a discount from the supermarket where he works.

(b) There is training opportunity and he can try different jobs. Also, there are a few workers from his hometown so he can chat with them about it.

Chapter 8

一、1. ❶ B ❷ B ❸ B, D ❹ A, C

2. ❶ 不是。是因为他整天坐在电脑面前工作，连午饭也是坐在电脑前吃。

❷ 不满意。他根本没有时间做其他的活动。

❸ 小花的爸爸觉得工作重要，但他觉得休息和休闲也同样重要。

❹ 他每天都要做半小时的运动，还跟家人一起做休闲活动。周末会出去游玩。

二、Summaries

(a) For example, when you have to look after young children or elderly relatives, or when you are preparing for a very important exam, or when you are starting a new business.

(b) You can discuss your problem with your superior and colleague. You can prioritise work according to their importance. You can switch off your mobile and computer when you finish work for the day.

Chapter 9

一、1. ❶ C ❷ B ❸ C ❹ C

2. ❶ 因为她去了欧洲旅游。

❷ 青菜炒年糕。

❸ 因为年糕的"糕"跟"高兴"的"高"读音一样，吃年糕就是希望孩子长得高，考试的分数高，天天高高兴兴。

❹ 讲究吉利。

二、Summaries

(a) They eat dumplings, look at lanterns and try to solve puzzles/riddles.

(b) Things are better nowadays as girls can go out every day and they can often see the boys they like.

Chapter 10

一、1. ❶ D ❷ B ❸ D ❹ C

Appendix II

    2. ❶ 播种和植树。

       ❷ 去他们附近的小山上植树。

       ❸ 小红要带蛋糕去扫她爷爷的墓，因为她爷爷生前最喜欢吃蛋糕。

       ❹ 星期日早上八点在南山公园大门口集合。

二、Summaries

    (a) Ming Dong took out the kites and found that his sister's kite was broken. So he made her a new one.

    (b) She said long long time ago Chinese people knew how to make and fly kites. They used bamboo, paper and wood strip to make kites.

Chapter 11

一、1. ❶ A   ❷ A   ❸ B   ❹ D

    2. ❶ 大虎居住的地区。

       ❷ 参赛者的亲友们。

       ❸ 上午小马帮他爸爸妈妈大扫除，下午学包粽子。

       ❹ 小马的妈妈。

二、Summaries

    (a) Making scented sachets which can be used to repel mosquitoes and flies.

    (b) She was making a heart-shape one for Wen Yue's younger sister; a fish-shape one for Wen Yue, and an apple-shape one for Wen Yue's grandma.

Chapter 12

一、1. ❶ B   ❷ C   ❸ B   ❹ C

    2. ❶ 因为中国很大，每个地方都有自己风味的月饼。

       ❷ 他们去买的月饼有豆沙、火腿、莲蓉和冰皮。

       ❸ 他们买月饼送给外公外婆、祖父母和父母。因为送他们，他们也吃得到。

       ❹ 冰皮月饼。

二、Summaries

    (a) All their lanterns are designed and hand-made by Mr Li and his staff, using traditional materials, unlike the ones mass-produced in factories.

    (b) They are in many different shapes, like fruit, animals, especially the Chinese zodiac ones.

Chapter 13

一、1. ❶ D   ❷ C   ❸ A   ❹ C

    2. ❶ 因为中国龙是中国文化的象征。

       ❷ 因为很久以前，中国各个地方崇拜不同的动物，这些被崇拜的动物叫图腾，后

来各地联合了，把不同的图腾合起来，就变成了龙。

❸ 在建筑上、家具上、皇帝穿的衣服上。

❹ 他们认为"九"是最大的数字，是一个吉祥的数字。

二、Summaries

(a) There was no cat when the Chinese zodiac animals were arranged for the list. The rat was put first on the list because rats were most active around midnight, which was the beginning of a day.

(b) The twelve animals included were rat, ox, tiger, hare, dragon, snake, horse, ram, monkey, rooster, dog and pig. In ancient China the twelve animals were used to represent the twelve periods of time, each animal represents one period.

Chapter 14

一、1. ❶ C ❷ B ❸ B ❹ B

2. ❶ 大明前后三次选的书是：《哈利波特》的最后一部书、《龙的传说》和《城南旧事》。

❷ 它被选为第二名。

❸ 他觉得这本书文字简单，图画有趣。

❹ 小兰觉得这本书里面的故事很感人。

二、Summaries

(a) Ms Wang started reading with her son when he was still quite young. They read picture books together and just talked about the pictures in the book. Her son became interested in reading not long after that.

(b) Ms Wang said the most important thing was to get children interested in reading first. Let them browse in libraries and bookshops and choose the books they like to read. Slowly you can start recommending books to them. At home, set aside 10-15 minutes everyday for reading quietly. Then talk about the book and how you feel about it. Let them see your enthusiasm for reading.

Chapter 15

一、1. ❶ B ❷ A ❸ C ❹ C

2. ❶ 在家阅读。

❷ 在家看电影会更放松。

❸ 沙发座位又宽大又舒服，还可以把沙发靠背放低。

❹ 连看三场，电影票会便宜一点，而且还免费提供小蛋糕、爆米花和饮料。

二、Summaries

(a) The Film Club has become a venue for promoting Chinese cultural activities

193

Appendix II

which include films, table-tennis, Chinese chess etc.

(b) Dr Lehman went to teach German in China 30 years ago. He lived in Shanghai for 5 years. He studied Chinese while teaching German, and married a Chinese medicine practitioner.

Chapter 16

一、1. ❶ B ❷ D ❸ C ❹ D

2. ❶ 因为明东的妈妈要看电视。
   ❷ 她要看一部功夫连续剧。
   ❸ 只在周末两晚播放，一连播 12 个周末。
   ❹ 他们看看电视上的烹饪节目，学一些基本技巧和一些不同的菜式。

二、Summaries

(a) The travel programme took the audience to an old fishing village in Hong Kong. It showed local customs, and an exhibition room displaying photos of the development of the village.

(b) He has to wait until after his exams before planning for a trip to Hong Kong. And then he has to work for a few months to earn enough money before he can go.

Chapter 17

一、1. ❶ C ❷ C ❸ C ❹ B, D

2. ❶ 他不想跟他姐姐一样弹钢琴；还有在电视里看到别人拉小提琴，好像很有趣。
   ❷ 他平常看着他姐姐弹钢琴，其实挺喜欢的。后来小提琴老师就介绍他学钢琴。
   ❸ 因为当他出外旅游时，只能带着他的小提琴，所以很多朋友以为他更喜欢小提琴。
   ❹ 他姐姐。

二、Summaries

(a) They have choirs, classes for instruments, pop music, classical music, as well as Beijing Opera.

(b) The performances included instrumental recitals, singing, and a Beijing Opera.

Appendix III: Useful expressions for speaking and writing

1. 这段英文说的是……   This English passage says that...
2. 我认为……   I think that...
3. 在我个人看来……   My personal opinion is that...
4. 我不认为……   I don't think that...
5. 我不反对……，不过……   I'm not against... but (however)...
6. 我的看法／观点／意见／想法是……   My opinion / view / idea / thinking is that...
7. 我来谈谈这么做的利与弊。利有……，弊有……   I'll discuss the advantages and disadvantages. The advantages are.... The disadvantages are...
8. 我觉得好的是……，不好的是……   I feel that the good things are..., the bad ones are...
9. 长处是……，短处是……   The strong points are (that)... , the weak ones are (that)...
10. 一方面……，另一方面……   On the one hand..., on the other hand...
11. 我承认这是事实／真的，可是……   I admit that this is true, but...
12. 请不要夸大事实，事情的真相是……   Let's not exaggerate the facts, the truth of the matter is...
13. 我被说服了，不过，……   I've been persuaded, although...
14. 我想要说的是……   I think what has to be said is...
15. 当我考虑的时候，我想到……   When I think about it, I realise...
16. 有人说……   Some people say...
17. 有些人觉得……   A few people feel that...
18. 多数人的看法是……，但是也有人认为……   Most people's opinion is that..., but there are people who think...
19. 最重要的是……   The most important thing is...
20. 主要的问题是……   The main issue / question is...
21. 主要的原因是……   The main reason is...
22. 这是我的看法。我们必须先……，然后……，最后……   These are my ideas, We must first of all..., then..., and finally...
23. 我建议……   I suggest...
     总而言之，……   In brief, ... / In a few words, ...

Appendix III

考官在口试时经常会问的问题
Optional generic questions by the examiner to promote discussion

1. 你可以举例说明……吗?
2. 你为什么这么说?
3. 你为什么有这个看法?
4. 我们可以由……得出什么结论?
5. 你可以举例来支持这个看法吗?
6. 为什么这很重要?
7. ……表示什么意思?

在口试问答中考生可以向考官提出的问题
Optional generic questions by the candidate to elicit points of view from the examiner or to check for understanding

1. 您同意我的看法吗?
2. 是不是可以认为……?
3. 我们可以说……吗?
4. 您是怎么看这个问题的?
5. 您对……有什么看法?
6. 您明白我的意思吗?

Appendix IV: Guide to tackling speaking exams

AS 的口语考试有两个。考生收到两份题卡后，到开始录音前，一共只有 15 分钟的准备时间。考生可以在一张 A4 纸的一面打草稿、列提纲，但务必记住：
1. 不能在 A4 纸的两面都写上笔记；
2. 不能在题卡上写字做笔记；
3. 在准备和口试期间，不允许用词典或其他任何工具，包括手机。

口试题一：主题是"当代华人社会的变迁"，录音时间 7—9 分钟。
口试题二：主题是"中国文化"，录音时间 5—6 分钟。

考生和考官的题卡一上有相同的主题、次主题和论点。不同的是，考官手里的那份，在论点下还有四个问题。考生和考官的题卡二上有相同的主题、次主题和论题。不同的是，考生的题卡上提供了三个要点，要求考生必须考虑；而考官的题卡上则有三个问题，与考生必须考虑的要点相对应。

无论是口试题一，还是口试题二，考官都必须按照题卡上问题的顺序，一字不差地逐句提问。如果考生答不出来，考官可以重复，但不允许有所改动。在问完规定的问题之后，考官可以在次主题的范围内，继续提问，展开讨论；而考生需要表达自己的观点和看法，提供相关论据，并得出结论，从而表明自己对文化和社会的理解。考官期待考生在讨论的过程中，能够向考官提出问题，来确认考生已经理解了他们的观点。

现在我们来举例谈谈口试题一。

考生的题卡如下：
主题一：当代华人社会的变迁
次主题：家庭

短文 在传统中国家庭中，通常都是"男主外，女主内"。丈夫在外工作，赚钱养家，而妻子则在家做饭、打扫、照顾孩子。现在男女平等，特别是在城市里，几乎每对夫妻白天都要工作。两人工作，家庭收入多了，可是下班回家做家务成了一个很大的负担。现在有些高收入家庭，妻子也会选择不出去工作，回归家庭。

论点 夫妻两人都工作对家庭好。

考官的题卡如下：
主题一：当代华人社会的变迁
次主题：家庭

短文 在传统的中国家庭中，通常都是"男主外，女主内"。丈夫在外工作，赚钱养

Appendix IV

家，而妻子则在家做饭、打扫、照顾孩子。现在男女平等，特别是在城市里，几乎每对夫妻白天都要工作。两人工作，家庭收入多了，可是下班回家做家务成了一个很大的负担。现在有些高收入家庭，妻子也会选择不出去工作，回归家庭。

论点 夫妻两人都工作对家庭好。

1. 短文的主要意思是什么？
2. 根据短文，丈夫和妻子都工作有什么问题？
3. "夫妻都工作对家庭好。"你同意这个论点吗？为什么？
4. 有钱的家庭妻子不出去工作了，你觉得这样好吗？为什么？

问题 1. 口试题一的第 1 个问题考官必定要问"短文的主要意思是什么？"考生不能只把短文照着读一遍，而是需要概括出主要意思。

考生：传统的中国家庭，通常是丈夫工作，赚钱养家；妻子做家务，照顾孩子。现在大多数家庭夫妻都工作，都有收入，做家务却成了一个负担。有些经济条件好的家庭，妻子就回家做全职太太。

问题 2. 口试题一的第 2 个问题总是从"根据短文"开始，根据短文涉及的内容提出问题。

考官：根据短文，丈夫和妻子都工作有什么问题？

考生：夫妻都工作的话，下班回家后，做家务就成了一个很大的负担。华人社会已经有所改变，随着家庭结构的变化，妻子的职责也发生了变化。过去妻子不工作，只要在家做贤妻良母，照顾好家庭就可以了；丈夫回家也基本不需要做什么家务，可以休息，或者吃妻子准备好的饭菜。现在妻子成了职业妇女，白天外出工作，下班回家还要煮饭、洗衣服、打扫、育儿等。妻子忙里忙外，特别累，精神上的压力也很大。丈夫与妻子共同分担家务很重要。这样，妻子的负担会小一些。否则，为了做家务，夫妻之间很可能会经常发生矛盾。比如夫妻两人下班回到家都很累，谁来做饭？谁来送孩子上补习班、兴趣班？孩子病了，谁留在家里照顾孩子？有的家庭，夫妻有一方要经常出差，做家务、看孩子和照顾老人就更成问题了。这些问题解决不了就会产生矛盾，发生争吵。（在这里，考生可以问考官：您同意我的看法吗？）

问题 3. 口试题一的第 3 个问题一定是在引用规定的论点后提出"你同意这个论点吗？为什么？"因此当考生拿到口试题后，这道题完全可以提前准备。如果你同意论点，就需要提出有力的论据来支持它；如果不同意，就需要提出足够的论据来反驳。论据无论是事实（具体事实、历史事实和统计数字等），还是理论（名言警句和科学公理等），都必须真实可靠、准确典型，这样才有说服力。

正方：

考官："夫妻都工作对家庭好。"你同意这个论点吗？为什么？

考生：我认为夫妻两人都工作对家庭好。中国人常说"贫贱夫妻百事哀"，过去不少家庭因为只有丈夫工作，收入少，无法保证家庭的基本生活，夫妻吵架甚至家庭破裂的事情时有发生。在有的家庭里，因为妻子没有工作，丈夫会认为是自己养活了妻子。有的甚至还有大男子主义作风，认为妻子就应该做所有的家务活。男女不平等的家庭是不会有真正的幸福的。但如果夫妻都工作，家庭有了双份收入，一家人的生活可以得到改善，家庭的幸福指数也会提高。比如，经济条件好了，全家可以一起外出度假旅行，居住环境也能变得更宽敞，还可以送孩子参加夏令营或游学团等。根据《2017—2018 年度留学白皮书》中指出，2017 年中国的自费留学生中，双职工子女占 65%。

夫妻都外出工作，共同赚钱养家；回到家也要共同承担家务，一起培养孩子。比尔·盖茨夫妻在 2016 年的年度公开信中提出，家务活不应该是女性的专利，这份工作需要夫妻共同承担。他们不但这么说，也是这么做的。丈夫与妻子一起做家务，能够体会到妻子日常的辛苦，会更体贴并尊重妻子。父母平等恩爱，让孩子生活在和谐民主的家庭中，也有利于孩子的成长。另外，我觉得如果夫妻收入都不错，也可以请家政做家务啊。（在这里，考生可以问考官：您对这个问题有什么看法？）

反方：

考官："夫妻都工作对家庭好。"你同意这个论点吗？为什么？

考生：有人认为夫妻两人都工作对家庭好，但是我不同意。正如我在回答第 2 个问题时谈到的，白天夫妻都工作，下班回家做家务就成了一个很大的负担。因此，不少夫妻经常为做家务发生争吵。另外，由于夫妻双方平日里工作家庭两头都忙，难免疏忽于对孩子的教育，缺少与孩子沟通的时间和机会，常常导致亲子关系淡漠。这对孩子的成长，尤其是叛逆期青少年子女的成长，非常不利。再则，现在双职工夫妻大多是独生子女，不但要照顾自己的小家庭，还要照顾年老的父母，夫妇还都要外出工作忙事业，难免给家庭带来很多问题。

我同学的父母都是职场上的成功者，收入很高。我同学要什么有什么，可就是回家见不到父母。最近这个同学被抓了。因为他不愿回到空荡荡的家，放学后就在街上逛，交了坏朋友，还吸毒了。根据上海社科院徐安琪研究员的调查，因为双职工夫妻的一方不能尽家庭义务的责任而离婚的比率已经占到 16%以上。

问题 4. 这个问题是在短文所属的次主题范围内设计的，期待考生能够拓展谈论与次主题有关的文化与社会话题。本书建议考生使用的句式，以及考试大纲建议

Appendix IV

考官问这道题时所用的句式，请参照本书的附录 3。

正方：

考官：有钱的家庭妻子就不出去工作了。你觉得这样好吗？为什么？

考生：刚才我已经说了，夫妻两人都工作对家庭并不好。如果经济条件允许，妻子回归家庭，在我看来，是一件很好的事情。

考官：你可以举例来说明这个看法吗？

考生：中国传统的家庭结构是"男主外，女主内"，我认为很有道理。现在不是也有一句流行语，说是"丈夫负责赚钱养家，妻子只管貌美如花"吗。

考官：你为什么有这个看法？

考生：因为有钱的家庭，丈夫通常是整天在外忙工作，妻子不出去工作了，就可以把家庭生活安排得有条理，把丈夫、孩子照顾好。家庭没有了后顾之忧，丈夫的事业可以更成功，可以赚更多的钱。再说妻子既要做职业妇女，又要做贤妻良母，太累，也不容易做到两全啊！（在这里，考生可以问考官：您同意我的看法吗？）

考官：我不同意。现在比丈夫挣钱多的妻子也有，丈夫在家做家务，你觉得怎么样？

考生：我认为，通常来说，妻子比丈夫适合做家务。男女平等，不等于男女一样啊。再说，妻子回归家庭，不是不工作，而是工作地点变成家里了。照顾家庭也是一份全职工作，而且还很辛苦。（在这里，考生可以问考官：您明白我的意思吗？

考官：那么，妻子不出去工作，没有自己的收入，她的家庭地位会不会降低？

考生：不会的。因为妻子把家收拾得干净舒适，丈夫回到家，就有饭吃，可以休息放松，丈夫会感谢妻子的。在我家，就是爸爸赚钱，妈妈管钱。爸爸用钱还要向妈妈申请，妈妈的地位比爸爸高啊！（在这里，考生可以问考官：您同意我的看法吗？

……

反方：

考官：有钱的家庭妻子不出去工作了。你觉得这样好吗？为什么？

考生：虽然这是个人的选择，但是我觉得不好，这是历史的倒退。从家庭来讲，妇女没有了自己的经济收入，就只能依附于丈夫，家庭地位容易降低。

考官：有人说，做家务也是工作。丈夫在外面赚钱，妻子也有功劳啊。

考生：这是事实。问题是全职太太通常以丈夫、孩子和家庭为中心，逐渐失去了自己的个性、初心，很容易脱离社会。特别是如果丈夫变心，离婚后的妻子，因为年龄问题，或者对专业的生疏，就很难再就业了。

这个问题就很严重了。（在这里，考生可以问考官：您明白我的意思吗？）

考官：你可以举例来说明这个看法吗？

考生：江苏律师左亮根据他接受的案例指出"现在 80 后全职太太成了一个危险职业"。这个阶段，妻子通常全心照顾年幼的小孩，而在外打拼的丈夫正处于事业的上升期。或因丈夫有情人，或觉得夫妻观点不一了，都可能导致离婚。我还觉得，现在的妇女几乎都受过不同程度的教育，有的还有高学历，有的很有工作能力，回归家庭，无论是对她自己来说，还是对社会来说都是一种浪费。

……

现在我们来举例谈谈口试题二。

如果考生的题卡如下：

主题二：中国文化

次主题：传统·端午节

你必须思考以下几点：
- 常见的端午节食品。
- 常见的端午节活动。
- 现代华人过端午节的原因。

那么，考官的题卡就可能如下：

主题二：中国文化

次主题：传统·端午节

按以下顺序向考生提问：
- 常见的端午节食品有哪些？
- 端午节经常有什么活动？
- 现代华人为什么要过端午节？

口试题二分为两个部分：

1. 必须逐一回答考官题卡上的这三道问题；
2. 在同一个次主题内，考官拓展开去问问题。例如：
   ❶ 为什么端午节要吃粽子？
   ❷ 在你介绍的端午节活动中选一个，做比较详细的介绍。
   ❸ 为什么人们说"端午"是一个坏日子？
   ❹ 你戴过香包吗？
   ❺ 你能介绍一个与端午有关的传说吗？
   ❻ 你知道中国还有哪些传统节日？

Appendix IV

❼ 提起华人习俗，你会想到什么？
❽ 你对中国的什么传统文化特别有兴趣？为什么？
❾ 你认为现代华人应该过传统节日吗？为什么？
……

　　以上谈的只是口语考试的内容。考官的提问是否听得懂，理解得对不对，发音、声调是否准确，表达是否流利，词语搭配、句子结构是否正确，词汇句式是否丰富，内容是否充实，有没有独到的见解，论据是否真实可靠，结论是否合理，等等，都会影响口语考试的得分。

Appendix V: Guide to writing responses to literary texts

写作试卷分成 B 和 C 两个部分。B 部分是根据三篇文学作品设两道考题，C 部分是根据两部电影各设一道考题，每年 AS 的写作考试总共有四道写作题，考生只需要在 B 部分或者 C 部分选择一道题来做就可以了。写作题用中文作答，建议字数为 225—300 字。

写作的语言要流畅明了，表达有连贯性，还要注意运用准确多样的句式和丰富恰当的词汇。根据 AS 考试大纲的要求，考生所写的内容必须从头到尾与论题有关，提出的观点得是经过深思熟虑的，并且要从作品中找出恰当的论据来支持自己的观点，辩论探讨能引出合理的结论。

下面我们来举例分析。

《一只叫凤的鸽子》（作者：曹文轩）
探讨夏望家的变故如何改变了夏望。
- 夏望的家庭情况。
- 夏望的家庭发生了什么变故？
- 发生家庭变故后，夏望有了什么变化？

一、动笔之前，先得审题

从五个写作考试题中选定一个后，得先把论题理解透彻。根据"探讨夏望家的变故如何改变了夏望"这个论题，可以分析出：

1. 人物是夏望；
2. 事件是夏望家的变故；
3. 题目的关键词是"变"。

二、扣住要点，选择材料

写作考试 B 部分，要求 written response to works (literary texts)。你的写作材料或用来证明你观点的论据，都必须从文学作品本身选取，就好像客户必须要到规定的商店去采购建筑材料一样。"巧妇难为无米之炊"，没有建材就造不了房子。写作材料一定要围绕试卷提供的三个要点来选择，要典型、充分、有说服力。否则，没有好材料就造不出质量好的房子，就通不过验收。

注意：如果从作品中直接引用，要用引号标明；如果是间接引用，就不需要，但内容必须符合作品的原意。

Appendix V

要点 1. 夏望的家庭情况

夏望家原来是小城首富，"秋虎家所有的家产加在一起，也抵不上夏望家一座鸽舍"。他家养了许多让人们惊叹、仰慕的"神鸽"，鸽子有佣人帮养，大狗看护。夏望父亲还按秋虎的赌徒父亲开的价买走了"凤"。

要点 2. 夏望的家庭发生了什么变故？

因为夏望的父亲拿高利息骗人，所以被判坐牢。家里的一切都被债主们哄抢一空，变得一贫如洗。

要点 3. 发生家庭变故后，夏望有了什么变化？

夏望的生活变得十分艰苦。以前隔两三天就会换一双名贵的新鞋，现在一连多天穿一双鞋头破、鞋带断了的鞋；过去"看都不看一下究竟是一些什么书，一买就是一大摞"，现在"手在口袋里不停地摸索，最终只摸索出几枚硬币，连一本最便宜的书也买不起，只好低着头走到一边去了"；过去是眉飞色舞、傲气十足，现在"看上去变矮了，眼睛也没以前亮了，整个人看上去灰突突的。""一双无神的眼睛，仿佛一个很疲倦的赶路人"；变故前他提起秋虎的土鸽"换我们家鸽子一根羽毛，我都不换"，可现在，他要把好不容易藏了起来的"凤"还给秋虎，还说"我不要你钱"，并拼命拦住大狗不要咬秋虎。

注意：写文章，在材料的处理上要有详有略。因为论题的关键词是"变"，这一段就应该写得详细，突出在家庭变故后夏望的变化。

三、文章结构

这是写作题，不是问答题。所以要在充分领会题意的基础上，对写作材料进行选择、加工和提炼，还要考虑全文的起、承、转、合，也就是谋篇布局。就这道写作题来说，到这儿，就需要考虑"合"，得出结论，使文章有完整的结构了：

总而言之，家庭的变故让夏望改变了。在我看来，他的变化不仅表现在他的穿着、动作、神情和语言上，而且他也变得真诚、善良、重友谊了。

注意：在上面有观点、有材料的分析后，现在可以很自然地得出结论，同时表明自己的见解。

Appendix VI: Guide to translating texts

从中文翻译成英文

　　从中文翻译成英文，就是要用英文写出中文原文的意思。这对英语为第一语言的学生来说不算太难，最重要的是学生阅读原文时，必须先理解原文的意思，然后用恰当的英文语言和修辞来翻译。翻译好的英文，学生还需要修饰，让它读来好像原文就是英文一样。

　　按照新考试大纲，考试的评分原则很"通融"。翻译后的英文如果拼写错了，只要意思不模糊，词句没有歧义，考官也会接受。例如：学生本来想写"accept"，可是写成了"acept"，这就当作"spelling mistake"；但如果写成了"except"，导致意思模糊了，就算作错。

　　如果英语母语者看翻译后的文章，不用懂中文原文就明白文意，这篇翻译就算成功了。

　　新大纲是以"逐点计分"的方式来评分的，就是说文章中的每一个小节如果翻译正确就得到一分。考官会按照考试局定下的评分方案来评阅试卷。学生在开始做题时，可以按照下面几个步骤进行翻译：

1. 仔细阅读原文并了解文意；
2. 再次读原文，分析它的结构；
3. 把句子拆开，分成词组；
4. 把词组翻成英文；
5. 把词组放回原来的句子，再把整句翻译出来；
6. 注意用词是否恰当，例如词语的单复数、时态等，句式是否顺畅，再把整句重新编排一下；
7. 利用学过的知识来改善句子的结构，并且让它符合原文的意思，同时保证句子不会有太重的"中文味"。

以下面的翻译题为例：

马明正一边做功课，一边戴着耳机听音乐，连他妈妈走进房间都不知道。妈妈并不反对马明这么一心二用，但是要他学好一门乐器，她认为这对马明将来申请大学会有好处。

1. 读完原文，我们知道这是一段关于马明对音乐有兴趣的短文。
2. 再次读原文，这次要看看它的结构。短文中的每个句子都不太长，但因为都用上了连词，所以翻成时要注意。
3. 现在把句子进行拆分：
　　　第一句我们可以拆成"一边……一边……""耳机""连……也不……""走进房间"；

Appendix VI

第二句可以拆成"并不……但……""一心二用""能学好""一种乐器""认为""将来""申请大学""有好处"。

4. 现在看看拆开的词组学生会怎么翻译。
   ❶ "一边……一边……"：根据语法，学生知道这组关联词对应的英文是"doing something on the one hand, and another thing at the same time"。
   ❷ "耳机"：学生可能会把它翻译成"ear machine"。
   ❸ "连……也不……"：根据语法，学生知道这组关联词对应的英文是"even...not..."。
   ❹ "走进房间"：学生可能会把它翻译成"to enter the room"或者"to go into the room"。
   ❺ "并不……但……"：根据语法，学生知道这组关联词是"not... but..."的意思。
   ❻ "一心二用"：学生可能已学过"一心"，会把它翻译成"whole-hearted"，至于加上"二用"之后，则要用想象力来翻译成"use twice"或者"distractedly"。
   ❼ "能学好"：学生大多会把它翻译成"can learn well"。
   ❽ "一种乐器"：学生大多会把它翻译成"a type of musical instrument"。
   ❾ "认为"：学生大多会把它翻译成"think"。
   ❿ "将来"：学生大多会把它翻译成"in the future"。
   ⓫ "申请大学"：学生大多会把它翻译成"to apply for university"。
   ⓬ "有好处"：学生大多会把它翻译成"has advantages"。

5. 现在把各词组放回原来的句子，看看会变成什么样子。
   Ma Ming is doing homework and wearing ear machine to listen to music at the same time.
   He doesn't even know his mother go into the room.
   Mother doesn't oppose to Ma Ming's distraction, but want him to learn well a type of musical instrument.
   Thinks this will have advantages when Ma Ming applies to university in the future.

6. 上面的句子虽然翻译成英文了，可是读起来并不通。要学生凭常用的英文语法和修辞，以及中文原文的大意来判断，并且把句子重新编排一下。学生现在可能会觉得"ear machine"其实就是"earphone"或者"headset"；"a type of musical instrument"翻译成"a musical instrument"就可以了。再看原文，这两句的时态应该是过去式，所以就要调整动词。

7. 重新整理句子以后，学生就要以他们熟悉的英文句式结构和修辞来重写翻译。现在的句子就变成：
   Ma Ming was doing homework while listening to music with his earphone on. He didn't even notice it when his mother entered his room. His mother didn't mind him multi-tasking, but wished he could learn to play a musical instrument well. She thought that would be advantageous for Ma Ming when he applied for university in the future.

注意：翻译人名的，就按照它们的普通话读音写成拼音。翻译地名时，如果是有名的地方，例如：国家（法国-France、意大利-Italy）、城市（巴黎-Paris、曼城-Manchester）等，就用它们已有的名字。

翻译练习

1. 在括弧内填上适当号码，连接下面意思相同的中、英文词语。

   ❶ 总算 • （ 3 ） simply
   ❷ 当然 • （ 6 ） obviously
   ❸ 简直 • （ 1 ） after all
   ❹ 也许 • （ 8 ） fortunately
   ❺ 几乎 • （ 7 ） even / go so far as
   ❻ 显然 • （ 4 ） probably / perhaps
   ❼ 甚至 • （ 5 ） almost
   ❽ 幸亏 • （ 2 ） of course / certainly
   ❾ 竟然 • （ 9 ） unexpectedly
   ❿ 经常 • （ 12 ） already
   ⓫ 左右 • （ 11 ） about
   ⓬ 已经 • （ 10 ） often
   ⓭ 偏偏 • （ 13 ） contrary to what was expected / unfortunately

2. 参考练习 1 的词语，把下列句子翻译成英语。

   ❶ 舅舅显然不相信自己的女儿被伦敦大学录取了，竟然问了一遍又一遍。
   翻译：Obviously the uncle can not believe that her daughter has been matriculated by London University, so he asks her again and again unexpectedly.

   ❷ 因为姑姑 80 岁了，所以经常会忘了钥匙在哪儿。
   翻译：Because my anti is 80 years old, so she often forgets where the key is.

   ❸ 当留学生正要去参加烧烤聚会的时候，偏偏下起了大雨。
   翻译：When students abroad are going to take part in a BBQ party, the sky is raining unfortunately.

   ❹ 这个英国姑娘会说法语和德语，甚至会说非常难的中国方言。
   翻译：This British girl can speak French and Germany, even can speak difficult Chinese dialect.

   ❺ 幸亏我没有迟到，那已经是今天最后一班火车了。
   翻译：Fortunately I didn't be late, that was the final train today.

   ❻ 英国同学简直不能相信，丽丽几乎一个中国字也不认识。
   Simply, 翻译：British students can not believe that Lily almost doesn't understand any Chinese.

   ❼ 德国的小田总算结婚了，她的父母当然很高兴。
   翻译：After all, a Germany girl Xiao Tian gets married certainly and her parents are happy.

   ❽ 明明从剑桥大学毕业后，也许会回美国当教师。
   翻译：After MingMing graduated from Cambridge University, he perhaps will return US and to be a teacher.

Appendix VI

3. 请将下面的中文短文翻译成英文。

张家乐是李美云的女儿，她和丈夫是在大学读书时相识相爱的。那时，大学毕业生的工作都是由国家负责分配的。她是一位化学工程师，丈夫是一位建筑师。他们在二十六岁时结婚，只有一个女儿。

现在他们住在一栋大楼的顶层公寓里，室内布置得非常现代化：一台电视机的大屏幕占了客厅三分之一的墙。每个人都很享受全家人在一起看电视的时间。

从英文翻译成中文

从英文翻译成中文，不仅要用中文写出原文的意思，还要语法及修辞准确。学生虽然阅读并理解英文一般不会觉得太难，但要翻成流畅的中文，还是会有一定的难度。

新的考试是以"逐点计分"方式来评分的。就是说文章中的每一个小节如果翻译正确就得到一分。考官会按照考试局定下的评分方案来评阅试卷。学生在开始做这题时，可以按照下面的几个步骤进行翻译。

1. 仔细阅读原文并了解文意；
2. 再次读原文，分析它的结构；
3. 把句子拆分成词组；
4. 把各词组翻译成中文；
5. 把词组放回原来的句子，再把整句翻译出来；
6. 注意用词是否恰当，例如量词、时态等，句式是否顺畅，再把整句重新编排一下；
7. 利用学过的知识来改善句子的结构，让它符合原文的意思，同时句子又不会有太重的"英文味"。

以下面的翻译题为例：

Although the majority of schools in China are state-run, there are now more than 70, 000 private schools, from pre-school through to higher education in China.

1. 读完原文，我们知道这是一句关于在中国的公校以及私校的情况的文字。
2. 再读原文，这次要看看它的结构，这句英文很长，有三个短句，翻译时不一定要用完全一样的结构。
3. 现在把句子拆开成词组。

   这句我们可以拆开成："although" "the majority of schools in China" "state-run" "more than 70, 000 private schools" "pre-school" "higher education"。

4. 现在看看拆开成的词组学生会怎样翻译。

   ❶ "although"：虽然（根据语法，学生知道"虽然"通常后面要加上"可是""但是"，或者"不过"）；

   ❷ "the majority of schools in China"：大多数的学校在中国；

   ❸ "state-run"：国家经营、国家管理；

   ❹ "more than 70, 000 private schools"：多过七万私家学校，多过七万私立学校；

❺ "pre-school"：学校前；

❻ "higher education"：高教育。

5. 现在把各词组放回原来的句子，看看会变成什么样子。

"虽然大多数的学校在中国国家经营，多过七万私家学校，学校前高教育在中国。"

上面是这句翻译的雏形，现在要把各个小节配上动词、连词，串起来，看看又是什么样子的。

"虽然大多数的学校在中国是国家经营，可是有多过七万私家学校，从学校前到高教育在中国。"

6. 上面的句子虽然翻译成中文了，可是读起来通不通，句子是否有很重的"英文味道"，就要学生凭借学过的语法和修辞，以及平时接触过的中文来判断了。这之后还要重新编排整句。学生可能会翻译成：

"在中国虽然大多数的学校是国家管理的，可是现在从学校前到高教育有多过七万私家学校。"

7. 重新整理译文后，学生就要从他们学过的关于学校类别、学校教育制度等知识，看看自己用的词语是否恰当。比如："private school"是"私立学校"；"state-run school"是"公立学校"；"pre-school"和"higher education"都是在讲教育的不同阶段，所以可以翻成"学前教育"和"高等教育"。于是，现在的句子就变成：

"在中国，虽然大多数的学校是公立的，可是现在从学前教育到高等教育阶段就有多过七万私立学校。"

要注意在把英文翻译成中文时，不要被原文的结构束缚，也不要随便想当然地编一篇中文。不要随便更换主语，也不要漏词。要注意细节和单复数，要选择正确的义项与句式，一步一步仔细考虑，然后再下笔成文。

一、根据要求把下列英文句子翻译成中文。

1. The health care service in China is much better now; and the life expectancy is much longer as well.（adjective + 得多）

   翻译：_____

2. Pollution is more serious in China than it in the West.（A 比 B + adjective）

   翻译：_____

3. An apartment in Shanghai is as expensive as in Beijing.（A 跟 B + adjective）

   翻译：_____

4. The sports facilities in the small town are not as good as those in the city.（A 没有 B + adjective）

   翻译：_____

Appendix VI

5. Some cities didn't even care about their own cultural heritage.（连……都／也）
   翻译：_____

6. Xiao Ming has no confidence in this year's final exams.（subject + 对 + object + verb / adjective）
   翻译：_____

7. Apart from being good at tennis, Da Ying plays football very well too.（除了……以外……）
   翻译：_____

8. No matter how busy Wang Ying is at work, when she comes home she still has to do all the house chores.（无论……还是……）
   翻译：_____

9. Grandma must go out to meet friends; otherwise she gets very bored at home and may even become ill.（不然／否则）
   翻译：_____

10. You can go out with your friends tonight only if you have done all your homework.（只有……才……）
    翻译：_____

11. The taxi driver will take you there as long as you tell him the name of the restaurant.（只要……就……）
    翻译：_____

12. Whilst all the adults are enjoying the moonlight, the children are playing with the lanterns.（当……的时候／之时；正在／在……）
    翻译：_____

13. Running to the workplace is liked by more and more people.（被；越来越）
    翻译：_____

14. The airport staff had this waiting area cleaned several times.（把）
    翻译：_____

15. We should regard this job offer as an opportunity to gain experience abroad.（视……为……）
    翻译：_____

二、完成下面的翻译题。

Although the majority of schools in China are state-run, there are now more than 70,000 private schools, from pre-school through to higher education in China. They cater for more than 14 million students. In the big cities there are many international schools.

三、把下面的英文短文翻译成中文。

I heard a story from a teacher at London University. A journalist asks three students from America, Britain and China: "what's your personal opinion about the international food shortage"?

The American replies: "What does international mean?"

The British student asks: "What is food shortage?"

And the Chinese student says: "What do you mean by personal opinion?"

Appendix VII: Vocabulary list

Chinese-English Vocabulary List

Chinese	Pinyin	English	Chapter
A			
安定	āndìng	stable	2
安分	ānfèn	be happy with	7
安享晚年	ānxiǎngwǎnnián	to enjoy old age	2
安心	ānxīn	to settle down	2
B			
白领	báilǐng	white-collar	8
白素贞	Bái Sùzhēn	Bai Suzhen, name of the white snake	11
百科全书	bǎikēquánshū	encyclopaedia	14
摆上	bǎishang	to put in front of	10
百姓	bǎixìng	people; general public	10
包办	bāobàn	arranged	2
保佑	bǎoyòu	to protect and bless	9
报答	bàodá	to repay a favour	11
报考	bàokǎo	to enter for an exam	6
报名	bàomíng	to enrol	4
爆竹	bàozhú	fire cracker	9
悲哀	bēi'āi	sorrow	13
悲剧	bēijù	tragedy	17
北宋	Běisòng	Northern Song Dynasty (960-1127AD)	10
贝多芬	Bèiduōfēn	Beethoven	17
彼此	bǐcǐ	one another	13
比如	bǐrú	for instance	6
必修	bìxiū	compulsory for study	5
编辑	biānjí	editor	1
汴河	biànhé	Bian River, a river within Kai Feng	10

变	biàn	to change	1
辩论	biànlùn	debate	5
标准	biāozhǔn	standard	8
表扬	biǎoyáng	praise	3
宾客	bīnkè	guest	17
病菌	bìngjūn	bacteria	11
拨打	bōdǎ	to dial	16
补习班	bǔxíbān	private tutorials	5
不断	búduàn	continuous	4
不够好	búgòu hǎo	not good enough	6
不仅	bùjǐn	not only	12
不透气	bú tòuqì	airless	8
不息	bùxī	non-stop; incessant	13
不知不觉	bùzhībùjué	without knowing	14
布置	bùzhì	to decorate	2
步步高升	bùbùgāoshēng	rising step by step	13
部门	bùmén	department (as in a company)	2

C

猜	cāi	to guess	15
才	cái	not until	1
苍蝇	cāngying	fly	11
曾经	céngjīng	once before	2
插柳	chāliǔ	to plant willows	10
蟾蜍	chánchú	toad	12
蟾宫折桂	chángōngzhéguì	It literally means plucking osmanthus flowers in the Palace of the Moon. It is used to describe someone succeeding in the imperial examination.	12
产品	chǎnpǐn	product	2
产生	chǎnshēng	to produce; to come into being	3
嫦娥奔月	cháng'ébēnyuè	Chang E running to the moon	12
场景	chǎngjǐng	scene	15
朝代	cháodài	dynasty	15
称呼	chēnghū	form of address	13
称作	chēngzuò	is called by	13

Appendix VII

成就感	chéngjiùgǎn	sense of achievement	7
成效	chéngxiào	result; effect	3
城镇	chéngzhèn	town	7
惩罚	chéngfá	to punish	11
宠坏	chǒnghuài	to spoil (a child)	3
抽空	chōukòng	to spare time	8
抽烟	chōuyān	to smoke	6
出差	chūchāi	be away on official business	4
出奇	chūqí	surprisingly	17
出色	chūsè	outstanding	8
出席	chūxí	attending	17
初中	chūzhōng	junior high school	5
除虫	chúchóng	to get rid of pests	7
除夕	chúxī	New Year's Eve	9
楚国	Chǔguó	the State of Chu	11
处理	chǔlǐ	to deal with	1
处世做人	chǔshìzuòrén	to conduct oneself in society	2
穿越片	chuānyuèpiàn	time-travel movies	15
传承	chuánchéng	to passed down and to inherit	16
传媒界	chuánméijiè	the media	16
传说	chuánshuō	legend	9
传统	chuántǒng	traditional	4
床位	chuángwèi	bed space	4
创办	chuàngbàn	to found	15
创业	chuàngyè	to start an enterprise	7
创意	chuàngyì	creativity	7
创作	chuàngzuò	making	15
春耕春种	chūngēngchūnzhòng	to grow crops in spring	10
春联	chūnlián	spring couplets	9
纯净	chúnjìng	pure; clean	13
辞旧迎新	cíjiùyíngxīn	to say farewell to the old and to welcome in the new	9
辞职	cízhí	resign	7
此起彼伏	cǐqǐ bǐfú	to rise or appear one after another	9
刺激	cìjī	exciting	6

匆匆	cōngcōng	hurriedly	8
存	cún	to save up (money)	2

D

搭建	dājiàn	to build	7
打败	dǎbài	to defeat	11
打发	dǎfā	to while away (one's time)	16
打麻将	dǎ májiāng	to play Mahjong	4
打太极拳	dǎ tàijíquán	to practise Tai Chi	4
打针	dǎzhēn	to give injection	4
《大闹天宫》	Dànàotiāngōng	Havoc in Heaven	15
大臣	dàchén	minister	11
大力	dàlì	vigorously	3
大棚	dàpéng	big shed	7
大蒜	dàsuàn	garlic	11
戴	dài	to wear	17
担心	dānxīn	to worry	6
单亲	dānqīn	single parent	1
当代	dāngdài	contemporary	15
荡秋千	dàngqiūqiān	to play on a swing	10
导演	dǎoyǎn	film director	15
捣药	dǎoyào	to pound medicine in a mortar	12
悼念	dàoniàn	mourning	10
得益于	déyìyú	benefited	15
登记	dēngjì	to register	14
登陆	dēnglù	to land	12
低落	dīluò	low	5
笛子	dízi	bamboo flute	17
点赞	diǎnzàn	"like it", it is an online network phrase, used to express "praise"	16
丁克族	dīngkèzú	a group of people with double income and no kids	2
叮嘱	dīngzhǔ	to urge someone to do or not to do something	2
顶	dǐng	(measure word for sedan chairs)	10
顶层	dǐngcéng	top floor	2

Appendix VII

动画片	dònghuàpiàn	cartoon movies	15
独处	dúchù	be on one's own	8
独居	dújū	to live alone	4
独生	dúshēng	single child	2
独生子女	dúshēng zǐnǚ	only child	3
独特	dútè	unique	15
读者	dúzhě	reader	14
锻炼	duànliàn	to exercise	4
对应	duìyìng	correspond	13
多子多福	duōzǐduōfú	the more children, the more benefits	4

E

俄罗斯	Éluósi	Russia	14
耳机	ěrjī	earphone	17
二胡	èrhú	a two-stringed bowed instrument	17

F

发达	fādá	developed	1
发行公司	fāxíng gōngsī	distributor	15
发挥	fāhuī	to develop	7
法海	Fǎ Hǎi	Fa Hai, name of the monk	11
法力	fǎlì	supernatural power	11
繁华	fánhuá	bustling; prosperous	10
繁殖	fánzhí	to breed	11
反对	fǎnduì	to oppose	6
反映	fǎnyìng	to reflect	16
方式	fāngshì	way	4
方位	fāngwèi	bearing	13
放宽	fàngkuān	to relax	3
放弃	fàngqì	to give up	16
放松	fàngsōng	to relax	4
放置	fàngzhì	to place	14
非	fēi	not	14
肥胖症	féipàngzhēng	obesity	3
分担	fēndān	to share (responsibility)	8
分配	fēnpèi	to allocate	2

分析	fēnxī	to analyse	7
坟墓	fénmù	grave	10
粉丝	fěnsī	fans	17
丰富	fēngfù	to enrich	16
丰富多彩	fēngfùduōcǎi	rich and varied	4
风格	fēnggé	style	10
佛教	fójiào	Buddhism	13
夫妻	fūqī	husband and wife	1
服饰	fúshì	costume	10
服装	fúzhuāng	clothing	4
福利	fúlì	benefit	3
负担	fùdān	burden	2
负面	fùmiàn	negative	3
负责	fùzé	be responsible for	2
负责	fùzé	responsible	1
妇女	fùnǚ	women	1
富贵	fùguì	riches and honour	9
富贵吉祥	fùguì jíxiáng	wealth, honour and luck	12

G

感恩	gǎn'ēn	thanksgiving	10
感恩	gǎnēn	to be thankful	12
高考	gāokǎo	college entrance examination	5
高铁	gāotiě	high speed rail in China	14
高中	gāozhōng	senior high school	5
格外	géwài	especially	5
格言	géyán	maxim; motto	16
根据	gēnjù	according to	3
耕地	gēngdì	cultivated land	7
工作量	gōngzuòliàng	workload	1
公立	gōnglì	state-run	5
公寓	gōngyù	apartment	2
公主	gōngzhǔ	princess	3
共享	gòngxiǎng	sharing	14
贡献	gòngxiàn	contribution	7

Appendix VII

供不应求	gōngbúyìngqiú	demand over supply	7
估计	gūjì	to reckon	4
孤独自闭	gūdú zìbì	solitary; unsociable	3
古装片	gǔzhuāngpiàn	costume / period drama	15
怪兽	guàishòu	monster	9
观音	Guānyīn	Guanyin (in Buddhism, it is called Avalokitesvara)	13
官	guān	court official	11
管理员	guǎnlǐyuán	person in charge	8
管弦乐团	guǎnxiányuètuán	orchestra	17
光盘	guāngpán	CD	17
广州	Guǎngzhōu	Guang Zhou, also known as Canton	14
逛街	guàngjiē	to window-shop	1
规定	guīdìng	to stipulate	13
柜子	guìzi	cabinet	14
桂花树	guìhuāshù	osmanthus tree	12
国际	guójì	international	5
过剩	guòshèng	excess; surplus	3
过时	guòshí	old fashioned	6

H

海外	hǎiwài	overseas	1
害虫	hàichóng	pest	11
寒食节	hánshíjié	Cold Food Festival	10
好评	hǎopíng	good comments/reviews	9
好问	hàowèn	inquisitive	12
喝醉	hēzuì	be drunk	11
合而为一	hé'érwéiyī	to combine into one	8
和尚	héshang	monk	11
和谐	héxié	harmonious	17
河蟹	héxiè	river crab	12
《红高粱》	Hónggāoliang	Red Sorghum	15
《红楼梦》	Hónglóumèng	The Story of the Stone, a classic Chinese novel	14
红绸舞	hóngchóuwǔ	red ribbon dance	9
红火	hónghuǒ	flourishing	7

胡同	hútòng	lane; alley	2
互动	hùdòng	to interact	16
化肥	huàféi	chemical fertiliser	7
怀疑	huáiyí	to suspect	6
欢天喜地	huāntiānxǐdì	wild with joy	9
缓解	huǎnjiě	to alleviate	3
换	huàn	to change	2
婚嫁	hūnjià	marriage	13
婚宴	hūnyàn	wedding banquet	17
婚姻	hūnyīn	marriage	2
活	huó	to live (Here the sentence means "only two survived".)	2
活力	huólì	energy	8
火焰	huǒyàn	flame	13
获奖	huòjiǎng	to win a prize	15

J

机构	jīgòu	organisation	4
极乐世界	jílè shìjiè	paradise	13
疾病	jíbìng	illness	11
集	jí	to incorporate	8
几乎	jīhū	almost	4
计划生育	jìhuà shēngyù	family planning	3
记录	jìlù	to record	16
纪录片	jìlùpiàn	documentaries	15
祭拜	jìbài	to worship	10
祭品	jìpǐn	offerings put in front of grave	10
祭祖	jìzǔ	to pay respect to ancestors	10
加快	jiākuài	to quicken	4
佳节	jiājié	festival	13
佳句	jiājù	well-turned phrase or saying	16
家庭	jiātíng	family	1
家乡	jiāxiāng	home country	5
嫁妆	jiàzhuang	dowry	13
坚决	jiānjué	determined	6

Appendix VII

减少	jiǎnshǎo	to reduce	1
建议	jiànyì	suggestion	1
建筑师	jiànzhùshī	architect	2
健儿	jiàn'ér	athlete	16
健康长寿	jiànkāngchángshòu	good health and longevity	12
讲解	jiǎngjiě	to explain	1
郊外	jiāowài	countryside	1
郊外	jiāowài	outskirt of a city	14
浇水	jiāoshuǐ	to irrigate; to water (plants)	7
骄傲	jiāoào	proud	2
轿子	jiào	sedan chair	10
教育	jiàoyù	education	3
接触	jiēchù	be in contact with	8
节省	jiéshěng	to save	8
节奏	jiézòu	rhythm	1
结伴	jiébàn	to do something together with others	10
金马奖	Jīnmǎjiǎng	Golden Horse Awards	15
金马影展	Jīnmǎ Yǐngzhǎn	Golden Horse Film Festival	15
金融界	jīnróngjiè	finance	6
金山寺	JīnshānSì	Golden Mountain Temple	11
金元宝	jīnyuánbǎo	gold ingot used as money in ancient China	9
尽早	jìnzǎo	as early as possible	7
进程	jìnchéng	process	4
禁止	jìnzhǐ	to forbid	10
经济	jīngjì	economy	3
经历	jīnglì	to experience	1
惊奇	jīngqí	surprised	17
惊喜	jīngxǐ	nice surprise	17
精力	jīnglì	energy	3
精力	jīnglì	vigour	8
精致	jīngzhì	delicate; exquisite	14
景象	jǐngxiàng	scene	10
敬茶	jìngchá	to offer tea respectfully	13
敬献	jìngxiàn	to present (respectfully)	10

救命之恩	jiùmìngzhī'ēn	the kindness of saving a life	11
就业	jiùyè	employment	3
居家	jūjiā	stay-at-home	4
居住	jūzhù	to live; to reside	1
巨响	jùxiǎng	huge noise	9
据说	jùshuō	it is said	9

K

K歌串烧	K gē chuàn shāo	singing a variety of songs	17
卡拉OK	kǎlā ŌK	karaoke	17
开	kāi	to run (Here the sentence means "to own and run a business".)	2
开播	kāibō	to begin broadcasting	16
刊登	kāndēng	to publish in a newspaper	7
砍	kǎn	to fell (a tree)	12
看望	kànwàng	to visit	1
靠窗	kàochuāng	by the window	14
科幻片	kēhuànpiàn	science fiction movies	15
空白	kòngbái	blank	13
枯燥	kūzào	dull and dry	14
会计师	kuàijìshī	accountant	1
苦恼	kǔnǎo	vexed	6
宽	kuān	wide	10

L

蜡烛	làzhú	candle	12
劳动力	láodònglì	manual labour	7
劳动者	láodòngzhě	manual worker	2
老龄化	lǎolínghuà	ageing	3
唠叨	láodao	be garrulous	2
了解	liǎojiě	to understand	1
雷峰塔	Léifēng Tǎ	Lei Feng Pagoda	11
类型	lèixíng	genre	15
离婚	líhūn	to divorce	1
李安	Lǐ Ān	Ang Lee	15
理发	lǐfà	have a haircut	2

Appendix VII

理论	lǐlùn	theory	14
连	lián	even	17
莲蓉	liánróng	lotus seed paste	12
联想	liánxiǎng	to associate; to imagine	17
《梁祝》协奏曲	Liáng ZhùXiézòuqǔ	Butterfly Lovers In italics	17
梁山伯	Liáng Shānbó	Liang Shanbo	17
俩	liǎ	both	2
亮点	liàngdiǎn	highlight	13
辆	liàng	(measure word for vehicles)	10
量血压	liáng xuèyā	to take blood pressure	4
邻居	línjū	neighbour	2
零食	língshí	snack	14
浏览	liúlǎn	to browse	14
留学	liúxué	to study abroad	2
留学生	liúxuéshēng	student studying abroad	5
流传	liúchuán	to hand down	12
隆重	lóngzhòng	grand; solemn	13
路边	lùbiān	roadside	14
乱七八糟	luànqībāzāo	messy	2
轮回	lúnhuí	reincarnation	13

M

麦草	màicǎo	straw	7
满意	mǎnyì	satisfactory	1
忙碌	mánglù	busy	8
毛病	máobìng	trouble; shortcoming	3
矛盾	máodùn	conflict	15
美满	měimǎn	perfectly satisfactory	8
汨罗江	Mìluójiāng	Miluo River, situated in northern Hunan Province	11
面积	miànjī	area of land	7
面临	miànlín	be faced with	3
面子	miànzi	face (as in reputation, prestige)	6
描绘	miáohuì	to depict	10
民以食为天	mínyǐshíwéitiān	food is everything to the common people	16

明清	míngqīng	the era of the Ming Dynasty and Qing Dynasty	14
《命运交响曲》	MìngyùnJiāoxiǎngqǔ	Symphony No.5	17
模拟	mónǐ	mock (exam)	5
陌生	mòshēng	strange	5
默默无闻	mòmò wúwén	little known	15
目前	mùqián	at present	4

N

耐心	nàixīn	patience	5
年末	niánmò	end of year	9
年夜饭	niányèfàn	meal eaten on New Year's Eve	9
农耕社会	nónggēngshèhuì	agricultural society	12
农历	nónglì	lunar calendar	9
农民	nóngmín	peasant	2

P

派	pài	to send	4
跑步通勤	pǎobùtōngqín	"runcommute" refers to a run between one's home and workplace	8
陪	péi	to accompany	1
培养	péiyǎng	to nurture; to foster	3
盆栽	pénzāi	pot plant	14
烹饪节目	pēngrènjiémù	cookery programme	16
批评	pīpíng	criticism	3
琵琶	pípa	a plucked string instrument with a fretted fingerboard	17
片商	piānshāng	film company	16
贫困	pínkùn	poor	7
频道	píndào	channel	16
聘礼	pìnlǐ	bride price	13
聘用	pìnyòng	to employ	2
平等	píngděng	equal	5
平衡	pínghéng	to balance	6
平均	píngjūn	on average	14
平台	píngtái	platform	15

Appendix VII

凭	píng	using something as proof of	14
屏幕	píngmù	screen	2
破旧	pòjiù	dilapidated	2
普洱茶	pǔěrchá	Pu'er tea	13
普及	pǔjí	becoming common	16
普通	pǔtōng	ordinary	2

Q

其实	qíshí	in fact	6
祈福	qífú	to pray for happiness	9
祈求	qíqiú	to pray for	12
企业	qǐyè	enterprise	7
起跑线	qǐpǎo xiàn	starting line	5
气氛	qìfēn	atmosphere	9
气色	qìsè	complexion	13
前世	qiánshì	previous life	11
强身健体	qiángshēnjiàntǐ	to strength the health and body	8
强调	qiángdiào	to emphasise	7
墙	qiáng	wall	2
敲锣打鼓	qiāoluódǎgǔ	to beat the gongs and drums	9
秦国	Qínguó	the State of Qin	11
青	qīng	blue green	13
青春期	qīngchūnqī	puberty	1
清醒	qīngxǐng	alert	8
情绪	qíngxù	mood	5
请教	qǐngjiào	to ask for advice	1
穷困	qióngkùn	poor	5
秋祭	qiūjì	offering to gods and ancestors in autumn	12
秋收	qiūshōu	autumn harvest	12
驱赶	qūgǎn	to expel; to banish	11
驱邪	qūxié	to drive away the evil spirits	9
娶	qǔ	to marry (a woman)	17
缺	quē	to lack; be short of	17
缺少	quēshǎo	lack of	3

R

热播	rèbō	to broadcast frequently	16
热线	rèxiàn	hotline	7
人类	rénlèi	human beings	12
人群	rénqún	cohort	16
人群	rénqún	group	3
任性	rènxìng	wilful	3
扔进	rēngjìn	to throw in	11
日复一日	rìfùyírì	day after day	8
日益	rìyì	increasingly	3
荣誉	róngyù	honour	15
如何	rúhé	how	15

S

洒	sǎ	to sprinkle	11
嗓音	sǎngyīn	voice	17
丧服	sàngfú	mourning clothes	13
丧礼	sànglǐ	funeral	13
扫墓	sǎomù	to sweep the grave	10
杀菌	shājūn	to kill germs	11
沙发上的土豆	shāfāshangde tǔdòu	couch potato	16
山茶花	shāncháhuā	camellia	10
山洞	shāndòng	cave	9
伤害	shānghài	to harm	11
商界	shāngjiè	the commercial world	14
商量	shāngliang	to talk over	6
商业化	shāngyèhuà	commercialisation	15
赏识	shǎngshí	appreciation	7
上级领导	shàngjílǐngdǎo	superior; leader	13
上门	shàngmén	to be delivered to the home	4
《舌尖上的中国》	Shéjiānshang de Zhōngguó	A Bite of China	16
社会	shèhuì	society	4
社交	shèjiāo	social	6
摄影	shèyǐng	photography	4

Appendix VII

伸手	shēnshǒu	to stretch out one's hand	3
生儿育女	shēng'éryùnǚ	to bear and rear children	2
生活指导师	shēnghuózhǐdǎoshī	life coach	8
生灵	shēnglíng	creature; living things	11
生气	shēngqì	to be angry	6
生前	shēngqián	before a person's death	10
牲畜	shēngchù	livestock	9
胜任	shèngrèn	competent	7
尸体	shītǐ	corpse	11
失去	shīqù	to lose	4
失望	shīwàng	disappointed	6
湿热	shīrè	hot and humid	11
十二生肖	shí'èr shēngxiào	12 Chinese zodiac	9
实际上	shíjìshang	in reality	9
实现	shíxiàn	to realise	1
实用	shíyòng	practical	2
实在	shízài	really	2
食脑族（靠智慧吃饭的人）	shínǎozú (kào zhìhuìchīfàn de rén)	people whose job involves the use of their brain, rather than their physical labour	7
事业	shìyè	career	1
视野	shìyě	horizon	16
是否	shìfǒu	is it not	6
收藏	shōucáng	be kept (as in a museum)	10
收藏	shōucáng	to collect	14
收成	shōuchéng	harvest	12
收入	shōurù	income	1
手艺	shǒuyì	craft	16
守着	shǒuzhe	to stick with	7
书生	shūshēng	a scholar	11
舒适	shūshì	comfortable	5
输	shū	to lose	5
熟食	shúshí	cooked food	13
属于	shǔyú	belong to	8
束	shù	a bunch (of flowers)	10

束腰带	shùyāodài	to tie a belt round one's waist	13
数量	shùliàng	quantity	15
数量庞大	shùliàngpángdà	great number	17
双方	shuāng fāng	both sides	4
说服	shuìfú	to convince by persuasion	11
私营	sīyíng	privately owned	7
思维范围	sīwéifànwéi	the scope in thinking	16
思想观念	sīxiǎng guānniàn	thinking; concept	1
死亡	sǐwáng	death	13
死者	sǐzhě	the dead	10
四合院	sìhéyuàn	courtyard house	2
艘	sōu	(measure word for ships)	10
俗语	súyǔ	common saying	16
素质	sùzhì	quality (of people)	5
随时	suíshí	anytime	14
随手	suíshǒu	not purposefully	14
随着	suízhe	in pace with; in the wake of	4
祟	suì	evil spirit	9
碎片时间	suìpiànshíjiān	small breaks in time	14

T

踏进	tàjìn	to step into	14
踏青	tàqīng	to do an outing	10
台北	Táiběi	Taipei, provincial capital of Taiwan	14
探春	tànchūn	to explore the spring scenery	10
唐朝	tángcháo	Tang Dynasty (618AD-907AD)	12
逃跑	táopǎo	to flee	9
提出	tíchū	to suggest	11
提灯笼	tí dēnglóng	to carry a lantern	12
体验	tǐyàn	to experience for oneself	17
《天龙八部》	Tiānlóngbābù	Tian Long Ba Bu, the title of one of the well-known martial art novels written by Jin Yong	14
《天注定》	Tiānzhùdìng	A Touch of Sin	15
天地	tiāndì	world	6

Appendix VII

天赋	tiānfù	natural gift	17
挑战性	tiǎozhànxìng	challenging	7
调查	diàochá	survey	3
铁观音茶	tiěguānyīnchá	Tie Guan Yin tea	13
同龄人	tónglíngrén	peer	3
统计	tǒngjì	statistics	4
痛苦	tòngkǔ	pain	13
投资	tóuzī	investment	15
投资	tóuzī	to invest	5
土地神	tǔdìshén	God of Earth	12
团圆	tuányuán	reunion	9
团圆节	tuányuánjié	Reunion Festival	12
推陈出新	tuīchénchūxīn	out with the old, in with the new	16
推广	tuīguǎng	to promote	15
推行	tuīxíng	to pursue	3
推销	tuīxiāo	sales	2
退休	tuìxiū	to retire	4
托老所	tuōlǎosuǒ	care centre for elderly people	4

W

外表	wàibiǎo	appearance	7
外地	wàidì	parts of the country other than where one is	4
外界	wàijiè	outside world	7
外佣	wàiyōng	foreign domestic helper	1
万物	wànwù	all things	13
微博	wēibó	Weibo (China's version of Twitter)	16
卫生	wèishēng	hygiene	11
文盲	wénmáng	illiterate	2
蚊子	wénzi	mosquito	11
《卧虎藏龙》	Wòhǔcánglóng	Crouching Tiger, Hidden Dragon	15
无论	wúlùn	regardless of	15
无所不谈	wúsuǒbùtán	to talk about anything whatsoever	6
吴刚	Wú Gāng	Wu Gang, the woodcutter on the moon	12
武侠小说	wǔxiáxiǎoshuō	martial art novel	14

X

行为举止	xíngwéi jǔzhǐ	behaviour	1
西红柿	xīhóngshì	tomato	4
吸毒	xīdú	to take drugs	6
喜气洋洋	xǐqì yángyáng	full of joy	9
系	xì	department (as in a university)	2
虾酱	xiājiàng	shrimp paste	16
下棋	xiàqí	to play chess	4
吓	xià	to scare	9
吓死	xiàsǐ	to scare to death	11
仙草	xiāncǎo	celestial grass	11
鲜美	xiānměi	tasty; delicious	12
鲜明的	xiānmíngde	distinctive	15
贤妻良母	xiánqīliángmǔ	virtuous wife and good mother	8
限制	xiànzhì	to limit	16
献上	xiànshang	to offer (such as flowers)	10
相爱	xiāng'ài	to fall in love	2
相处	xiāngchǔ	to get along with	3
香包	xiāngbāo	scented pouch	11
香菜	xiāngcài	coriander	4
香草	xiāngcǎo	herb	11
享受	xiǎngshòu	to enjoy	2
项	xiàng	(a measure word)	3
象征	xiàngzhēng	to symbolise	12
消毒	xiāodú	to sterilise	11
消息	xiāoxi	news	10
小皇帝	xiǎo huángdì	little emperor	3
小曲	xiǎoqǔ	arias	17
孝顺	xiàoshùn	filial obedience	13
效果	xiàoguǒ	result, effect	17
效率	xiàolǜ	efficiency	8
心理	xīnlǐ	mentality	3
辛苦	xīnkǔ	hard	1
新潮	xīncháo	trendy	6

Appendix VII

新婚	xīnhūn	newly wed	13
新款	xīnkuǎn	new style	6
薪水	xīnshuǐ	salary; wage	7
兄弟姐妹	xiōngdìjiěmèi	brothers and sisters; siblings	1
兴高采烈	xìnggāocǎiliè	in high spirits; in great delight	9
幸福	xìngfú	happy	2
幸好	xìnghǎo	luckily	1
性别	xìngbié	gender	7
性格	xìnggé	personality	3
雄黄	xiónghuáng	realgar, a mineral	11
修车	xiūchē	to repair cars	2
许仙	Xǔ Xiān	Xu Xian, name of the scholar	11
选修	xuǎnxiū	opitional for study	5
学区房	xuéqūfáng	catchment area housing	5
寻找	xúnzhǎo	to look for	7

Y

压	yā	to press down	11
"压力山大"	yālì shāndà	pressure as big as a mountain	6
压岁钱	yāsuìqián	money given to children as a Chinese New Year gift	9
淹	yān	to flood	11
严	yán	strict	6
严重	yánzhòng	serious	3
养成	yǎngchéng	to form (a habit)	3
养儿防老	yǎng'érfánglǎo	to have children to prepare for old age	4
养家	yǎngjiā	to provide for the family	2
养老	yǎnglǎo	to provide for old age	2
养老院	yǎnglǎoyuàn	old people's home	4
养育	yǎngyù	to raise (a child)	3
妖	yāo	evil spirit; demon	11
摇滚乐	yáogǔnyuè	rock music	17
野兽	yěshòu	wild animal	9
一栋	yídòng	a block of (building)	2
一石多鸟	yìshí duōniǎo	to kill many birds with one stone	8

Vocabulary list

医护人员	yīhù rényuán	medical staff	4
医疗条件	yīliáo tiáojiàn	medical condition	2
仪式	yíshì	ceremony	13
移民	yímín	to emigrate	5
亿	yì	a hundred million	4
义务	yìwù	obligation	4
艺人	yìrén	artist	17
阴阳	yīnyáng	Yin and Yang, the two opposing principles in nature, with Yin representing the feminine and Yang the masculine	12
音色	yīnsè	timbre	17
隐隐约约	yǐnyǐnyuēyuē	indistinct	12
营养	yíngyǎng	nutrition	3
影视娱乐	yǐngshìyúlè	film / TV entertainment	14
拥挤	yōngjǐ	crowded	8
幽雅	yōuyǎ	quiet and tastefully decorated	14
幽怨	yōuyuàn	resentment; bitterness	17
有机	yǒujī	organic	7
有节制地	yǒujiézhìde	controlled; disciplined	16
有声书	yǒushēngshū	audio book	14
有意义的	yǒuyìyì de	meaningful	16
余	yú	surplus	9
娱乐	yúlè	entertainment	4
语文	yǔwén	language and literature	5
玉兔	yùtù	Jade Rabbit	12
预防	yùfáng	to prevent	11
欲望	yùwàng	desire	16
遇到	yùdào	to encounter	1
元素	yuánsù	element	15
园林	yuánlín	landscape architecture	6
圆梦	yuánmèng	to make a dream come true	4
愿望	yuànwàng	wishes	1
愿望	yuànwàng	wishes	12
月坛	Yuètán	Temple of the Moon	12

Appendix VII

粤剧	yuèjù	Cantonese opera	17

Z

杂货	záhuò	groceries	2
暂时	zànshí	temporarily	3
则	zé	a measure word, it's used for an item of news or an advertisement	7
责任	zérèn	responsibility	4
占	zhàn	to occupy	2
战争	zhànzhēng	war	2
张口	zhāngkǒu	to open one's mouth	3
长辈	zhǎngbèi	older generation	9
长生不老	chángshēngbùlǎo	immortality	12
掌握时尚	zhǎngwòshíshàng	follow the new trend	16
招聘	zhāopìn	to advertise for a job vacancy	7
照顾	zhàogù	to look after	1
着重	zhuózhòng	with emphasis on	16
侦探片	zhēntànpiàn	detective movies	15
真实	zhēnshí	realistic	15
争论	zhēnglùn	to argue	2
政策	zhèngcè	policy	3
政府	zhèngfǔ	government	3
政治运动	zhèngzhìyùndòng	political movement	2
支持	zhīchí	support	1
支配	zhīpèi	to have control over	8
直接	zhíjiē	directly	8
职场	zhíchǎng	world of employment	7
职位	zhíwèi	job; position	7
植树造林	zhíshù zàolín	to plant trees to make a forest	10
植物园	zhíwù yuán	botanical garden	6
纸马	zhǐmǎ	paper horse (horse made with paper and bamboo strips)	10
指导	zhǐdǎo	to guide	16
质量	zhìliàng	quality (of product)	5
中西合璧	zhōngxīhébì	Chinese and Western combined together	17

种	zhòng	to grow	4
种瓜种豆	zhòngguāzhòngdòu	to grow melon and bean	10
种植	zhòngzhí	to grow; to cultivate	7
重点大学	zhòngdiǎndàxué	key university (similar to Russell Group or Ivy League universities)	5
重视	zhòngshì	to see as important	14
《周礼》	Zhōulǐ	the Rites of Zhou Dynasty	13
主任	zhǔrèn	person in-charge	2
主色调	zhǔsèdiào	main colour	13
住宿	zhùsù	boarding	5
住宿学校	zhùsùxuéxiào	boarding school	4
祝英台	Zhù Yīngtái	Zhu Yingtai	17
专门	zhuānmén	specialised	10
专业	zhuānyè	specialised; subject; discipline	6
转型期	zhuǎnxíngqī	transition period	7
状况	zhuàngkuàng	situation; condition	1
追求	zhuīqiú	pursuit	16
追求	zhuīqiú	to pursue	1
准许	zhǔnxǔ	to allow	3
资讯	zīxùn	information	1
资源	zīyuán	resource	5
自动售货机	zìdòngshòuhuòjī	automatic sales machine	14
自理	zìlǐ	to take care of oneself	4
自杀	zìshā	to commit suicide	11
自身	zìshēn	oneself	3
自私	zìsī	selfish	3
字幕	zìmù	subtitled	15
综合症	zōnghézhēng	syndrome	3
总经理	zǒngjīnglǐ	general manager	2
总算	zǒngsuàn	on the whole	5
走读	zǒudú	day pupil	5
租借	zūjiè	to rent	5
组织者	zǔzhīzhě	organiser	15
作法	zuòfǎ	to use magic	11

English-Chinese Vocabulary List

English	Pinyin	Character	Chapter
A			
(a measure word)	xiàng	项	3
a measure word, it's used for an item of news or an advertisement	zé	则	7
(measure word for sedan chairs)	dǐng	顶	10
(measure word for ships)	sōu	艘	10
(measure word for vehicles)	liàng	辆	10
"runcommute" refers to a run between one's home and workplace	pǎobùtōngqín	跑步通勤	8
12 Chinese zodiac	shí'èr shēngxiào	十二生肖	9
A Bite of China	Shéjiānshang de Zhōngguó	《舌尖上的中国》	16
a block of (building)	yídòng	一栋	2
a bunch (of flowers)	shù	束	10
a group of people with double income and no kids	dīngkèzú	丁克族	2
a hundred million	yì	亿	4
a plucked string instrument with a fretted fingerboard	pípa	琵琶	17
a scholar	shūshēng	书生	11
A Touch of Sin	Tiānzhùdìng	《天注定》	15
a two-stringed bowed instrument	èrhú	二胡	17
according to	gēnjù	根据	3
accountant	kuàijìshī	会计师	1
ageing	lǎolínghuà	老龄化	3
agricultural society	nónggēngshèhuì	农耕社会	12
airless	bú tòuqì	不透气	8
alert	qīngxǐng	清醒	8
all things	wànwù	万物	13

almost	jǐhū	几乎	4
Ang Lee	Lǐ Ān	李安	15
anytime	suíshí	随时	14
apartment	gōngyù	公寓	2
appearance	wàibiǎo	外表	7
appreciation	shǎngshí	赏识	7
architect	jiànzhùshī	建筑师	2
area of land	miànjī	面积	7
arias	xiǎoqǔ	小曲	17
arranged	bāobàn	包办	2
artist	yìrén	艺人	17
as early as possible	jìnzǎo	尽早	7
at present	mùqián	目前	4
athlete	jiàn'ér	健儿	16
atmosphere	qìfēn	气氛	9
attending	chūxí	出席	17
audio book	yǒushēngshū	有声书	14
automatic sales machine	zìdòngshòuhuòjī	自动售货机	14
autumn harvest	qiūshōu	秋收	12

B

bacteria	bìngjūn	病菌	11
Bai Suzhen, name of the white snake	Bái Sùzhēn	白素贞	11
bamboo flute	dízi	笛子	17
be away on official business	chūchāi	出差	4
be drunk	hēzuì	喝醉	11
be faced with	miànlín	面临	3
be garrulous	láodao	唠叨	2
be happy with	ānfèn	安分	7
be in contact with	jiēchù	接触	8
be kept (as in a museum)	shōucáng	收藏	10
be on one's own	dúchù	独处	8
be responsible for	fùzé	负责	2
bearing	fāngwèi	方位	13

Appendix VII

becoming common	pǔjí	普及	16
bed space	chuángwèi	床位	4
Beethoven	Bèiduōfēn	贝多芬	17
before a person's death	shēngqián	生前	10
behaviour	xíngwéi jǔzhǐ	行为举止	1
belong to	shǔyú	属于	8
benefit	fúlì	福利	3
benefited	deyìyú	得益于	15
Bian River, a river within Kai Feng	biànhé	汴河	10
big shed	dàpéng	大棚	7
blank	kòngbái	空白	13
blue green	qīng	青	13
boarding school	zhùsùxuéxiào	住宿学校	4
boarding	zhùsù	住宿	5
botanical garden	zhíwù yuán	植物园	6
both sides	shuāng fāng	双方	4
both	liǎ	俩	2
bride price	pìnlǐ	聘礼	13
brothers and sisters; siblings	xiōngdì jiěmèi	兄弟姐妹	1
Buddhism	fójiào	佛教	13
burden	fùdān	负担	2
bustling; prosperous	fánhuá	繁华	10
busy	mánglù	忙碌	8
Butterfly Lovers In italics	Liáng ZhùXiézòuqǔ	《梁祝》协奏曲	17
by the window	kàochuāng	靠窗	14

C

cabinet	guìzi	柜子	14
camellia	shāncháhuā	山茶花	10
candle	làzhú	蜡烛	12
Cantonese opera	yuèjù	粤剧	17
care centre for elderly people	tuōlǎosuǒ	托老所	4
career	shìyè	事业	1
cartoon movies	dònghuàpiàn	动画片	15

catchment area housing	xuéqūfáng	学区房	5
cave	shāndòng	山洞	9
CD	guāngpán	光盘	17
celestial grass	xiāncǎo	仙草	11
ceremony	yíshì	仪式	13
challenging	tiǎozhànxìng	挑战性	7
Chang E running to the moon	cháng'ébēnyuè	嫦娥奔月	12
channel	píndào	频道	16
chemical fertiliser	huàféi	化肥	7
Chinese and Western combined together	zhōngxīhébì	中西合璧	17
clothing	fúzhuāng	服装	4
cohort	rénqún	人群	16
Cold Food Festival	hánshíjié	寒食节	10
college entrance examination	gāokǎo	高考	5
comfortable	shūshì	舒适	5
commercialisation	shāngyèhuà	商业化	15
common saying	súyǔ	俗语	16
competent	shèngrèn	胜任	7
complexion	qìsè	气色	13
compulsory for study	bìxiū	必修	5
conflict	máodùn	矛盾	15
contemporary	dāngdài	当代	15
continuous	búduàn	不断	4
contribution	gòngxiàn	贡献	7
controlled; disciplined	yǒujiézhìde	有节制地	16
cooked food	shúshí	熟食	13
cookery programme	pēngrènjiémù	烹饪节目	16
coriander	xiāngcài	香菜	4
corpse	shītǐ	尸体	11
correspond	duìyìng	对应	13
costume / period drama	gǔzhuāngpiàn	古装片	15
costume	fúshì	服饰	10
couch potato	shāfāshangde tǔdòu	沙发上的土豆	16

Appendix VII

countryside	jiāowài	郊外	1
court official	guān	官	11
courtyard house	sìhéyuàn	四合院	2
craft	shǒuyì	手艺	16
creativity	chuàngyì	创意	7
creature; living things	shēnglíng	生灵	11
criticism	pīpíng	批评	3
Crouching Tiger, Hidden Dragon	Wòhǔcánglóng	《卧虎藏龙》	15
crowded	yōngjǐ	拥挤	8
cultivated land	gēngdì	耕地	7

D

day after day	rìfùyírì	日复一日	8
day pupil	zǒudú	走读	5
death	sǐwáng	死亡	13
debate	biànlùn	辩论	5
delicate; exquisite	jīngzhì	精致	14
demand over supply	gōngbúyìngqiú	供不应求	7
department (as in a company)	bùmén	部门	2
department (as in a university)	xì	系	2
desire	yùwàng	欲望	16
detective movies	zhēntànpiàn	侦探片	15
determined	jiānjué	坚决	6
developed	fādá	发达	1
dilapidated	pòjiù	破旧	2
directly	zhíjiē	直接	8
disappointed	shīwàng	失望	6
distinctive	xiānmíngde	鲜明的	15
distributor	fāxíng gōngsī	发行公司	15
documentaries	jìlùpiàn	纪录片	15
dowry	jiàzhuang	嫁妆	13
dull and dry	kūzào	枯燥	14
dynasty	cháodài	朝代	15

E

earphone	ěrjī	耳机	17
economy	jīngjì	经济	3
editor	biānjí	编辑	1
education	jiàoyù	教育	3
efficiency	xiàolǜ	效率	8
element	yuánsù	元素	15
employment	jiùyè	就业	3
encyclopaedia	bǎikēquánshū	百科全书	14
end of year	niánmò	年末	9
energy	huólì	活力	8
energy	jīnglì	精力	3
enterprise	qǐyè	企业	7
entertainment	yúlè	娱乐	4
equal	píngděng	平等	5
especially	géwài	格外	5
even	lián	连	17
evil spirit	suì	祟	9
evil spirit; demon	yāo	妖	11
excess; surplus	guòshèng	过剩	3
exciting	cìjī	刺激	6

F

Fa Hai, name of the monk	Fǎ Hǎi	法海	11
face (as in reputation, prestige)	miànzi	面子	6
family planning	jìhuà shēngyù	计划生育	3
family	jiātíng	家庭	1
fans	fěnsī	粉丝	17
festival	jiājié	佳节	13
filial obedience	xiàoshùn	孝顺	13
film company	piānshāng	片商	16
film director	dǎoyǎn	导演	15
film / TV entertainment	yǐngshìyúlè	影视娱乐	14
finance	jīnróngjiè	金融界	6

Appendix VII

fire cracker	bàozhú	爆竹	9
flame	huǒyàn	火焰	13
flourishing	hónghuǒ	红火	7
fly	cāngying	苍蝇	11
with emphasis on	zhuózhòng	着重	16
follow the new trend	zhǎngwòshíshàng	掌握时尚	16
food is everything to the common people	mínyǐshíwéitiān	民以食为天	16
for instance	bǐrú	比如	6
foreign domestic helper	wàiyōng	外佣	1
form of address	chēnghū	称呼	13
full of joy	xǐqì yángyáng	喜气洋洋	9
funeral	sànglǐ	丧礼	13

G

garlic	dàsuàn	大蒜	11
gender	xìngbié	性别	7
general manager	zǒngjīnglǐ	总经理	2
genre	lèixíng	类型	15
God of Earth	tǔdìshén	土地神	12
gold ingot used as money in ancient China	jīnyuánbǎo	金元宝	9
Golden Horse Awards	Jīnmǎjiǎng	金马奖	15
Golden Horse Film Festival	Jīnmǎ Yǐngzhǎn	金马影展	15
Golden Mountain Temple	JīnshānSì	金山寺	11
good comments/reviews	hǎopíng	好评	9
good health and longevity	jiànkāngchángshòu	健康长寿	12
government	zhèngfǔ	政府	3
grand; solemn	lóngzhòng	隆重	13
grave	fénmù	坟墓	10
great number	shùliàngpángdà	数量庞大	17
groceries	záhuò	杂货	2
group	rénqún	人群	3
Guang Zhou, also known as Canton	Guǎngzhōu	广州	14
Guanyin (in Buddhism, it is called Avalokitesvara)	Guānyīn	观音	13
guest	bīnkè	宾客	17

H

happy	xìngfú	幸福	2
hard	xīnkǔ	辛苦	1
harmonious	héxié	和谐	17
harvest	shōuchéng	收成	12
have a haircut	lǐfà	理发	2
Havoc in Heaven	Dànàotiāngōng	《大闹天宫》	15
herb	xiāngcǎo	香草	11
high speed rail in China	gāotiě	高铁	14
highlight	liàngdiǎn	亮点	13
home country	jiāxiāng	家乡	5
honour	róngyù	荣誉	15
horizon	shìyě	视野	16
hot and humid	shīrè	湿热	11
hotline	rèxiàn	热线	7
how	rúhé	如何	15
huge noise	jùxiǎng	巨响	9
human beings	rénlèi	人类	12
hurriedly	cōngcōng	匆匆	8
husband and wife	fūqī	夫妻	1
hygiene	wèishēng	卫生	11

I

illiterate	wénmáng	文盲	2
illness	jíbìng	疾病	11
immortality	chángshēngbùlǎo	长生不老	12
in fact	qíshí	其实	6
in high spirits; in great delight	xìnggāocǎiliè	兴高采烈	9
in pace with; in the wake of	suízhe	随着	4
in reality	shíjìshang	实际上	9
income	shōurù	收入	1
increasingly	rìyì	日益	3
indistinct	yǐnyǐnyuēyuē	隐隐约约	12
information	zīxùn	资讯	1

Appendix VII

inquisitive	hàowèn	好问	12
international	guójì	国际	5
investment	tóuzī	投资	15
is called by	chēngzuò	称作	13
is it not	shìfǒu	是否	6
it is said	jùshuō	据说	9
It literally means plucking osmanthus flowers in the Palace of the Moon. It is used to describe someone succeeding in the imperial examination.	chángōngzhéguì	蟾宫折桂	12

J

Jade Rabbit	yùtù	玉兔	12
job; position	zhíwèi	职位	7
junior high school	chūzhōng	初中	5

K

karaoke	kǎlā ŌK	卡拉OK	17
key university (similar to Russell Group or Ivy League universities)	zhòngdiǎndàxué	重点大学	5

L

lack of	quēshǎo	缺少	3
landscape architecture	yuánlín	园林	6
lane; alley	hútòng	胡同	2
language and literature	yǔwén	语文	5
legend	chuánshuō	传说	9
Lei Feng Pagoda	Léifēng Tǎ	雷峰塔	11
Liang Shanbo	Liáng Shānbó	梁山伯	17
life coach	shēnghuózhǐdǎoshī	生活指导师	8
"like it", it is an online network phrase, used to express "praise"	diǎnzàn	点赞	16
little emperor	xiǎo huángdì	小皇帝	3
little known	mòmò wúwén	默默无闻	15
livestock	shēngchù	牲畜	9
lotus seed paste	liánróng	莲蓉	12
low	dīluò	低落	5

luckily	xìnghǎo	幸好	1
lunar calendar	nónglì	农历	9

M

main colour	zhǔsèdiào	主色调	13
making	chuàngzuò	创作	15
manual labour	láodònglì	劳动力	7
manual worker	láodòngzhě	劳动者	2
marriage	hūnjià	婚嫁	13
marriage	hūnyīn	婚姻	2
martial art novel	wǔxiáxiǎoshuō	武侠小说	14
maxim; motto	géyán	格言	16
meal eaten on New Year's Eve	niányèfàn	年夜饭	9
meaningful	yǒuyìyì de	有意义的	16
medical condition	yīliáotiáojiàn	医疗条件	2
medical staff	yīhù rényuán	医护人员	4
mentality	xīnlǐ	心理	3
messy	luànqībāzāo	乱七八糟	2
Miluo River, situated in northern Hunan Province	Mìluójiāng	汨罗江	11
minister	dàchén	大臣	11
mock (exam)	mónǐ	模拟	5
money given to children as a Chinese New Year gift	yāsuìqián	压岁钱	9
monk	héshang	和尚	11
monster	guàishòu	怪兽	9
mood	qíngxù	情绪	5
mosquito	wénzi	蚊子	11
mourning clothes	sàngfú	丧服	13
mourning	dàoniàn	悼念	10

N

natural gift	tiānfù	天赋	17
negative	fùmiàn	负面	3
neighbour	línjū	邻居	2
new style	xīnkuǎn	新款	6

Appendix VII

English	Pinyin	Chinese	Page
New Year's Eve	chúxī	除夕	9
newly wed	xīnhūn	新婚	13
news	xiāoxi	消息	10
nice surprise	jīngxǐ	惊喜	17
non-stop; incessant	bùxī	不息	13
Northern Song Dynasty (960-1127AD)	Běisòng	北宋	10
not good enough	búgòu hǎo	不够好	6
not only	bùjǐn	不仅	12
not purposefully	suíshǒu	随手	14
not until	cái	才	1
not	fēi	非	14
nutrition	yíngyǎng	营养	3

O

English	Pinyin	Chinese	Page
obesity	féipàngzhēng	肥胖症	3
obligation	yìwù	义务	4
offering to gods and ancestors in autumn	qiūjì	秋祭	12
offerings put in front of grave	jìpǐn	祭品	10
old fashioned	guòshí	过时	6
old people's home	yǎnglǎoyuàn	养老院	4
older generation	zhǎngbèi	长辈	9
on average	píngjūn	平均	14
on the whole	zǒngsuàn	总算	5
once before	céngjīng	曾经	2
one another	bǐcǐ	彼此	13
oneself	zìshēn	自身	3
only child	dúshēng zǐnǚ	独生子女	3
opitional for study	xuǎnxiū	选修	5
orchestra	guǎnxiányuètuán	管弦乐团	17
ordinary	pǔtōng	普通	2
organic	yǒujī	有机	7
organisation	jīgòu	机构	4
organiser	zǔzhīzhě	组织者	15
osmanthus tree	guìhuāshù	桂花树	12

out with the old, in with the new	tuīchénchūxīn	推陈出新	16
outside world	wàijiè	外界	7
outskirt of a city	jiāowài	郊外	14
outstanding	chūsè	出色	8
overseas	hǎiwài	海外	1

P

pain	tòngkǔ	痛苦	13
paper horse (horse made with paper and bamboo strips)	zhǐmǎ	纸马	10
paradise	jílè shìjiè	极乐世界	13
parts of the country other than where one is	wàidì	外地	4
to passed down and to inherit	chuánchéng	传承	16
patience	nàixīn	耐心	5
peasant	nóngmín	农民	2
peer	tónglíngrén	同龄人	3
people whose job involves the use of their brain, rather than their physical labour	shínǎozú(kào zhìhuìchīfàn de rén)	食脑族（靠智慧吃饭的人）	7
people; general public	bǎixìng	百姓	10
perfectly satisfactory	měimǎn	美满	8
person in-charge	zhǔrèn	主任	2
personality	xìnggé	性格	3
person in charge	guǎnlǐyuán	管理员	8
pest	hàichóng	害虫	11
photography	shèyǐng	摄影	4
platform	píngtái	平台	15
policy	zhèngcè	政策	3
political movement	zhèngzhìyùndòng	政治运动	2
poor	pínkùn	贫困	7
poor	qióngkùn	穷困	5
pot plant	pénzāi	盆栽	14
practical	shíyòng	实用	2
praise	biǎoyáng	表扬	3
pressure as big as a mountain	yālì shāndà	"压力山大"	6

Appendix VII

previous life	qiánshì	前世	11
princess	gōngzhǔ	公主	3
private tutorials	bǔxíbān	补习班	5
privately owned	sīyíng	私营	7
process	jìnchéng	进程	4
product	chǎnpǐn	产品	2
proud	jiāoào	骄傲	2
Pu'er tea	pǔerchá	普洱茶	13
puberty	qīngchūn qī	青春期	1
pure; clean	chúnjìng	纯净	13
pursuit	zhuīqiú	追求	16

Q

quality (of people)	sùzhì	素质	5
quality (of product)	zhìliàng	质量	5
quantity	shùliàng	数量	15
quiet and tastefully decorated	yōuyǎ	幽雅	14

R

reader	dúzhě	读者	14
realgar, a mineral	xiónghuáng	雄黄	11
realistic	zhēnshí	真实	15
really	shízài	实在	2
red ribbon dance	hóngchóuwǔ	红绸舞	9
Red Sorghum	Hónggāoliang	《红高粱》	15
regardless of	wúlùn	无论	15
reincarnation	lúnhuí	轮回	13
resentment; bitterness	yōuyuàn	幽怨	17
resign	cízhí	辞职	7
resource	zīyuán	资源	5
responsibility	zérèn	责任	4
responsible	fùzé	负责	1
result; effect	chéngxiào	成效	3
result; effect	xiàoguǒ	效果	17
Reunion Festival	tuányuánjié	团圆节	12

reunion	tuányuán	团圆	9
rhythm	jiézòu	节奏	1
rich and varied	fēngfùduōcǎi	丰富多彩	4
riches and honour	fùguì	富贵	9
rising step by step	bùbùgāoshēng	步步高升	13
river crab	héxiè	河蟹	12
roadside	lùbiān	路边	14
rock music	yáogǔnyuè	摇滚乐	17
Russia	Éluósī	俄罗斯	14

S

salary; wage	xīnshuǐ	薪水	7
sales	tuīxiāo	推销	2
satisfactory	mǎnyì	满意	1
scene	jǐngxiàng	景象	10
scene	chǎngjǐng	场景	15
scented pouch	xiāngbāo	香包	11
science fiction movies	kēhuànpiàn	科幻片	15
screen	píngmù	屏幕	2
sedan chair	jiào	轿子	10
selfish	zìsī	自私	3
senior high school	gāozhōng	高中	5
sense of achievement	chéngjiùgǎn	成就感	7
serious	yánzhòng	严重	3
sharing	gòngxiǎng	共享	14
shrimp paste	xiājiàng	虾酱	16
singing a variety of songs	K gē chuàn shāo	K歌串烧	17
single child	dúshēng	独生	2
single parent	dānqīn	单亲	1
situation; condition	zhuàng kuàng	状况	1
small breaks in time	suìpiànshíjiān	碎片时间	14
snack	língshí	零食	14
social	shèjiāo	社交	6
society	shèhuì	社会	4

Appendix VII

solitary; unsociable	gūdú zìbì	孤独自闭	3
sorrow	bēi'āi	悲哀	13
specialised	zhuānmén	专门	10
specialised; subject; discipline	zhuānyè	专业	6
spring couplets	chūnlián	春联	9
stable	āndìng	安定	2
standard	biāozhǔn	标准	8
starting line	qǐpǎo xiàn	起跑线	5
state-run	gōnglì	公立	5
statistics	tǒngjì	统计	4
stay-at-home	jūjiā	居家	4
strange	mòshēng	陌生	5
straw	màicǎo	麦草	7
strict	yán	严	6
student studying abroad	liúxuéshēng	留学生	5
style	fēnggé	风格	10
subtitled	zìmù	字幕	15
suggestion	jiànyì	建议	1
superior; leader	shàngjílǐngdǎo	上级领导	13
supernatural power	fǎlì	法力	11
support	zhīchí	支持	1
surplus	yú	余	9
surprised	jīngqí	惊奇	17
surprisingly	chūqí	出奇	17
survey	diàochá	调查	3
Symphony No.5	MìngyùnJiāoxiǎngqǔ	《命运交响曲》	17
syndrome	zōnghézhēng	综合症	3

T

Taipei, provincial capital of Taiwan	Táiběi	台北	14
Tang Dynasty (618AD-907AD)	tángcháo	唐朝	12
tasty; delicious	xiānměi	鲜美	12
Temple of the Moon	Yuètán	月坛	12
temporarily	zànshí	暂时	3

thanksgiving	gǎn'ēn	感恩	10
the commercial world	shāngjiè	商界	14
the dead	sǐzhě	死者	10
the era of the Ming Dynasty and Qing Dynasty	míngqīng	明清	14
the kindness of saving a life	jiùmìngzhī'ēn	救命之恩	11
the media	chuánméijiè	传媒界	16
the more children, the more benefits	duōzǐduōfú	多子多福	4
the Rites of Zhou Dynasty	Zhōulǐ	《周礼》	13
the scope in thinking	sīwéifànwéi	思维范围	16
the State of Chu	Chǔguó	楚国	11
the State of Qin	Qínguó	秦国	11
The Story of the Stone, a classic Chinese novel	Hónglóumèng	《红楼梦》	14
theory	lǐlùn	理论	14
thinking; concept	sīxiǎng guānniàn	思想观念	1
Tian Long Ba Bu, the title of one of the well-known martial art novels written by Jin Yong	Tiānlóngbābù	《天龙八部》	14
Tie Guan Yin tea	tiěguānyīnchá	铁观音茶	13
timbre	yīnsè	音色	17
time-travel movies	chuānyuèpiàn	穿越片	15
to accompany	péi	陪	1
to advertise for a job vacancy	zhāopìn	招聘	7
to alleviate	huǎnjiě	缓解	3
to allocate	fēnpèi	分配	2
to allow	zhǔnxǔ	准许	3
to analyse	fēnxī	分析	7
to argue	zhēnglùn	争论	2
to ask for advice	qǐngjiào	请教	1
to associate; to imagine	liánxiǎng	联想	17
to balance	pínghéng	平衡	6
to be angry	shēngqì	生气	6
to be delivered to the home	shàngmén	上门	4

Appendix VII

to be thankful	gǎnēn	感恩	12
to bear and rear children	shēng'éryùnǚ	生儿育女	2
to beat the gongs and drums	qiāoluódǎgǔ	敲锣打鼓	9
to begin broadcasting	kāibō	开播	16
to breed	fánzhí	繁殖	11
to broadcast frequently	rèbō	热播	16
to browse	liúlǎn	浏览	14
to build	dājiàn	搭建	7
to carry a lantern	tí dēnglóng	提灯笼	12
to change	biàn	变	1
to change	huàn	换	2
to collect	shōucáng	收藏	14
to combine into one	hé'érwéiyī	合而为一	8
to commit suicide	zìshā	自杀	11
to conduct oneself in society	chǔshìzuòrén	处世做人	2
to convince by persuasion	shuìfú	说服	11
to deal with	chǔlǐ	处理	1
to decorate	bùzhì	布置	2
to defeat	dǎbài	打败	11
to depict	miáohuì	描绘	10
to develop	fāhuī	发挥	7
to dial	bōdǎ	拨打	16
to divorce	líhūn	离婚	1
to do an outing	tàqīng	踏青	10
to do something together with others	jiébàn	结伴	10
to drive away the evil spirits	qūxié	驱邪	9
to emigrate	yímín	移民	5
to emphasise	qiángdiào	强调	7
to employ	pìnyòng	聘用	2
to encounter	yùdào	遇到	1
to enjoy	xiǎngshòu	享受	2
to enjoy old age	ānxiǎngwǎnnián	安享晚年	2
to enrich	fēngfù	丰富	16

to enrol	bàomíng	报名	4
to enter for an exam	bàokǎo	报考	6
to exercise	duànliàn	锻炼	4
to expel; to banish	qūgǎn	驱赶	11
to experience for oneself	tǐyàn	体验	17
to experience	jīnglì	经历	1
to explain	jiǎngjiě	讲解	1
to explore the spring scenery	tànchūn	探春	10
to fall in love	xiāng'ài	相爱	2
to fell (a tree)	kǎn	砍	12
to flee	táopǎo	逃跑	9
to flood	yān	淹	11
to forbid	jìnzhǐ	禁止	10
to form (a habit)	yǎngchéng	养成	3
to found	chuàngbàn	创办	15
to get along with	xiāngchǔ	相处	3
to get rid of pests	chúchóng	除虫	7
to give injection	dǎzhēn	打针	4
to give up	fàngqì	放弃	16
to grow crops in spring	chūngēngchūnzhòng	春耕春种	10
to grow melon and bean	zhòngguāzhòngdòu	种瓜种豆	10
to grow	zhòng	种	4
to grow; to cultivate	zhòngzhí	种植	7
to guess	cāi	猜	15
to guide	zhǐdǎo	指导	16
to hand down	liúchuán	流传	12
to harm	shānghài	伤害	11
to have children to prepare for old age	yǎng'érfánglǎo	养儿防老	4
to have control over	zhīpèi	支配	8
to incorporate	jí	集	8
to interact	hùdòng	互动	16
to invest	tóuzī	投资	5
to irrigate; to water (plants)	jiāoshuǐ	浇水	7

Appendix VII

to kill germs	shājūn	杀菌	11
to kill many birds with one stone	yìshí duōniǎo	一石多鸟	8
to lack; be short of	quē	缺	17
to land	dēnglù	登陆	12
to limit	xiànzhì	限制	16
to live (Here the sentence means "only two survived".)	huó	活	2
to live alone	dújū	独居	4
to live; to reside	jūzhù	居住	1
to look after	zhàogù	照顾	1
to look for	xúnzhǎo	寻找	7
to lose	shīqù	失去	4
to lose	shū	输	5
to make a dream come true	yuánmèng	圆梦	4
to marry (a woman)	qǔ	娶	17
to nurture; to foster	péiyǎng	培养	3
to occupy	zhàn	占	2
to offer (such as flowers)	xiànshang	献上	10
to offer tea respectfully	jìngchá	敬茶	13
to open one's mouth	zhāngkǒu	张口	3
to oppose	fǎnduì	反对	6
to pay respect to ancestors	jìzǔ	祭祖	10
to place	fàngzhì	放置	14
to plant trees to make a forest	zhíshù zàolín	植树造林	10
to plant willows	chāliǔ	插柳	10
to play chess	xiàqí	下棋	4
to play Mahjong	dǎ májiāng	打麻将	4
to play on a swing	dàngqiūqiān	荡秋千	10
to pound medicine in a mortar	dǎoyào	捣药	12
to practise Tai Chi	dǎ tàijíquán	打太极拳	4
to pray for	qíqiú	祈求	12
to pray for happiness	qífú	祈福	9
to present (respectfully)	jìngxiàn	敬献	10
to press down	yā	压	11

to prevent	yùfáng	预防	11
to produce; to come into being	chǎnshēng	产生	3
to promote	tuīguǎng	推广	15
to protect and bless	bǎoyòu	保佑	9
to provide for old age	yǎnglǎo	养老	2
to provide for the family	yǎngjiā	养家	2
to publish in a newspaper	kāndēng	刊登	7
to punish	chéngfá	惩罚	11
to pursue	tuīxíng	推行	3
to pursue	zhuīqiú	追求	1
to put in front of	bǎishang	摆上	10
to quicken	jiākuài	加快	4
to raise (a child)	yǎngyù	养育	3
to realise	shíxiàn	实现	1
to reckon	gūjì	估计	4
to record	jìlù	记录	16
to reduce	jiǎnshǎo	减少	1
to reflect	fǎnyìng	反映	16
to register	dēngjì	登记	14
to relax	fàngkuān	放宽	3
to relax	fàngsōng	放松	4
to rent	zūjiè	租借	5
to repair cars	xiūchē	修车	2
to repay a favour	bàodá	报答	11
to retire	tuìxiū	退休	4
to rise or appear one after another	cǐqǐ bǐfú	此起彼伏	9
to run (Here the sentence means "to own and run a business".)	kāi	开	2
to save up (money)	cún	存	2
to save	jiéshěng	节省	8
to say farewell to the old and to welcome in the new	cíjiùyíngxīn	辞旧迎新	9
to scare to death	xiàsǐ	吓死	11
to scare	xià	吓	9

Appendix VII

English	Pinyin	Chinese	#
to see as important	zhòngshì	重视	14
to send	pài	派	4
to settle down	ānxīn	安心	2
to share (responsibility)	fēndān	分担	8
to smoke	chōuyān	抽烟	6
to spare time	chōukòng	抽空	8
to spoil (a child)	chǒnghuài	宠坏	3
to sprinkle	sǎ	洒	11
to start an enterprise	chuàngyè	创业	7
to step into	tàjìn	踏进	14
to sterilise	xiāodú	消毒	11
to stick with	shǒuzhe	守着	7
to stipulate	guīdìng	规定	13
to strength the health and body	qiángshēnjiàntǐ	强身健体	8
to stretch out one's hand	shēnshǒu	伸手	3
to study abroad	liúxué	留学	2
to suggest	tíchū	提出	11
to suspect	huáiyí	怀疑	6
to sweep the grave	sǎomù	扫墓	10
to symbolise	xiàngzhēng	象征	12
to take blood pressure	liáng xuèyā	量血压	4
to take care of oneself	zìlǐ	自理	4
to take drugs	xīdú	吸毒	6
to talk about anything whatsoever	wúsuǒbùtán	无所不谈	6
to talk over	shāngliang	商量	6
to throw in	rēngjìn	扔进	11
to tie a belt round one's waist	shùyāodài	束腰带	13
to understand	liǎojiě	了解	1
to urge someone to do or not to do something	dīngzhǔ	叮嘱	2
to use magic	zuòfǎ	作法	11
to visit	kànwàng	看望	1
to wear	dài	戴	17

to while away (one's time)	dǎfā	打发	16
to win a prize	huòjiǎng	获奖	15
to window-shop	guàngjiē	逛街	1
to worry	dānxīn	担心	6
to worship	jìbài	祭拜	10
toad	chánchú	蟾蜍	12
tomato	xīhóngshì	西红柿	4
top floor	dǐngcéng	顶层	2
town	chéngzhèn	城镇	7
traditional	chuántǒng	传统	4
tragedy	bēijù	悲剧	17
transition period	zhuǎnxíngqī	转型期	7
trendy	xīncháo	新潮	6
trouble; shortcoming	máobìng	毛病	3

U

unique	dútè	独特	15
using something as proof of	píng	凭	14

V

vexed	kǔnǎo	苦恼	6
vigorously	dàlì	大力	3
vigour	jīnglì	精力	8
virtuous wife and good mother	xiánqīliángmǔ	贤妻良母	8
voice	sǎngyīn	嗓音	17

W

wall	qiáng	墙	2
war	zhànzhēng	战争	2
way	fāngshì	方式	4
wealth, honour and luck	fùguì jíxiáng	富贵吉祥	12
wedding banquet	hūnyàn	婚宴	17
Weibo (China's version of Twitter)	wēibó	微博	16
well-turned phrase or saying	jiājù	佳句	16
white-collar	báilǐng	白领	8
wide	kuān	宽	10

Appendix VII

wild animal	yěshòu	野兽	9
wild with joy	huāntiānxǐdì	欢天喜地	9
wilful	rènxìng	任性	3
wishes	yuànwàng	愿望	1
wishes	yuànwàng	愿望	12
without knowing	bùzhībùjué	不知不觉	14
women	fùnǚ	妇女	1
workload	gōngzuòliàng	工作量	1
world of employment	zhíchǎng	职场	7
world	tiāndì	天地	6
Wu Gang, the woodcutter on the moon	Wú Gāng	吴刚	12

X

Xu Xian, name of the scholar	Xǔ Xiān	许仙	11

Y

Yin and Yang, the two opposing principles in nature, with Yin representing the feminine and Yang the masculine	yīnyáng	阴阳	12

Z

Zhu Yingtai	Zhù Yīngtái	祝英台	17